GOD OF THE SUN

ANJALI CHANDA

authorHOUSE®

AuthorHouse™ UK
1663 Liberty Drive
Bloomington, IN 47403 USA
www.authorhouse.co.uk
Phone: 0800 047 8203 (Domestic TFN)
+44 1908 723714 (International)

Published by AuthorHouse 11/19/2019

ISBN: 978-1-7283-8242-5 (sc)
ISBN: 978-1-7283-8241-8 (e)

Print information available on the last page.

Cover Artwork by Lauren Kelly

This book is printed on acid-free paper.

Dedicated to B & L

To all the Lost Souls that Come Home to Themselves

Chapter 1

THE SOAP OPERA BEGINS

At the request of some of my friends, I'm now starting a diary to record the details of my dream of setting up a hotel in Goa. This will be my personal account of my big adventure, recording my highs and lows and the general craziness that occurs here in the land of the coconut.

Well, I have actually been here two weeks now. I will try to recall the events to date. It's been a bit of an emotional roller coaster.

So, on day one I arrived at the Arabian Waters resort in Shakthar, severely jet-lagged because I hadn't really slept on the plane for any of the three legs of the journey (London → Abu Dhabi → Mumbai → Goa). I can't remember the chronological order of things, but the trip didn't start in the best of ways. Firstly, a damn cockroach flew and landed on my dinner (Meditation salad, cauliflower, mozzarella, and boiled eggs swimming in olive oil—maybe Mr Cockroach did me a favour). I ended up having my old faithful, lentil dhal and roti. Then the candle in the glass holder tipped and the glass smashed. I had dinner and went straight to bed before anything else happened. I woke up at 1 p.m. the next day. I relaxed for the next few days, which were uneventful. In addition, there was no Wi-Fi anywhere! I used my data allowance for Facebook updates and WhatsApp and to speak with Harry, my new business partner.

Harry advises me that one of his friends is coming to pick me up to take me to Hansari. A dude called Jai texts to say he'll pick me up on the morning of 9 September. He speaks good English, so it's all good. I was hoping he was going to be a fittie. Anyways, Jai arrives and meets me at the Arabian Waters restaurant. First impressions: not a fittie; a bit shy and soft-spoken. We have a little time to kill, so Jai shows me around Light of Moon Shakthar—first time I've seen the place in real life. I had only seen pics Harry had sent me and those on Bookings.com. The outside is covered in blue plastic sheeting and palm leaves to protect the building from the monsoon rains. The restaurant inside is dark with all the furniture piled up. It's miserable and smells of mould. The rooms are the same. The landlord has put up some of his guests in a couple of the rooms. There are lots of empty bottles. I see some of Harry's "antique" furniture. It's hideous! So, not the best first impression, but definitely a lot of potential. We talk about how improvements can be made, for example by opening a side entrance into an office for guests to check in and clearing the path to the beach to make it prettier and more accessible. Yep, the place definitely has potential, and I am feeling a little excited. ☺

Then Jai takes me to Glamour, a swanky hotel resort. It is a bit rough around the edges, but otherwise it's a nice-looking place. It's where the "rich" Indians go. Not my cup of tea, it has a characterless corporate feel, even if there are a lots of Laughing Buddha statues and engraved wooden signs. I also meet Hanu and just say hi to him. Jai and Hanu rattle on in Hindi, I think. I catch the odd word. We then go to the bank to do some money exchanging for me.

Sometime later, we load up Harry's car with my huge suitcases and head off on our three-hour road trip to Hansari. We're having trouble understanding each other with both our accents, with a lot of "whats", "ers", "come again" s, and confused looks, but our communication is good. We chat about where we're both from (yes, I'm English with an Indian face. One of my favourites is when a local asks me, "Are you half milk and half chocolate?" I reply, "No, I'm fully chocolate." LOL :D). We discuss how we know Harry and make the usual small talk. Anyways, small talk turns into more personal stuff. Indians don't seem to have any boundaries when it comes to asking about personal details. I am used to this from previous experience, but this conversation differs slightly. Jai is a modern Indian kind of a guy. But one thing is strange: I don't feel uncomfortable at all, and I end up telling this random dude, whom I've only known a few hours, very personal stuff about my past. I mean, I don't even talk about this kind of stuff to some of my closest friends. Seriously, go figure! I am shocked at myself to say the least. I tell him that what I've said is top secret, and I'm pretty sure I can trust him. He does seem like a really cool guy.

So, after a hell-raising passenger experience with a few buttock-clenching moments with a head-on near miss from playing chicken with other vehicles, we arrive at Hansari. I meet Harry again after four or so months following a few Skype calls and loads of WhatsApp messaging. We sit down to have a good hot cup of sugary chai (my nerves are shot to buggery from the road trip). We sit and chat, have a general catch-up. Jai has gone off lurking in the background somewhere. He's done his chauffeuring duties. Harry helps to get me a room around the corner from Light of Moon (LOM), Hansari. The room is a bit manky, but surprisingly it has hot water. Results! So, after a bit of a lie down and a shower, I saunter down for dinner. All fine and dandy. I say to Harry that we'll talk business tomorrow.

To be perfectly frank, I wasn't really looking forward to coming to Hansari, worried I'd bump into some of the faces from previous visits, namely the Kovvi guys. But I keep my head down and don't wander too far. But I do go to see the guys at

Café Inn and say hi to Freddy, but he isn't there. Probably for the best, right? ☺

The next day I get up go down to breakfast. Great, the Wi-Fi is working. I do a bit of a Facebook update, posting that I have arrived safely and all that. I send messages to Cheryl, Andy Bro, and Lucy, my main contact points back home. The lads are busy with customers, so I just generally watch the world go by and make notes of discussion points to go through with Harry on my laptop. I see Jai, who says good morning, and the washing-up woman greets me like royalty, bless her rubber chappals. I have a Skype chat with my cousin Kathy in France. I needed to see a familiar face especially from the fam!

So eventually I sit down with Harry and go through the plan of who's doing what, who's investing what, and how we will share profits—a general high-level plan. Yep, all seems good, even if he does give me the thousand-yard stare once or twice.

I meet one of Harry's mates, Kamel, who I suspect may be batting for the "other team". We all sit down for dinner and chat. Kamel is an interior designer and had his first horse-riding lesson yesterday. Harry says we'll go and visit Kamel's place tomorrow. Which we do, and it's absolutely amazing. It's a little Portuguese villa which he has done up impeccably with a definite Indian flavour, but modern art deco pieces thrown in here and there. Tea is served in a copper-type teapot, and two little Indian women in saris are wandering around, tending to the gardens and the laundry. Very inspirational stuff; it's what I aspire to build. Harry's boss, who is the landlord for LOM Hansari, is there also. He's hiding from his wife, who has called him numerous times. He, too, is suitably impressed with Kamel's place.

Having had a lovely couple of days in Hansari, I am mostly feeling positive.

Now, I can't remember if Jai had mentioned something in the car or not about whether Harry is of disreputable character. But over the course of the next three days in Hansari, Jai somehow mutters the odd comments to me about Harry. On one occasion was when we went to Sindi to buy me an Internet dongle for me to take back to Shakthar. So, I listened, and I am fully aware that I don't really know either of them very well at all, but I try to keep an open mind. Still, Jai's words have sunk in and have made me very cautious.

On the return journey to Shakthar, Harry is my designated driver, and it isn't a bad drive at all—a lot calmer that Jai's kamikaze style. As people do on road trips, we chat about life. No secrets are divulged this time. Harry does most of the talking this time, telling me about his family, Jasmine, his baby, his background, how far he's come in his life, and how he left his small village at the age of twelve to go to the big bright-lights city of Hindavi, one of the most affluent cities in India. From there he worked in various restaurants and hotels. Then he came to Goa to try his hand at making it big there. On my previous visit, he told me he was one of the live-in help for a rich family when he was seventeen. The woman of the house seduced him. He stayed there until he was bored of her advances. I think then that's when he headed to Hindavi.

I talked about my family, how my grandad is the love of my life. I talked about my personal values, saying that truth and honesty are paramount to any relationship, just to make a point. Jai's comments were still playing on my mind.

We arrive late in Shakthar and order some dinner and drinks at Arabian Waters. We're joined by Hanu. Hanu, Jai, and Harry all know each other from Glamour days. I listen to them rattle on in Hindi, I think it is, catching the odd word. Harry translates some of the conversation into English for me, and I put in my two cents' worth. Hanu leaves, and then Harry gives me the rundown on Hanu, saying that he came from Dubai to run Glamour and didn't really have any business acumen. He basically lost a bunch of money to Glamour's owner and is now trying to get it back. It sounds like Harry is slagging Hanu off as well. That doesn't sit well with me. The guy has barely left, and

Harry's going on with himself—this is actual red flag number one, as opposed to gossip or hearsay.

Now this where I start to doubt that he is telling me the truth. Again, I barely know any of these guys. My gut instincts say that Hanu is a good guy. I thought Harry was a good guy too, but I have no point of reference in relation to him except Jasmine, his wife, who seems lovely from the WhatsApp messaging and Skype calls.

Note to self: keep my wits about me, smile, listen, and nod at the right places. Keep my initial thoughts to myself. Make relevant points when I must, and do not be completely passive. Just watch, listen, and learn!

So, I check back in at Arabian Waters. The guys at Arabian Waters—what a miserable bunch! Especially the two younger lads who manage the bookings and restaurant.

The next day, I meet Harry back at Arabian Waters. He had stayed with a friend. He shows me Light of Moon again. I feel a tad more positive. He says he'll get a room cleaned for me, so I don't have to pay for a room at Arabian Waters. I am a bit reluctant as I don't want to be alone in a big building by myself.

We meet the landlord. Harry hands him a wad of cash. The older woman and man remind me of my grandparents. Only the other day I was messaging with my real cousins about Pops and his Sootie (walking stick). I feel a tinge of affection for these two old strangers.

Later that day, there is an emergency at Hansari. One of the waiters has absconded. Harry left to go back to deal with the emergency.

A lot still needs to be updated, but today is officially meltdown day. After a few days of being stressed and angry, I finally break down and cry on the phone to Harry. He says all the right things. I don't particularly feel better, but what more can I do? It all started with a text message Jai sent to Harry. I am upset and angry to say the least. I thought he was my friend.

Jai showed me a text he had sent to Harry about the money transfer, including his reply, which reads, "She is weird." And then he has the gall to look at me and say, "Are you angry about that?" Damn right I am. He said that I was weird just because I so happened to get a cab myself to get breakfast. If that's what he's saying to Harry about me, then is there any truth to all the stuff he's said about Harry to me? Anyway, I speak to Harry on the phone. If he's blagging me, then he's very convincing. I tell him that if he wants something, he should come to me direct instead of messaging Jai.

I am feeling all alone! I can't trust anyone, not even people who make out to be my friends! Another side note: I am seeking legal advice to find out how binding this legal contract will be.

I still haven't transferred money into Harry's account.

Also, I have packed my suitcases just in case I need to make a sharp exit. I need to look at flights to Hindavi, but Yatu, an old friend from London, has invited me as his plus-one to a wedding in Kerala in the second week in October. I might just cut my losses and go. There is still time. However, the longer I stay, the harder it will get. But my own stubbornness is keeping me here! I am not a quitter! I want to make this work.

Maybe I'm extra sensitive because of the impending moons. I don't know, they're all fucked up anyway.

OK, I'll try to get back to where I left off, where Harry had to leave Shakthar because of a waiter crisis at LOM Hansari, which was around 10 September just to put a timeline on events.

So, I'm left alone in Shakthar, back at Arabian Waters, and before leaving Harry says he will speak to someone about starting work at LOM, i.e. painting, cleaning up, and generally getting things ready.

The following day, nothing happens—no phone call, nothing, nada, zilch. OK, perhaps the waiter crisis is keeping Harry busy. I'm patient, and I wait, chill, and watch beautiful sunsets. The next day I give Harry a quick call, and he tells me he's phoned his friend Mango, who will come and talk about renovations. I get Mango's number and call him, and he says he'll be here in the evening. So, more chilling. Mango arrives later that day. He seems like a very nice person, very chatty and friendly. We walk round LOM and discuss ideas. There is an amazing view from the roof of the beach. I have a little fantasy about having secret drinks with a fittie. ☺ Everything seems positive. I'm happy. Mango's real name is Madhav, but I say I will call him Dave. He's happy about that.

This Ganesh festival is still going on, so it's still quiet. And I just hang fire for now, but I am getting a tad impatient. Anyway, a couple of days pass, and nothing happens. I phone Harry. He says he is sending down Jai, who turns up on Thursday. The next couple of days are taken up with the painters, who have finally arrived, and discussing what their costs are going to be and how much paint will be needed for painting each room, the stairwell, and the exterior. Nothing was discussed with Harry, so I make a decision and agree to the amount and method of payment. It will be coming out of my pocket anyway. Jai acts as translator. The painters do not speak English or understand Punjabi, but they seem like good guys. They all are from Karnataka, Harry and Jai's home state. They're proper rural Indians. I think I intimidate them, but I try to put them at ease. They are shy! Bless them!

Also, I have to buy the guys provisions so they can cook for themselves, rather than them eating out, which would be costly for them. I have no issues with this even though Harry hadn't even mentioned it.

Anyways, work has started on LOM. Rooms are being painted white with grey borders on the architrave and one grey wall. It looks very stylish. Jai is managing the painters, buying the paint, taking the money from Miss Money Bags here, and coordinating what needs to be done. Everything seems to be going smoothly enough, and the painters are working quite swiftly.

In the evening Jai takes me to Anjaru beach. We sit at a beach restaurant called Angel, where we have a couple of drinks, order dinner, and chat. I can't really make out the beach because it's night, but the sound of the sea is soothing. A little later, and as if by magic, Hanu turns up with his little chef friend. The usual jibber-jabber occurs.

So, it's Saturday, 17 September, and it's the weekend. I'm still a little grumpy and stressed. I've found out more about Harry's lack of responsibility when it comes to paying his bills and the mountain of money he owes. I'm still reluctant to transfer money directly into his account. But the day goes on. I mill about with Jai, go for lunch, and meet the new housekeeping boy Jalan, a sweet boy with a cheeky smile. He is shy with me! Bless him!

In the evening, after much discussion, we head to Chatu, which is party central. I must be presentable and not wear jeans! Yeah, whatever! Anyway, I get ready and wear a skirt and a black T. I put some nice make-up on and do my hair. It's nice to actually get dressed up a bit, rather than living in shorts and flip-flops, although I still end up wearing flip-flops. It's been raining, so I don't want to wear my nice gladiator sandals just yet and ruin them on their first outing.

I am getting used to Jai's driving. As we arrive in Chatu, it's absolutely chocka with traffic. There are cars, scooters, and motorbikes all vying to get through the tiniest gap, and all the while it's lashing with rain. The air con in the car is broken, so seeing out of the windscreen is near impossible. We finally get through the gridlock and park up outside Nick's Italian restaurant. We each have a vodka and Coke to calm our nerves.

As we walk up, I recognise a couple of the places from the first time I was in Chatu with the Global Adventures crew. I recognise the place where a blue shot drink came out of my nose due. I do not mention this to Jai—obviously! Walking, walking, walking, we finally make it to Mambo's bar. It's a big place that would not be out of place in any big city. It's full of young (and not so young) Indians having a good time, drinking, smoking, and having a bit of a boogie. Again, it's no different from any major city or resort in Europe. The only difference is that it's full of brown faces with literally a handful of white faces, which I find quite fascinating. Jai says during peak season the ratio will change and will be mostly white faces and a handful of brown faces, which is what I'm used to back home. I order a Red Bull and vodka. I don't know what Jai drinks, whisky of some sort. Tunes are playing, and it's all modern stuff, all the latest dance tunes, including Justin Bieber's "Sorry". The beat is getting to me now, and I feel the urge to make some shapes. We head into the dancing room, and some funky tunes are playing. It's a bit like "We're not in Kansas anymore, Toto!" It is hard to have a conversation over the loud music. Jai is speaking too softly and with his accent. There is a lot of "What?" "Er?" and "Come again."

I drink more Red Bull and vodka. We move outside to the bar area again so we can chat. I am a bit tipsy now! I can't remember much of the conversation, but we pinkie-swear on something. I think it might have been about sticking together and looking out for each other—something like that. He talks about when he wants to get married and to whom, basically someone who understands him. Which is what we all want, right?

After more making of shapes, it's now 3 a.m. We head back to car. On the way home we stop off to get something to eat. I have tomato soup, but I'm feeling sick after too many Red Bull and vodkas.

We engage in more general conversation about life on the way home. Jai asks me what I want out of life. I say that I want to fall in love and be happy. He asks too many questions, and it takes me off guard. But I answer as honestly as I can without giving everything away. I am still feeling sick. Anyway, I get back to the Arabian Waters in one piece. Once I'm in my room,

I get a text from Jai saying he had fun watching me dance. I reply with "Thanks. Good night, and sweet dreams". Sleep!

The next day, Sunday, a room has been cleaned for me at LOM, and I move in. Yay, I don't have to pay £30 a night at the Arabian Waters. It is the only time I see the bookings boy smile, after I hand him a wad of cash when I check out.

The painting is progressing well; the guys are fast workers. I am a little grumpy today, just a bit tired from the late night. I go to Palm Tree Vista (PTV) for lunch, which is the nearest place where the Internet dongle will work. I'm still grumpy. After a multitude of discussions about Harry's credit status, I transfer money into Jai's account to pay the 50 per cent advance for the painters, plus a bit extra for me, as I am out of hard cash. I have palak paneer, the perfect hangover food.

I don't want to go out tonight. Jai gets Mango to bring us takeout. We sit out on my balcony for dinner. I can't see the view yet as the covers are still on the outside of the building, but I can hear the sea. It's cosy. Jai has smokeage, so we skin up, listen to tunes, and generally chit-chat until 2 a.m. Where does the time go?! After one last joint (well, two) "for the road", I chuck Jai out of my room.

We talked about lots of things. He asked me about previous relationships, and he told me about his. I talked about my house, my cat, work, my partying history, my friends, and my car. He said he would have bought my car off me if he had known. I say I didn't even know you then. He told me about how Harry had told him to pick me up, and he had imagined that I would be a fifty-year-old woman because of Harry's previous encounter with a woman called Marie, who had basically set Harry up with money and an apartment in Hindavi, and the Light of Moon up in Hansari. She sounded like a sugar mummy, but who knows the actual reality? Maybe there was a physical relationship or not. I don't know. Jai had assumed he would be picking up someone of the same ilk. I didn't ask him what he thought when he saw me. However, Jai had texted me previously while I was at Arabian Waters and asked if Harry and I had dated. I answered no, which is true. It's best not to have love relationships with people you're going to work with.

We engaged in more gossip, including Harry's alcoholic brother's relationship with the landlord's daughter, which was one of the sickest things I'd ever heard. It started with Harry's brother taking up residence in one of the rooms at LOM. Whether he was meant to be working there or not is not 100 per cent clear, but he essentially started to date one of the landlord's daughters. One evening, they must have gotten it together after a bit of a drink-fest and basically ruined the mattress. Don't even ask for details; I did not want to know! So, the next day Harry's brother threw the mattress out in front of the landlord's yard. I mean literally, what the fuck?! I don't know what happened to the daughter, but I do know that she works as a receptionist somewhere, and according to Jai she isn't even all that.

That night, even after the nightmare story of Harry's brother, I had a damn good sleep. The smokeage had done its job.

On Monday, 19 September, Jai and Mango are heading to Hansari to pick up Harry. I hadn't assumed I'd be going, but I got invited along for the ride. Luckily, I am sitting in the back seat, so I don't have to experience playing chicken with oncoming vehicles. Mango talks nonstop, and Jai is getting annoyed, but he secretly enjoys the banter. They are brothers from other mothers, even if Mango is old enough to be Jai's dad. I'm just listening to them and enjoying the banter between them. Mango occasionally asks if I'm all right. Bless him! We talk about Mango's transition to Christianity, how he used to be a drunken mess, passing out on the side of the road or in jungles. Two years ago, God spoke to him, and he accepted Jesus Christ as his Saviour. He is now starting his political career and is in the process of raising funds to run in the next local elections. He's selling fish to raise funds. I ask him about his policies and campaign. He says that he wants to stand up for and defend local poor people, who are not represented by the corrupt political system. A right little Goan Jeremy Corbyn. Any man (or woman) who can change his life, literally coming out of the gutter to build a life not only for himself but also for the people around him, deserves everything he dreams of. Mango is such a sweet, big-hearted man. I am full of admiration for him.

Now just before we head off, Jai asks me for four thousand rupees (£45) for fish and other stuff for Hansari. I am a bit pissed off about this. I'm not here to support Hansari. I'm setting up Shakthar. I express my annoyance to Jai. He says Harry will give me the money back. Yeah, right. Harry already owes me fifteen hundred rupees. Anyway, I give him the money. Fucking soft touch!

We reach Hansari, and when Harry turns up, he shakes my hand but doesn't even have the gall to look me in the eye. He has not even texted/messaged me once over the last few days to see how I am. I had spoken to him briefly about how the landlord was being a dick and saying that he needed six and a half lakhs by Tuesday; otherwise, he would throw all the paint away. Anyway, that has not happened.

Harry, however, is being shady as fuck. He does not even sit with me. The three men all sit together on a separate table. This fucks me off severely, and I glare at Jai as if to say, *What the fuck, dude?!* Jai asks what I want for lunch, and I eat my lunch on my own. I can feel the fury brewing inside.

Eventually Harry walks past, and I ask him to come and sit and talk. Jai sits down also, so I ask him to leave us for a few minutes, which he does.

I tell Harry how I've been feeling, pissed off and left alone. He has not even checked if I'm OK. He says he is sorry—that's why he sent Jai. I also request the money he owes me, and he's all sheepish. I ask again so I can get ciggies. He doesn't give me the money, but he does get a packet of cigarettes for me. We talk about how Shakthar is going and how it's my responsibility; he will not get involved. He says that if I want anything, I should come to him direct and not ask Jai. I'm telling you, this guy has the gift of the gab! But I'm onto him!

Anyway, the others join us at our table. We have some dinner. I get a free cocktail, which I've technically I've already paid for. Things seem to be smoothed out.

Harry gets all chatty and tells me a secret. He says he's going to star in a film which he is going to invest in. By the sounds of it, it's an independent film. He tells me about the director and how he made a film with one crore (about £100,000) and made so much back, blah, blah, blah. I smile and look all interested. All the while I'm thinking, *Just wait till I tell Jai.* I get shown a nice dinner plate and the new staff T-shirts for Hansari, which are actually quite nice.

We start heading back to Shakthar at about 9.30 p.m. A half hour into the journey, Jai turns around and asks for petrol money, at which point I'm seething. I am low on cash anyway, which is why I was asking for the four thousand rupees. I say no and have a mini rant, but I don't want to talk in front of Mango, as apparently, he can't hold his water when it comes to gossip (previously Jai said that I had told him that I had a husband in Punjab, which I don't! Why would I say that? I put Jai straight on that one). Anyway, I say we would talk when we got back, Jai and I.

We get back to Shakthar, and I'm still fuming. Jai comes to my room, and I have a rant at him. He's stuck in the middle, but I need to vent and have a little smokeage to chill. I go to wash my face and brush my teeth, but the water runs out. I call Jai as am beyond annoyed. He gets Mango to speak to the landlord to turn the water on. Mango says the landlord is out and can't turn the water on. Jai comes to my room and says he'll get me a bucket of water. I basically slam the door in his face.

The next day I wake up still angry and starving. Queue meltdown day! See above!

I am still annoyed with Jai. Basically, I feel betrayed. I

thought he was my friend. He comes and picks me up from Palm Tree Vista, to where I have retreated. We're still talking, but it's awkward to say the least. I'm generally quiet today, but I try to keep myself busy. I get to know Jalan the housekeeping boy a bit more and help him make up a room for some guests of Harry's who are staying at LOM Shakthar. I'm not sure if anyone else is picking up on the atmosphere. The painting is continuing; the place will look amazing when it's finished. Later I go for lunch with Jai in Obrah. I wander around a couple of places and find an organic beauty spa. I go in to ask for prices, and a young Indian woman comes out. I speak to her about the place and the products and massages they offer. She's a really nice young woman. I tell her I will be working at LOM, and she says she knows it. She owns the spa. Finally, I've met an Indian businesswoman. I say, "We women need to stick together." We exchange numbers, and I say I will pop down soon for a massage. God knows I need it; my neck still hurts. Jai has previously mentioned my hunched shoulders and said if I hunch my shoulders while wearing a one-piece, i.e. a dress, I will look like a lesbian. He's got a way with words, the fucker!

Jai and I go for lunch. It's still awkward, but the frozen atmosphere is slowly thawing. I never do get an apology. Hanu makes a passing appearance. It wouldn't be a night out without his shiny face turning up. We discuss what we need to buy tomorrow. I make a list of what is needed, pillows, bedding, etc.

In the evening we head to Laksara for drinks. Drinking and driving is the norm here. It scares the shit out of me. By the time we head back, the roads are clear, but there's random groups of cows in the roads. The beasts just do not move!

In Laksara we go to Charlie's. It's quite famous apparently. I am sure I have walked past it when I was on holidays the last couple of times. It's a two-storey permanent structure with a terrace section at the top. Inside it is like a dingy techno club with low ceilings and fluorescent scribbles. I like it. We sit on the terrace overlooking the beach. There is something so calming about the sound of the ocean. The moon is high and partially covered by clouds. Drinks are ordered. I have a small kingfisher. Jai has his whisky drink. I still don't know what it is. I need a beer after yesterday and today. It's dark, and there's only candlelight to illuminate our faces. The music is playing, electronic dance stuff, which is good. Loads of small groups of people are sitting round, chilling, having drinks, and smoking shishas.

Whenever we sit at tables, we never sit opposite each other; the opposite seat is always empty. Maybe we need to keep that distance between us. As the night progresses, we chill and chat. Even though we say we won't talk about business, we often end up taking about Harry and what's going on, so I am making a concerted effort not to talk shop. I ask Jai why he said I was weird—just had to. He says it was because Harry was bugging him about transferring the money, adding that if he had meant it, would he really have shown me the text conversation? He asked why I had left by myself the previous morning. I told him that I was hungry, and I didn't want to disturb him just to get breakfast. I think we cleared that up.

Jai says that when he saw me leave, he thought, *Oh shit.* He says that he would not have been happy had I left, but he would have been even more unhappy for Harry, who would have had a Diwali (Festival of Light—firework shows and stuff), which is quite amusing. We talk about general stuff. He asks what qualities I want in a man. I ask, "Physical or personality?" He laughs. I say, "Funny, intelligent, and kind." I don't ask him what he wants in a woman. At times I'm quiet, just taking in the scenery. He asks why I'm I silent. I tell him I don't want to talk just for the sake of talking. He says I should be more normal. I say, "What is that supposed to mean?" He just laughs.

I don't know if I am picking up on anything, but he seems to have moved closer. And with the candlelight and the sound of the ocean, it's the perfect romantic setting.

I ask what he thought when he first saw me. After considering

Harry's history with Maria, he says he thought I was dumb! I mean, what the fuck?! This guy! I ask why. Basically, he thought that Harry had snared me into one of his dodgy deals. I say I'm not dumb, but I accept that I might have been naive. He doesn't know what that means, so I explain that it means sort of innocent, adding that because I believe in the goodness of humanity, I'm taking this risk. He says that Harry keeps saying "my girl" whenever referring to me "My girl" will do this" or "Ask my girl." That's why he had asked me previously if I had dated Harry, which I had say No to.

I talk about taking this risk and not wanting to be in the same job for the rest of my days even though I was damn good at my previous occupation.

He says something and finishes by telling me I look nice with my hair up and wearing glasses. I just say thanks. He looks nice, too, in his jumper, but I don't say anything. This is a business relationship, and after the last couple of days I'm not even contemplating any other kind of relationship. Regardless, there's lots of eye contact, and he lights my ciggies for me.

It's getting late, and I'm getting tired, so we decide to head back. He suggests a smoke and says, "On the beach." I say OK, but then he says that would be very dangerous for him.

I say, "OK, why?" He says that there are some things he will not say. I say, "OK, I'm not nosy!"

We head back to Shakthar, but the roads are blocked. We drive around for ages trying to find the right road. On the way back he suggests I drive. I say, "*No way.*" He says he wants to make sure I am independent, just in case the time comes when he is too drunk, and I have to drive. I reply, "So, I will be your personal taxi service?" I can't tell if he is flirting or not, but I do not entertain the look. Still, he gives me lots of cheeky looks and continues lighting my ciggies.

Eventually we get back to Shakthar. It's late. I don't want a smoke, so we retire to our respective rooms.

Wednesday, 21 September

Having slept like a log, I awake to the top covers being taken down and my room being filled with sunlight. I am starving. After I quickly wash and dress, I go downstairs and ask Jalan where I can get tea. He takes me on his scooter to the bakery in Shakthar Market, but they only do pastries and have no coffee to take away. So, I ask him to take me to Palm Tree Vista. I think the guys there are getting used to me turning up for breakfast with my laptop. I sort out my accountant's invoice from home, and I read an email from Michelle at Kirkham's (my mortgage broker) saying the money should be to me by next week. Excellent news.

I decide to just put the three lakhs into Harry's account even though I still don't have any contract. I know I am being a fool, but I'm too emotionally committed to this project. I've paid my share of the season's rent. Whatever Harry does with it is not my problem. Well, it is! But the place looks good, and the rooms are coming together. I am just praying and keeping faith that it will all work out. Jai turns up to help with the missing info for Harry's account. Over a coffee he tells me that Harry wants him to go to Unjaan to meet him and bring him here, then we head back to LOM.

I go around with Jalan to check the rooms to see what is missing and make a list. Then I potter about for a bit. My balcony view is amazing, looking out over the beach with the Arabian Sea a couple of hundred metres away. I sit and have a ciggie.

I catch up with Jai later on. He says that he and Mango met Harry in Unjaan. Harry took the car from them and sent them back by taxi. Harry was going to Chatu to meet a woman who is going to give him fifty thousand rupees. No one knows who this woman is. Harry will come back and meet us later. He eventually turns up in the car. The three of us go to Anjaru for dinner. Harry talks his usual bullshit, generally wittering on to himself. Jai is quiet during dinner. Harry is insistent on going to Hindavi to get the new furniture we need. I don't see the point in going to Hindavi when we'll have to pay for flights and hotel bills. Jai previously said that Harry expects me to foot the bill for him. No fricking chance!

We get back from dinner and park up. The landlord is waiting for us. Immediately he starts shouting at Harry. Jai tells me to go to my room. I feel like a child being told what to do, but I think he's trying to save me from getting dragged into any arguments. I hear a lot of shouting coming from outside.

Jai texts later to say that there was a fight. I ask, "Did the landlord hit Harry?"

He replies, "No, baba, just lots of shouting from the mouth (LOL). Jai is very much stressed out from all of this. ☹"

The next morning, I wake up and find that it is very quiet outside. I can't hear the painters doing their thing. There are no sounds of Jai, Jalan, or even Mango, who sometimes visits Jai in the morning. Considering the rooms are full, it's deadly quiet. I am a bit concerned, but then I think that maybe rain has called off play and everyone is having a lie-in. I say a little prayer to help resolve this situation; to help Harry, the landlord, and me to make the right choices; and to guide use through this. I get ready and ask Jalan to take me to PTV.

Jalan says that something is going on with Harry and the landlord. The landlord has said painting has to stop. Hence the reason it is so quiet. I try not to think about it. I feel beyond stressed now and conclude that what will be, will be.

I have breakfast at PTV—pancakes, banana, and honey. I am eating too much starchy, sugary stuff. ☹ I am wearing my Nicorette patch—not smoking today.

I try to cancel the international transfer to Harry's account. I can't get through to HSBC, so I send them a message. I will see what happens. I feel like I'm living on blind faith.

I message Yatu about going to the wedding in Kerala and how to get down to Cochin via Hindavi. We have a lovely phone conversation. I haven't spoken to him in so long. I give him a rundown of the situation. He gives an outsider's perspective on the situation and provides a pragmatic view. He messages a lovely saying from his dad: "It's better to try and fail than to sit and dream. Failure is closer to success." I'm definitely trying. We discuss my plans B, C, D, and E.

I do a Facebook catch-up. Dice, the beautiful little rescue kitten, is looking gorgeous. I love her! I watch a panda video on Facebook. I want a panda! :D

I have come to the realisation that I have been extremely stupid in all of this. I have been taken in by Harry and his banter. I don't know anything about him and have taken him at face value. I haven't done any due diligence with regards to background checks. I'm kicking myself over this. Big mistake. But what was I supposed to do? I suppose that maybe I have been dumb and very naive. I've wanted this for so long and so badly that I've been making bad decisions.

From now on, I need to stand my ground. This is not like me! Being away from my real friends and family, it's like I've lost touch with reality and my own perspective. I'm surrounded by people whom I don't know and possibly can't trust. One person is saying one thing, and another person is saying another thing. But one thing is consistent: between Jalan and the painters, and with the landlord having a "Diwali" at Harry, Harry has a habit of not paying his way and not paying back what people are owed. One thing is for sure: the people who work for me will be looked after. They are the ones who will really make this work for me. Without them I cannot do it. I cannot do it alone.

I message Jai to see if he is wake. He is. He asks if I'm at my office (PTV), I say yes. He says there is a meeting happening, adding that he is hungry and hasn't been sleeping because of the stress he's been under about the situation. He also advises me to think properly and not to waste my money. He's a good lad. I appreciate that he is trying to look out for me.

It's lashing down with rain now. I ask Jalan to come pick me up. He is such a sweet lad, too, with a cheeky smile. He says the meeting is still going on and that the landlord wants all his money. He says he knows everything about LOM, including how to top up Wi-Fi and do laundry. I tell him I will need him if things work out. We get soaked riding back on the scooter. Jai is standing around outside LOM, waiting for the meeting to finish, I suppose. He doesn't look happy. I tell him to message me about what's happening. I go to my room.

He was a bit aloof with me at dinner last night, and he was aloof me with again just now. I am not sure how I feel about that.

Now I am just chilling in my room, feeling slightly apprehensive about the meeting that is going on. We'll see what happens. The best option for me would be to buy Harry out. I know it can work if he is not around. Will Jai stick around? I don't know. If all goes pear-shaped, I will go to Kerala, meet Yatu and his friends (some from London and other parts of the UK), and just have fun for a couple of months. I'll enrol in a yoga school and just enjoy myself. Why am I putting myself through this?

Currently it's 2 p.m. on Thursday, 22 September.

This morning I wake up to torrential rain. The heavens have really opened up today. I put on my black hoodie—so glad I brought it with me—and go to breakfast at Arabian Waters on my own. No one was up yet. The painters were starting their day's work. Nice chilly morning, actually. I order breakfast, watch the angry grey Arabian Sea lashing against the grey sand, and listen to some 1980s electronic chill-out tunes. I am really loving "Hey, Little Girl" by Icehouse. There are workers at Arabian Waters building bamboo fencing on the restaurant's terrace. One of them checks me out. I check him out. Nice broad muscly back and shoulders. The guys here are dark-skinned. I think I might like it. ☺ It's a nice way to start the morning.

After breakfast one of the managers comes and sits with me. He is the brother of Munni (a nice guy—we have spoken extensively in Punjabi. They are from the state next to Punjab in North India). He asks the usual questions: "Where are you from? What do your mum and dad do? Do you have brothers? Are they married? Are you married?"

To this last question I reply, "No, I am independent!" I don't stay long after that. The guy creeps me out a little.

I get back to LOM and say hi to the landlord and his daughter. I see their cat, and the daughter says she has had kittens. OMG, kittens! :D I go and see them. *I love kittens!* I show them a picture of my fur baby Lizzie. I don't stay long. Everyone was up by the time I got back to LOM. Harry seems his chirpy self. Jai is grumpy. Jalan is smiley. I feel happy and am back to my usual friendly self. My mood has definitely improved from the last few days. Things are a lot clearer now.

Right, let me give you more updates from yesterday. Around 4 p.m. I was called to see Harry at Arabian Waters. Hmm ... OK! I was pretty much still in the dark as to what had happened with the landlord. Anyway, I sat with Harry, and he started telling me what I needed to do, asking me when I was going to buy the rest of the furniture. I firmly stated my two conditions for moving forward with the situation. I was still pretty much ready to leave following the slanging match between the landlord and Harry.

My two conditions are as follows: (1) Before I buy any furniture or invest any more money, I want a written contract. (2) The three lakhs that I transferred must go to the landlord for this season's rent. If these two conditions are not met, then I cannot see the partnership working.

I stated that for me there are two options: (1) I cut my losses and leave outright. (2) I buy Harry out of the business. (I am not sure if the landlord would agree to this, but I had to say it.) I could see Harry's head whizzing to take all this in. He didn't say anything further about buying any new furniture. Also, I stated it would be advisable for Harry, the landlord, and me to sit down and clear the air. We also discussed how the rent and the profits would be split between the rooms and the restaurant. He babbled on, which confused me. I needed to see things written in black and white. We fleshed out who would pay what and when.

To summarise, my three lakhs will go directly to the landlord once my transfer clears. Then the landlord has agreed that the remaining six lakhs can be paid in instalments over the rest of the season. Three lakhs will come from the restaurant, and three lakhs will come from Harry's share. Any balance/credit that Harry has from the previous endeavour will be cleared by him, independent of this season. This is very important, as I am not here to clear Harry's debt. This seems reasonable to me. I had made it clear to him that I was aware of the situation. The next step for us is to sit with the landlord and ensure he is happy with me. He hasn't even talked to me properly. And then we'll need to draw up the contract. Harry will arrange a meeting with the advocate (a legal person) later this evening and another with the landlord. In general conversation, I told him I was ready to leave last week. I need to keep these guys on their toes. I think they need me more than I need them. At the end of the day I'm the one with the cash, but I will stand my ground. Harry admitted that he has made mistakes and that he is working to fix them, which I appreciate.

After things were cleared, we moved on to chat about Harry's movie career (to my amusement). He stated that his director was coming to Hansari to meet him and arrange a photoshoot. He will be playing a villain in the movie (LOL). He then made several calls to someone to give his height, clothes size, and various other measurements, while standing up, walking around the restaurant, and talking loudly, ha ha ha! This guy does crack me up. :D I have to laugh now. It's just pure comedy! I had lunch and then headed back to my room, leaving Harry to sort out his photo opportunity and five minutes of fame, which he so craves!

Around 6 p.m. I am summoned again, this time to sit and

talk with the landlord. I go downstairs. The landlord is none the wiser as to what is happening. We all sit in the landlord's living room. A small congregation of children have joined us. Harry and the landlord begin to talk in local dialect. I catch the gist of it. Basically, the landlord is pissed because Harry has been avoiding his calls and has been nowhere in sight. The landlord says that this is what caused the tension which resulted in the fight the other night. I nod and agree, saying "Same" to let the landlord know I have been feeling the same way. Harry profusely apologises and says he should have been honest, but he has been working to sort his finances out (I think he's in a lot of debt). I start to feel sort of sorry for him. He's trying his damnedest to fix things—but not on my time and with my money, dude!

We discuss the rent with the landlord. Basically, he wants my three lakhs now (pending international transfer clearance), three lakhs at the end of December, and the final instalment of three lakhs at end of March. I confirm that Harry will pay his outstanding balance separate from this season's money. I write all of this down in my book (meeting minutes, bitches!) and write the same in the landlord's book. We confirm the bills that will need to be paid going forward: electricity, bar licence, restaurant licence, rubbish disposal, Wi-Fi, and a couple of other bits, and who will be responsible. The landlord actually says he is happy that I am here! Results! That is exactly what I want to hear. He is going to be our neighbour, and therefore I want to ensure we set off on the right foot. So, the landlord and his brother are happy. I'm happy, and Harry—well, I think he has resigned himself to the fact that he's not going to get away with his little schemes. He seems positive enough.

At the end of the meeting, Harry pops out with the landlord's brother to show him some work that we'll be doing. The landlord's daughter explains that previously Harry had advised that he was getting three lakhs to clear some of his debt, whereas now he has changed his tune. I nod and say I understand. I still need to watch this fella. Shady as fuck! But no one messes with the Sabitron, aka Madam Boss Lady! Ha ha ha! :D

Later on, I go to Arabian Waters for dinner. I can't be arsed waiting for anyone. It's pissing it down, and I'm wearing a hoodie and trainers. I'm all in black! I have lentil dhal and roti and one kingfisher. The sea is roaring in the darkness. I sit and relax, listening to tunes on my headphones, feeling relieved after today's events. Harry joins me later on and says he can't get a hold of the advocate. I say OK and reiterate the point I'd made earlier. He is still talking about his director. I just laugh at him. He rabbits on. I wonder where Jai is. Half an hour later he appears out of nowhere, looking rather grumpy still. We all sit and chat for a bit about some famous South Indian film star. Jai shows me pics of this star. In real life he's bald as a coot (I don't even know what a coot is), but in films he has a full head of hair. I laugh at the difference. Harry goes off to make a call to some random dude in Dubai. Jai asks what I had for dinner and tells me he's been to Unjaan with Mango. He took Mango to a Mall because he had never been to one before. We talk a little about what's been happening today. I say, "We'll talk more once Harry has left." He's still weird with me when Harry is around. I feel drawn to him. I think it's mutual, although I could be imagining it!

We all leave. Harry is still rattling on about playing the villain. He's leaving for Hansari tomorrow.

It's Friday, 23 September. Harry has left, and Jai is off doing chores. Jalan advises that the electrician and plumber will arrive when the rain stops. The next mini crisis no doubt will happen when Clive the chef arrives. Never a dull moment. I am feeling good, like I'm back to my usual self. My mind is clearer and more focused on the task in hand. I need to start sorting all the bookings and doing other admin stuff. I will do that at the office (PTV) tomorrow.

Chapter 2

MADAM BOSS LADY

It's Saturday, 24 September. I have been here nearly three weeks. I'm starting to pull things together. Harry has gone back to Hansari to meet his director. It was a very miserable day yesterday, the rain lashing down most of the day and into the evening. I was pretty much confined to my room—had a bit of a headache. I think the week's events were taking a toll on me. I tried to sleep it off, but no luck. I was starving and had to get Jai, who was out, to organise takeout for me. I hate having to rely on other people to even feed me. If the weather was OK, I would have gone to PTV, but it was shitty. I got paneer tikka and garlic naan. It was *fit*, and I wolfed it down. I'd ordered chocolate for afterwards. I have not been eating much over the last week because of stress, I imagine. I needed a good feed.

The plumber had arrived to check a leaky pipe but had no keys to get into the room. He felt a bit surplus to requirements.

Jai has returned from his trip to Nimpura and Unjaan to get samples. He has been out most of the day and evening. He has bought some nice stuff, keeping to the white and grey theme. I think we need some colour also, some bright pinks, reds, and blues just to break up the whiteness.

In the evening, Jai and I sit on my balcony to have a

catch-up. I think he's knackered. The fucker takes the piss out of me because I'm new to this and because I don't even know the basics. He's doing my head in. We have a smoke, so my head is a bit frazzled. It is not the nice mellow resin we had previous nights but really old green which was in his wallet.

Clive the chef hasn't arrived yet. Harry keeps saying he's coming in two days, then another two days. Jai offers up some other options if Clive the chef doesn't arrive. I could just run the rooms as a bed and breakfast. But the landlord will still need his remaining six lakhs. I cannot make that just on the rooms. Another option is for me to take up the restaurant. If I do, I want Jai to run it. Even though he is a piss-taker, he will be good at the job. I'm impressed with him in terms of his work history and design ideas, and obviously he ran the place before, so he has the experience. He says he's not sure what he is doing or what is going to happen. However, if I finance the restaurant, I know he can make it great. He'll have sole responsibility. I'll need to come up with the three lakhs' rent and give him a cut of the profits, obviously. He wants 10–12 per cent of the profits. And I think he is emotionally committed to making it work. He doesn't seem to be the type of guy to just walk away. But we'll see.

I would need to see the numbers on how much investment is needed. This morning he said about £2,000. Time is short to make an impact on the start of the season; there's only a week left until the start of October. I am seriously thinking about this but will need to make the decision fast. Luckily, I have the money to invest. But I haven't said anything to Jai. I've just made faces! I'm sure he would be seeing pound signs in his eyes if I were a bit more open.

The landlord pulled me aside again earlier this morning. He is feeling a lot more comfortable with me, I think, and I am feeling more comfortable with him. It's important to have a good relationship with him. One of his daughters translated, but I got the gist of what he was saying. They reiterated that I should watch out for Harry. I need to check to see if the bank transfer went through. If Harry doesn't give the landlord that money, I will seriously lose my shit at him.

Jai also mentioned that the contract should state who will keep the items according to what that they have invested. For example, I will keep all the light fittings if I leave LOM. Good point.

So, the next morning I message Harry about Clive the chef. I also message and phone Clive the chef myself. I receive no answer to either.

If I want this to work—and goddam I do, even if it kills me—I need to fund the restaurant.

I speak to the other landlord's daughter. She is the receptionist at a hotel (OMG. I know her from Harry's brother's antics). She says she knows a Russian woman who runs a Chatter group which recommends places in Goa. I ask her to contact the Russian woman and get me an introduction. She says she will phone the woman. It's nice just to speak to women. I'm surrounded by men all day. I am missing my girlfriends at home.

The electrician is coming today, and hopefully we will have Wi-Fi. God! I am feeling a bit isolated from the outside world. What did we do before social media?

I have moved out of the big room on the third floor to a smaller room on the second floor. It's cosy, but it has no curtains. The third-floor room is going to get painted. I want to get one floor complete at least. It's all bitty at the moment. The ground floor hasn't even been started yet. I need to start moving stuff out of the storeroom and into another room.

Jai has come back with a sample of the Light of Moon business card. It looks good. I need to know the cost. I also need to start with the building of the step for the office (the current storeroom). Fuck! So much to do!

It's now Monday, 26 September. I have a few days to catch up on. Work has been progressing. One room is nearly ready with new lights having been fitted and new bedding having been put on bed, with just the curtains to go up. I am recycling an existing pair as they fit in with the colour scheme. I have a discussion with Jai about adding a splash of colour because at the moment it's just white and grey. Jai says that all hotels are simple, just one or two colours. However, I don't want just a standard style. I want some character to the rooms by adding some coloured cushions and accessories. I am Madam Boss Lady after all. We both agree we like purple. But Jai has done a really good job.

OK, just to recap on events from last Friday through to the weekend.

On Friday evening, we sat out on my balcony to catch up on what's been happening and to talk about what is going to happen. It was like our end-of-day rundown. We were chilling with drinks and smokes, and Jai was taking the piss out of me. I also got some more juicy gossip and a lot of the backstory regarding Harry, Harry's wife Jasmine, Jai, and his previous escapades. So, there used to be a gang of lads who all worked at LOM in previous seasons. They all hung out and partied as lads do. Jai also sheepishly said he was with someone at the time. Harry had met Jasmine when she was doing her yoga training. And as yoga mostly involves nubile females, Jai became friends with Jasmine also. At the time Harry was dating another woman, but he ditched her to go out with Jasmine. This other woman then ended up going out with the owner of Glamour, the swanky place down the road. The owner is married, and both this new woman and his wife got pregnant at the same time. So, Harry has a very personal grudge against this guy. I had wondered why Harry kept slagging off the owner of Glamour, saying he's a nasty man and that his wife is a horrible woman. This stuff just gets better and better. :D

I swear, people have this idea that India is full of high morals, but Goa, fricking hell, is on a whole other level. I love it! :D

Now, Jasmine. I haven't met her yet. I am looking forward to meeting her and getting to know her side of the story and how she and Harry got together. I had messaged her over the summer when I was in contact with Harry. She seems like a lovely young woman. Jai says she's really sweet but a bit like a baby. I don't understand what that means as she's a grown woman in her forties! :o Harry is thirty-five or thereabouts. Jasmine is of Middle Eastern heritage. I think she was born in the United States, and the family are originally from Egypt. She had spent about twelve years in London. Over the summer both she and Harry, along with their baby, were in Abu Dhabi. Her father was pretty wealthy and had bought houses in all the countries they lived in. He passed away recently. So, from the sounds of it, Jasmine has led a pretty sheltered life without a want in the world. Jai says Jasmine and Harry have a pretty strange relationship, considering they are man and wife. When Harry was staying with Jai in Hindavi, Jai never heard or saw any phone calls between them. I am so intrigued by this whole situation. And there is another factor to consider in all of this: the child! How will this affect the dynamic? It's going to be exciting to watch.

Jai also mentioned another couple from back in the day. An older woman in her fifties, covered in piercings and tattoos, was going out with a twenty-five-year-old. She rents the small house at the back of LOM. OMG, I can't wait to meet all these people. :D

Jai and I ended up chatting till the early hours again. I chucked him out and went to sleep.

Saturday, 24 September

Work at LOM continues, and the day goes smoothly enough. I am feeling restless. I need to get out as I have been pretty much confined to LOM for a couple of days. The weather is still not great; it's grey and overcast.

Over lunch Jai and I discuss options for what to do if Clive the chef doesn't arrive. We agree that I would take up the restaurant and bar and Jai would run it. My only condition is that Jai would run the show, and all I would want is the three lakhs to pay the landlord. He would be his own boss, which is what he wants. We mull over the numbers briefly and leave it at that. One thing about Jai is that he's very impatient and focuses on the negative. I try to have faith. But Clive the chef hasn't even been in touch. Neither has Harry. No surprise there.

We discuss plans for later on.

So, it's Saturday night. I want to go out. We decide to go to Charlie's in Laksara. The landlord takes us in his taxi (Harry has taken the car). It's busy, and we can't get a table outside. We sit inside, and it's not as romantic as last time, which is fine with me. It's a lot busier today, and dance music is playing loudly. I am really liking this place. We order drinks. While I check my messages, we sit in silence. I decide just to stick to vodka today as I don't want to get bloated. The measures here come in three sizes, thirty millilitres, sixty millilitres, and ninety millilitres. I get the sixty millilitres with soda and lime. Jai gets his usual Blenders Whisky (I now know his brand). We chat about Harry but then decide it's time to relax and not talk shop. Jai seems a bit quiet, but then the conversation starts getting easier as we relax. We talk about personal stuff and relationships. He asks personal questions again. I tell him I will talk in a general sense but not give specifics.

As the drinks flow, so does the conversation. We end up talking about sex as one does! He says something to the effect of, if something were to happen between us (me and him), it shouldn't affect our working relationship. I tell him nothing is going to happen. And even if it did, I am not a stupid teenager who would get all gooey and possessive. I tell him that the fact that he said "if something were to happen" means that he is attracted to me. He laughs. I ask him what his pulling techniques are, he states, "basically, I start asking personal questions, which steers the conversation towards sex". Hmm …

I think I'm getting pulled here. The guy is smooth to say the least. I ask him if he's ever been in love. He says yes, with his first girlfriend at college. He talks about marriage and how he's getting pressure from family to get hitched as he will be thirty next year. I tell him my advice is to do whatever makes him happy. Life is short. I tell him that even though I am proud of my Indian heritage, I do not let it define me as a person. I enjoy talking to him, and I think he gets what I'm talking about. We're getting to know each other.

I ask him why he is weird with me when Harry is around. He says that he doesn't want Harry to know that we're close. Harry gets jealous and may try to mess things up.

At the next table a young Indian woman is absolutely mortalled. She can't walk or even stand up. Her friends are trying to fix her, but she is too far gone. While Jai is in the washroom, one of the lads at the table starts to talk to me. He asks where I'm from, then says something about my eyes. He backs off as soon as he sees Jai sit down at the table. The lad apologises and leaves, but intermittently as he is walking past, he gives me a look. I just smile politely.

By now, I'm getting a bit tipsy, and the music is getting to me. A young woman walks past and puts flyers for a bar/club on the table. We each take one and see it's just a five-minute walk away. Jai asks if I want to go. I say we could check it out. He says I might not like it. We have another drink and then decide to go. We're both merry now, any thoughts of shop having been dropped a few hours ago.

The UV Bar is a small place with a bar and a dance floor. It's not packed, but there are people standing at the bar. Some of them are throwing "big fish, little fish" shapes even though it's raining. The music is pretty hard techno stuff. And I can see a few gurning faces. It's weird seeing mostly Indians off their tits, ha ha! :D

A random guy walks past with some UV paint. He paints the arm of a young woman who is sitting at the bar. I want to be painted. I ask him to paint my leg. Jai says the guy is lucky to paint my leg. Jai is laughing at me, but he likes my leg paint and takes a picture.

It's loud, so we have to get pretty close to talk to each other. As I'm a happy drunk, I want to give Jai a hug just coz he's been looking out for me and making sure I'm OK. He's tall and generously built, and I have to reach up to put my arms around him. It's nice to have a big, strong hug. He kisses me on the cheek.

I feel like getting close to him.

Some other guys try to dance with me, including an older guy. We call him "Uncle". Then these other weirdos start chatting with us. Jai is telling them about LOM. I say to Jai that we make a good team. I attract them, and he gives them the spiel. I kiss Jai on the cheek but say I will not kiss him properly. I have to keep saying this to him, and he says I'm making him crazy.

I will not kiss him. Coz if I do, I won't be able to hold back. I will not kiss him! I will not kiss him!

Fuuuuckkk! I kissed him!

The next morning is now officially Goa hangover #1. I wake up late, and the electrician is on his way. Out of the blue, Clive the chef calls. I'm still pissed, so I am super happy to hear from him. He says he's been stuck in Gandabaan and has been shopping for provisions for the restaurant. He is going to Hansari and then will be coming to Shakthar in a couple of days.

I quickly wash and get dressed for the electrician. Jalan takes me downstairs to meet him. We do a walk-around of the jobs that need doing and point out where the new lights are to be fitted in the sample room (currently Jai's room).

I'm fading and am feeling sick. I go to Arabian Waters for breakfast. I'm bored of that place now, but it's only a minute away.

The electrician goes away to get parts, and then when he returns, Jai takes over showing him where to fit the new lights.

I go to my room to lie down. I still feel sick, but I can't sleep. So, I get showered and get Jalan to take me to PTV so I can check my Internet stuff. I check my account and see that the three lakhs have cleared my account. The money is now with Harry, who needs to give it to the landlord. Let's see how that goes.

I message Dave back at home and pressure him to come out to Goa. He's seriously thinking about it.

Jalan comes to pick me up again to go back to LOM. Little sweetheart, he is.

After a little nap in the evening, I wake up to the sound of voices. Everyone is in Jai's room. The electrician is nearly finished, and Jai has put out the sample new bedding. It really does look like a proper hotel bedroom now. It's lovely, in fact. The landlord, his brother, some kids, Jalan, the electrician, and Jai are all there. I'm the only female. They all stand around talking in the local dialect. I can understand bits and bobs. Strangely, I didn't know any of these people three weeks ago, but now it's like they're turning into an extended family. A short while after they all leave, it's just me and Jai in the room. We take some pictures of the room to send to Harry.

I don't feel uncomfortable, and there doesn't seem to be any awkwardness between us considering the previous night. We're cool, and I'm happy about that. I'm glad we got closer and that it's our little secret. I think it will help in that if Jai feels closer to me, then he'll look out for me even more and have my best interests at heart.

Later, Jai asks Jalan to get pizza and garlic naan bread for us. We chill in my room and have a little smoke to take the edge off the hangover. He is wearing the most hideous vest top, all pink and yellow swirly patterns. It hurts my eyes to look at it. I ask him if it's a woman's top, ha ha! ☺ We chat, eat, and listen to music, and then I send him off to his room. I need to sleep!

This morning I wake up and go to Nimpura with Jai and the landlord. We need to get more paint. I need cash. I go to the bank to see if I can open an account. it seems I cannot open an account; one of the visa conditions is that I cannot exceed my visa by 180 days, which is six months. I need to try another bank. We go for breakfast, and I tell Jai off. Earlier he came up to me and said, "Give me six thousand rupees for the paint." I didn't like his tone. I know he has no bad intentions; it's just the way they all speak. But I want to be spoken to with a bit of decorum. He said, "Sorry, boss," and "Why do girls make a thing of these things?" I will teach him. Ha ha! I don't think he likes to admit when he is wrong. A little please and a thank you goes a long way.

He is still wearing the hideous top. My attraction to him is waning. Ha ha!

At lunchtime we hang out in his room, and then we go sit on the balcony. The landlord is giving him stick because he needs the three lakhs to pay some of his bills. He cancelled a ticket to Hindavi because Harry won't answer our calls and we don't know when he'll get here.

Jai says the landlord told him that I should just take up the place. We discuss the contractual implications. From a financial perspective, it's doable for me. But it's still a lot of money, and it means a bigger commitment. However, if I want to make money out of running LOM, I won't get a serious return until next season. I will think about it. I will only do it if Jai sticks around to run the restaurant side. I cannot do that myself.

I also make a fuss about being asked to pay for Jasmine's scooter that is in the garage, which needs to be paid for. I say No. It's that bloody Harry asking Jai to ask me. He says it's a company scooter. So fricking what? It's not mine, and I can't even ride the thing. I'd rather buy a nice little car. I'm not paying for it. Also, the cost of new mattresses works out to be about £250 each. Fuck that! That's high even by UK standards. I am stamping my foot down now.

I wish Jai wouldn't wear that hideous top. I might have to borrow it and burn it accidently on purpose.

It's now Wednesday, 29 September, and the craziness ensues. But first, here's a little recap of the last couple of days:

On Monday evening Jai and I went to dinner at the Tiki Bowl in Obrah. I didn't want to dress up, but I did want to go out, so I kept it neat and casual. We didn't have a car, so we went on a scooter. The night was cool, and it wasn't raining. I love being a passenger on a scooter, feeling the wind in my hair and just watching the scenery go by. Jai pointed out a few places of interest.

There is Wi-Fi at the Tiki Bowl, so I spent the first half hour catching up on messages. We both sat in silence on our phones. The place was empty; we were the only ones in there. It was nice and relaxing with the sounds of crickets and other night creatures. Jai was getting bitten by mozzies. For whatever reason, the mozzies had been laying off me for the last week or so. Maybe they were bored of my blood. Fine with me! :D

We ordered food, and the hot and sour soup was nice, but the spring rolls were not crispy. Jai didn't like his soup. We talked about general stuff, just chilling while enjoying each other's company. After finishing dinner, we headed back. Conversation on a scooter is not the best, but we talked about Saturday night. I said I had no regrets. He didn't either.

It was late, but we hung out in my room for a while. He knows I'm writing a diary, so he asked if he could read some. I reluctantly cut and paste a couple of paragraphs for him to read. Obviously, he features heavily, so I didn't want to show too much, as it's my personal account of my experience so far and how I felt at the time. I let him read the "Official Meltdown" extract and the first few introductory paragraphs. The Official Meltdown includes the "she is weird" message episode and how I was feeling: "I am feeling all alone! I can't trust anyone, even people who make out to be my friends!" He again said that wasn't true, the "I can't trust" comment. I said it's OK, as we have moved on since then.

He didn't say much other than "It's "good." We were lying on my bed while he read. He skinned up, and shortly after he asked if he could stay back, i.e. stay in my room with me. I feel close to him, and I know he feels close to me, but I wasn't sure. I didn't want to get into the habit of sleeping together. I know myself, and if we continue, my feelings for him will grow! He went to his room but messaged me, saying that he didn't want to just leave me alone and that he only wanted to hug and sleep. He came back, and we hugged and slept.

In the morning, I woke up early. I woke him up and told him he needed to go to his room. It won't be good for either of us if people start talking. I am Madam Boss Lady, and it will affect how people see me. Jai doesn't want to be the talk of the town either. Plus, the secrecy makes it all the more exciting and erotic.

I went to PTV for breakfast. Jalan took me on the scooter. I got cash to buy stuff for the plumber. Jai went with the landlord to Nimpura. He completely blew the money I gave him. FFS!

Around midday, Harry, Clive the chef, and another dude, Karan, arrived at LOM from Hansari. I showed them around the newly decorated room and the rest of the rooms. Harry seemed suitably impressed. We all went to Arabian Waters for tea. But Clive and Karan wanted beer. We hung out there for a bit. Jai joined us.

My first impressions of Clive? He looks Nepalese, but says he is half Indian, half Chinese and that he is from a Christian background. He seems nice enough.

Karan is one of Harry's friends. He's from Lebanon. He's out here to set up something with Harry. (Oh dear God, how can we warn him?!) He's a bit of a fittie, and obviously nothing is going to happen. He's friendly and chatty.

Harry was being his usual bullshitting self and tried to be the big man with Karan and Clive.

When Jai and the landlord arrived, it kicked off again with Harry and the landlord. All the family seemed to be involved—the landlord, his brother, and the old woman. I could hear the shouting from the side balcony but could not make out what was actually being said. But I heard something to the effect of "Leave here," along with "Dubai this" and "Dubai that". Apparently, the last fight involved Harry going on about his life in Dubai and Hindavi. The landlord wasn't impressed. He had said to me during our one-to-one chat that if Harry loves Dubai so much, he should go and live there and get away from here.

Jai told me to go to my room again. I think he just didn't want me to become involved or get dragged into the shouting. Like a good little obedient Miss Money Bags, I went to my room, but still listened from my balcony.

Later, after the shouting subsided, I was invited to hang out with the boys on the new room's balcony. I got invited as an afterthought, and only because Jai had said something. I asked what was happening for dinner; it was already eight-ish in the evening. We chatted, drank, and listened to music on my Bluetooth speaker. Clive was sharing some of the food items he had brought with him, fish and beef snacks, and they stank! Gross. Clive was pissed! I chatted with Karan about music, London, and his background. He is Christian too.

Harry was intermittently dishing out his wisdom and talking about the progress of his movie career and photo shoot. I asked him about what happened downstairs. He said that the landlord is now a bad guy and has become greedy for money. I nodded but didn't say anything. Jai was in the corner, chatting with Karan.

Later, around 10.30 p.m., we headed out to Anjaru for dinner. We went to Angel, where Jai had taken me that first time. Clive was sitting next to me talking shit. He kept calling me Lady Diana! Ha ha! What the fuck? She was killed in a car accident. I don't want to fall to the same fate, however unlikely. I told him he is the weirdest man I have ever met and that he is rude.

My food arrived, and I was starving. I hadn't eaten since breakfast twelve hours prior, apart from a few peanuts on the balcony earlier. I had ordered veg momos, which are little steamed pastry parcels. Clive asked if he could have one. I said yes. He proceeded to feed my precious momo to the beach dog beside him. I was fricking annoyed but tried to keep the lid on my temper, with only a "Jeez, you fed it to the dog!" I finished my food and turned my back to him. The others were sitting round on their phones.

Karan wanted weed, so one of Jai's acquaintances turned up, a big black dude! Clive muttered something racist about black people. I was really not liking this guy now but decided to reserve judgement until tomorrow, after he had sobered up. Karan went off with the black dude and came back a bit worse for wear and didn't say anything for the rest of the evening.

Jai messaged a little hello from across the table. Cute! ☺ I told him I was annoyed with Clive coz he gave my food to the dog! He got the brunt of my temper most of the time.

We started to head back to the car to get back to LOM. On the way, we lost Clive. Harry said, "Fuck it. Leave him. It's his life!" So, we just left him there. :D Ha ha!

Once we got back to LOM, Clive had the key to his and

Karan's room. I can't make this shit up! Karan was out of it. We didn't know what he'd smoked. Harry, Jai, and Karan all crashed out in the other room.

It's Wednesday, 28 September. I wake up and go to the office for breakfast. I'm still starving from last night. I treat myself to paratha. It is lush; I need it. Bloody Internet connection is shit.

Jalan comes to pick me up as I have been summoned by Harry to Arabian Waters. I get there, and there are two other random Indian dudes sitting with Harry, Jai, and Clive. Clive doesn't even acknowledge me. Yep, still weird. Harry asks if the money has been transferred. I say yes as it's gone from my account. I confirm the account number. Alarm bells are ringing! I had no issue with moving money to Jai's account to buy all the samples, etc.

Harry starts wittering on with himself as he does and is holding court with his friends. I'm the only female again. I don't interact much, as I don't know who these guys are. I'm just glad Jai is here.

The two new random Indian dudes are some Bollywood film director and some politician from what Harry says. Jai and Clive leave to discuss restaurant/kitchen stuff. We all chat about some South Indian actor. I am not really interested, but I join in on the conversation. Karan turns up with Clive and Jai, and then Harry, the two random Indian dudes, and Jai leave.

I acknowledge Clive and ask how he's feeling. He says he's fine but doesn't even look up. Yep, still rude! I chat with Karan a bit and then leave. I am so bored of these guys, to be honest. I just want to chill out with Jai.

I go back to my room just to get some space. I knock on Jai's door, and when I open it, I see he's lying on his bed. I ask about the plumber, and he says we'll deal with it later. He puts on a top, and then we go to my balcony. He starts saying that Clive was trying it on with me and that Harry said something about me in their language. Jai had replied to them that I wouldn't do what they were suggesting and that I wouldn't put up with it. Who the fuck do they think I am? Harry really doesn't give a shit about anyone but himself.

Also, today Harry had also asked Jai to arrange for girls for the two Indian guys. I am dumbfounded. Jai said he said no. Basically, Harry was asking Jai to pimp some girls. I haven't mentioned this before, but I am sure Jai said that Harry spent a brief period in Hindavi as a pimp. *Who the fuck am I mixed up with?!*

We order lunch via Jalan, and Jai goes back to his room. I chill on the balcony, mulling things over. There's still tension with the landlord, and we cannot do any other work without his permission.

I call Jai when lunch arrives. He comes back in with some A4 sheets of paper. It's a copy of the official contract between Harry and the landlord. I read it, and it gives the outline of the terms. Point 11 mentions that permission is needed from the landlord for any works to be carried out. Point 16 says that three months' notice needs to be given for the termination of the contract. I don't know why Jai has given me this. And it's seriously fucking with my head.

I need to get out! The walls seem like they are closing in on me. I go to Arabian Waters, order a kingfisher, and hide on the beach for a couple of hours. I'm smoking too many cigarettes. The beach dogs keep me company and want me to pet them. Two of the dogs take turns trying for my affections. I put my headphones on and try to block out everything. The beach is quiet. Two men are walking their cow with big horns on the beach. A couple of people are horse riding. A random guy walks past, and the beach dogs start barking at him. The dogs are protecting me at least.

The sun is bright orange in the sky, and it's beautiful, shining over the calm sea. I say a little prayer. The beauty of this world is amazing.

I think about Lizzie, and it makes me cry. I tell one of the dogs I have a fur baby at home, saying that she is my Queen. I'm missing her so much. The dog seems to understand. I look into the dog's old eyes and ask him what he has seen. All he wants is love and affection. He just wants me to pet him.

I swear, animals are more honest about their emotions than humans. I feel more comfortable with these beach dogs than I do with most people

I head back to my room. Karan is at Arabian Waters by himself. I say hi, but I can't be arsed making conversation. I get back to my room and have a little snooze.

While I am in the shower, Jai knocks on my door. I poke my head around the corner, and he says he has given the landlord the cheque from Harry for the three lakhs. He has sorted it! He says they (all the men) are going out, and it would be better if I were just to ask Jalan to get me some dinner. I say, "Fine. I don't want to talk to anyone anyway."

I don't want to be around the type of men who think women are commodities. It makes me sick to the stomach. I don't want to be here. I want to go home!

I ask Jalan to go get me dinner, two kingfishers, a packet of fags, and some crisps and chocolate. He is such a sweetheart and restores my faith a little bit.

Jai texts and calls to make sure I'm OK. He says, "Don't be angry please, madam. It doesn't suit you." I don't know how to take this. Am I not allowed to be angry and upset?! He thinks he's not being a good friend to me. But I tell him I'm not angry at him. He is so sweet and kind to me.

The next day I wake up refreshed. It's a new day, and the weather is lovely. I go to the office (PTV) for breakfast. The network is horrendous—keeps hanging! I try to make Jai a little bit richer by transferring money, but I don't think it's working. He has been using his own money to buy things. I need to sort his money as he isn't even getting paid and is using his family's money. His mum is calling him to ask what is happening.

He arrives at the office to come pick me up. The Internet banking site is still hanging! The money for the three lakhs' rent is out of my account, but Harry is still saying it's not in his account. Hmm, I'm not sure what to make of this.

Jai orders breakfast. We chat about general things that are happening at LOM. I say sorry to him, apologising for having taken my anger out on him. We're good! He tells me about last night's boys' night out. He says that the two Indian guys are not a director and a politician; they are drug peddlers or something like that, and they were wanting to get cocaine and "brown sugar". I can't believe what I'm hearing. I clarify: "Brown sugar as in heroin?" He says yes. I am gobsmacked. I make him promise me that he will never get involved with anything like that.

He says, "Nah, baba!" and promises me. And how dare Harry bring that kind of people to LOM? There are families and small children around. I'm in shock!

Jai also explains that Clive the chef doesn't have any money to invest in the restaurant. I cannot run the rooms without a restaurant. I won't be able to make the full year's rent without a restaurant.

The best option would be for me to fund the restaurant and, after all expenses are paid, keep the profits. We had briefly discussed this before.

I get back to LOM, and I go to meet Harry at Arabian Waters. He's sitting with Clive the chef and Karan. I ask Harry if I can have a word in private. After he finishes his breakfast, we sit in my room. I explain that as an option, I can fund the restaurant, as he is in financial difficulties and as Clive cannot invest. He says that everything's OK, saying he is getting money (from God knows where). We leave it at that with nothing really resolved.

We all go downstairs. I bid a casual farewell to the "director" and his jangly jewellery with a limp handshake. He is wearing more jewellery than most women I've seen. Indian guys are so lame when it comes to a handshake—just comes across as feeble. It's not like they're going to catch cooties or anything. Or maybe I'd be catching cooties from them. Yuk! The "politician" walks past without saying a word. Good riddance to the pair of them.

A random black dude with dreads walks out of LOM. I glare at him and just say hi.

As Harry is about to leave, he and Jai have a heated discussion. Jai later says that if I hadn't have been there, he would have ripped Harry a new one. But as Jalan and I were watching from the side-lines, he kept his composure. He should have ripped Harry a new one!

I go back to Arabian Waters. Karan and Clive are there. I say to Karan, "Was he not meant to leave with Harry?"

He says, "Yes."

I tell him they left for Hansari ten minutes ago. What's up with this, Harry?! He keeps leaving his people behind. In the end Jalan drops Karan off at an agreed meeting spot in Thairi.

With Karan gone, Jai has joined us. I leave Jai and Clive the chef to discuss all matters of the restaurant. I get myself a bottle of water and chill on the beach for a while. I look back a couple of times and see that Clive is very animated. Jai will let me know the score later.

So later on, Jai and I hang out on my balcony. He lets me know what's happening with Clive. Clive is essentially penniless and cannot fund the restaurant, which is what we suspected. Jai explains what Clive has said to me. So, I can hear it for myself, we go to Clive's room for a meeting. Harry has basically told Clive a bunch of lies about the whole set-up. Surprise, surprise! Harry has told him that he has funded all the work that is happening. I put Clive straight! He is dumbfounded. He cannot believe it's muggins here who has already paid out something in the region of six lakhs, including rent.

I can't remember the full details of the discussion, but I know we decided that if the restaurant is to work, I will fund it and cut Harry out. I explain that I have already proposed this option to him. Clive and I shake hands (his handshake is not feeble) to commit to his working with me. Jai is sitting and listening. We agree we will go to Hansari tomorrow to have a meeting with Harry.

So that's the plan of action!

I go back to my room and create a template for the October 2016 season's room rates. It looks good on LOM letterhead. I will send this tomorrow to the couple enquiring about the second weekend in October. Yay, my first booking! :D

In the evening I'm feeling a bit wired! I just want to get out of my head. All this scheming and the coup attempts are just too much for my little brain. I just need some light relief. Jai, Clive, and I hang out on Clive's balcony. I'm drinking and smoking too much. Jai goes off somewhere in the car. He says he has a business meeting. Hmm, at this hour? Clive and I chat about general shit and talk about Harry.

Jai comes back, and he's a bit smiley. I wonder what he has been up to. It transpires that he went to get smokeage. We chat about going partying, the three of us. But the chef isn't up to it. The beers are making me a little sleepy, but I still feel a bit hyper. I need to do something not work related. I and Jai decide to go to the beach. I'm glad Clive doesn't want to come.

It's pitch-black now. Jai and I walk through the overgrown bushes to the beach behind LOM, Jai lighting the way with his phone. We sit on a rock and chat. I tell him how the beach dogs were keeping me company yesterday when I had to retreat. One of the dogs comes to say hello to us. I say that animals sense things about human emotions. I give the example of the one time I awoke from a bad dream and was upset and crying, and Lizzie came up to my face and put her face to mine. I miss her so much, my little fur queen.

We don't stay long, as something is biting Jai's bum. We go back to my room and smoke the joint. We're sitting on the floor of the balcony, and Harry phones. He's been calling Jai almost every half hour most of the day. Jai says he's freaked about what's happening. He tells me that I had upset Harry about the whole restaurant debacle and because I hadn't offered him any of the profit from the restaurant. FFS, it's a business, not a charity.

Later, sitting on my bed, Jai tells me about when he went to see the numerologist (a psychic of some sort), who told him about his future and marriage. The numerologist told him that if he were to have an arranged marriage, it would not work. It would end up in divorce, and the would not live beyond the age of thirty-two. I just listen. This is quite intimate stuff he is telling me. I'm not sure why he is sharing it with me. Is he trying to tell me something? I don't know.

It's late again, and I'm very tired and stoned. Jai stays back. This guy is too much!

In the morning, I awake up from a restless night at sunrise. There are still no curtains in my room. I wake Jai and throw him out to go to his room before anyone else wakes up. I manage to get around three hours' more sleep. After waking again and showering, I go to Arabian Waters for breakfast. I'm starving again. Again, I had no dinner last night.

Harry phones to say someone is trying to contact me about a booking. I call the person back. Halfway through the phone call, my credit runs out. I try to find Jalan, but he's gone to Nimpura as he has a bad eye. The landlord ends up taking me to Shakthar Market to charge my phone. He also requests the ten thousand rupees for the electric bill. He is going to Hindavi later. He shows me the undated cheque Harry has given him and says he has been to the bank and there is no money in the account. He's getting psyched.

The landlord also collars Clive the chef, and they have somewhat of a heated conversation about Harry. I text Jai to tell him and to ask him to come back from wherever he's gone off to. The landlord says he wants to slap Harry. Clive advises him not to. Ha ha! I can't help chuckling to myself, but I keep a straight face.

Harry phones again and says the money is still not in his account. He also explains that he was upset that I had said that

I would take all the profit from the restaurant, and that I had hurt his heart. I apologise and say that was not the intention, adding that it was only an option. He says he can get money from other sources, namely Jasmine, if he needs it. I say OK. He tells me to check the money transfer. I said I will.

There is no Internet at Arabian Waters. My dongle isn't working. FFS! What's up with this place?

Jai, Clive, and I head to the office (PTV) to try to get access there. The Internet is working but is very slow. Eventually I am able to speak to someone at HSBC International, who is based in Hyderabad (India). I call a UK number, and they put me through to an Indian call centre. Fortunately, I had put one thousand rupees on my phone recharge. The guy explains that HSBC have been trying to contact me as they have queries regarding the transfer. He says they left me voicemail. I can't access VMs here. He advises that the money has left my account but is pending queries from HSBC India, where the money is currently sitting. I answer the queries and request the money be transferred ASAP.

So, it's not Harry's fault after all. The money is stuck in HSBC India. I'm assuming it's down to security purposes within international banking. Security is high in India since the Hindavi terrorist attack about ten years ago.

I phone Harry back and let him know. I also tell the landlord once we get back to LOM. He seems to be placated. I explicitly tell him it's not Harry's fault. For all of Harry's faults, I don't want to apportion blame where it's not warranted.

Another head fuck of a day!

We get back to LOM, and there's a flurry of activity. The restaurant is being cleared out by Jalan (on his own). Some old dude with wonky eyes and his chubby companion have turned up to look at reupholstering some of the furniture. They cannot negotiate a good price, so the wonky-eyed man and his chubby friend leave in a huff.

The plumber has been and has fitted new showerheads.

Some are not flush with the wall, so I'm not happy about that. That's one of the things that I hate—untidy workmanship. I show Jai, and he has a go at Jalan for not telling the plumber about the caps that fit over the wall bracket thing. The plumber will come back tomorrow to finish.

My head is done in, so I go hide in my room for a bit and play my music loudly. Jai knocks on my door and pretends to tell me off.

Jai has been doing some wheeling and dealing of his own. He has been to see a place in Obrah, the next beach down from Shakthar. The next day he takes me and Clive to look at the place. There's a large bar and dining area, and a hillside to build shacks. Initially he'll build a handful, but there is the potential to build up to forty huts up the hillside in terraces. I'm not sure if he wants to take this place on his own for this season or if he wants to take it with Harry. Jai is stressed because the landlord of this place needs some money up front.

We also see another place called Home. It's a large complex of beach huts overlooking the beach. Originally it must have looked really nice, but the owner has not maintained it. It's rough around the edges with a hideous gold mermaid statue as you approach, which for me is wrong on so many levels. There's another statue, a six-foot-high Buddha. The owner wants to sell it for three crores (three million rupees, or £300,000). Apparently, according to Jai, Harry loves this place.

When we come back, we all retreat to our respective rooms to de-stress. Later I get showered, and then we all hang out on Clive's balcony. Jai joins me and Clive later. We listen to tunes and eat another very late dinner brought to us by Jalan.

Jai takes a call and speaks with a soft voice. I don't know if he is dating anyone. We're not exactly dating. I don't know what we are. I feel a bit melancholy. We listen to Justin Timberlake's "What Goes Around ... Comes Around". I mentioned a few days ago that I like this song. I can feel myself become introverted;

I don't say much. Jai, when Clive isn't around, asks why I am silent. I say I am tired, which I am.

Jai's head is fucked from everything. My head is fucked from everything. Clive is lucky that he's not committed to anything. He can walk away without losing a bean.

I've had enough. I leave and go to bed. But I can't sleep. Jai knocks on my door to get his smokes left in my room from the night before. Then he leaves A few minutes later my phone buzzes. It's Jai. He's really stressed, poor guy. I want to create some distance between us, but I can't leave him in his room all stressed. He comes back to my room.

We start to talk about why he's stressed. Harry has been pestering him pretty much nonstop for the last couple of days, talking about new places he wants Jai to invest in, which Jai doesn't want to do, not with Harry anyway. Jai also says that he hadn't expected we would get so close. Neither had I. He asks why I had said on the very first night we went to Charlie's that he was like my brother. He tells me that it has been playing on his mind. I don't remember saying it, but I surmise it might have been to create some distance between us. It didn't exactly work out that way.

I don't know what's happening with us. I am trying not to get attached. I really don't understand how we got to this point. Never in a million years had I expected to meet someone pretty much in my first week of being here. It's not just a physical thing. I can't explain it; it's like we're drawn towards each other. I really care about him, and I know he cares about me. Even on that first road trip to Hansari, I felt completely comfortable with him. I can be myself with him. I don't feel apprehensive about sharing my feelings or showing my emotions with him, which is not like me at all. I'm usually very closed off. Maybe I am learning to be freer.

But one day, and I think it will be soon, he will leave, if Harry pushes him enough. I tell him that if he wants to leave, I would be upset, but I wouldn't hold him back.

Chapter 3

TRUST NO ONE!

A couple days have passed since my last update. Shortly I will bring you up to speed on the things leading up to today's events.

It's Tuesday, 4 October. It is a new day, and it's time to play hardball with these people. I've come to the realisation that even if someone is nice to your face, you never really know what their true intentions are—no matter what they tell you. Previously I was Madam Boss Lady, and now it's Madam Boss Bitch. I will not be taken for a mug. People underestimate me. They think that just because I'm small and have a pretty face, I will not fight back. I will fight to the death if I must, if I feel that people are taking the piss and taking me for a fool. I might be small, but I have the heart of a lioness. I have not come this far in my life, having come from absolutely *nothing* and having worked my balls off, just to lie down and take shit.

Today I am clear-headed and ready to fight!

OK, so just to provide some information about the development of our relationship: Jai and I have gotten really close. We spend most of our time together, both professional and personal. We have a good working relationship. I care about him very much. I'm not in love or anything, but I do care about him. I think he cares about me too.

The last couple of days have seemed to just roll together in a big blur, but the consistent factor is that I can't get my money to India quickly enough.

I made an international transfer on Saturday to Jai's account and transferred money into Cheryl's account to do a Western Union.

The money I transferred to Jai's account will take approximately four to five days to clear. The Western Union transfer can take a half an hour apparently, from a UK outlet to anywhere in the world.

Cheryl is busy, so she will do this on Monday after work. I'm trying to find an outlet for her to do the transaction, but there doesn't seem to be any around.

I manage to withdraw twenty thousand rupees from local ATMs.

Saturday evening, we go to Anjaru for dinner. This is the place where I left off in the previous chapter.

Sunday, I go to the office and check the Bookings.com site. There is a booking for today, 3 October. I message the guest to confirm if they are still coming.

Later at Arabian Waters the guest calls, but we have trouble understanding each other. His English isn't great, and my Hindi is just as bad. I try speaking in Punjabi, but to no avail. But I understand that they will not be arriving until Tuesday, 4 October.

I get back to LOM, and the painters are just lounging around. I'm not paying them to sit on their arses. I have a look around with Jalan and discover that there's a big spill of black paint in the downstairs room. I get the painters to clear some of the mess that they have made and then get them to do a few other jobs. I ask Jalan to start tidying up the top floor.

The electrician is also here, starting to put in the wiring for the new lights. He's brought his little friend with him, who looks like an Indian Oompa Loompa. He's smiley. I like him. The electrician proper is younger but a bit moody. Jai has been dealing with him.

In the evening we hang out on Clive's balcony. We order dinner. Clive is playing music, ranging from Metallica to Mozart and Beethoven. Never in a million years did I think I would be listening to classical music in Goa. It's actually a refreshing change. Clive pretends to do the waltz.

Jai plays some cheesy romantic Western music, including Bryan Adams. I pull a face. He then plays Justin Timberlake again. He knows I like that one.

After eating another late dinner, I stay out a little longer and then go to bed. I'm exhausted.

Jai messages. We both say we're tired and just want to sleep in our own rooms. However, he comes to my room. I'm wide awake now. He's like electricity!

We talk about his plans for the place in Obrah and how he is going to fund it initially. I jokingly say I could be a silent partner. He doesn't know what that means, so I explain. A silent partner funds the project and, while not involved in the running of the business, takes a cut of the profit. I can see his mind working. I'm not going to invest. I'm not that stupid.

Monday morning, I wake up refreshed. Even though it was a late one the night before, I had a good sleep. Jai sneaks out to go to his room.

The electrician arrives to continue with the wiring. I give Jai money to go buy light fittings. The painters are asking for the remainder of what I owe them. I tell them I will pay them tomorrow as I need to go to an ATM. The money I have to pay them with is the Western Union money being transferred by Cheryl. But she is having a bad day. She tries, but it's not possible today.

The pressure is building!

Clive is just milling around doing fuck all and generally getting in the way.

I knock on Clive's door for a light. He opens the door, and it stinks of weed. I don't say anything, but I am annoyed. At least smoke on the balcony.

Clive moves out of the sample room. He chooses one of the deluxe rooms upstairs which isn't complete yet.

Jai returns early in the evening with some hideous light fittings. I hate them. They are way too big and a dark brass colour. He's also got some clay white clamshell ones. They too are hideous but not as ugly as the brass ones. They are expensive also. He says they will go with the antique furniture. I explain that not everything has to be antique.

He is also asking why Clive is in one of the best rooms. I say it is so the guests booked for tomorrow can have his room. Jai says he's going to put those guests on the third floor. He hadn't fricking told me before now! Also, he is waiting on confirmation of another booking for three deluxe rooms. Clive can bloody move back round. Clive makes a face, and I tell him that paying guests take priority.

Jai goes back to the shops to return the hideous light fittings.

People are beginning to do my head in.

Jai sends some pics of different light fittings on WhatsApp. I choose some modern-style ones and a really nice standing lamp. I'm going to take that one home for sure once I finish with this place.

Jai comes back with some nicer fittings, and we watch the electrician fit them in the third-floor deluxe room. The painters had painted the bed frame earlier, and it looks nice.

Jai gives me grief for having put Clive in one of the best rooms. I repeat that he can move back down again. Jai says that if he had a smart boss, she wouldn't have done that. I say, "Are you calling me dumb again?"

He says, "No, that's not what I said." I explain that he might have used different words, but they imply the same thing. He disagrees.

I say, "No, you're saying the same thing." He's getting on my nerves. He says something about “his place”, meaning LOM. I realise this a few minutes later and pull him up on it. It’s not his place! I’m getting wound up now.

I am now starving. It’s 9.30 p.m. I quickly change because I am still in scruffs. We go to Anjaru for dinner with Clive in tow.

I receive a message from Cheryl. She is getting annoyed and cannot do the transaction because the outlet is closed. I’m stressed as fuck now. I show Jai the message, and he says he won’t be able to buy the bedding. I snap back at him, “Don’t you think I know that?!” The physical distance between us is huge. I purposely didn’t sit close to him. We order food, and I have vodka, lime, and soda, a large one. It goes to my head as I haven’t eaten since lunch.

My head is whirling, I’m stressed, and I leave the table to go have a cigarette by the beach. I don’t want them to see me cry. I’m on the verge.

When I return, there is a message on my phone from Jai asking, “What happened? Why did you go?” I can’t talk; I’m too upset. I eat my dinner momos in silence. The atmosphere is so thick that you can cut it with a knife. I feel a bit sick, so I feed half the momos to a beach dog, probably the same one from last time. He’d sniffed me out, the sad-faced dog.

I order another drink. I’m feeling very fuzzy now. Both Clive and Jai eat their food in virtual silence. Jai messages to tell me not to drink too much. Who the fuck does he think he is, telling me what to do?!

A random drunk white dude approaches the table. He is seriously smashed and probably not just from drink alone. There are more tourists now, and they all look dirty. Anjaru is a bit of a shithole really. It seems a lot of people come to Goa to get smashed/high. I’m realising there is a dark side to Goa. It can swallow you up and spit you out if you’re not careful. Jai had said that some tourists lose everything, and they resort to selling trinkets like beggars just to get a flight back home. I will not be one of them! I don’t want to be in Anjaru anymore.

We drive back in silence. Jai is driving like a manic. I don't say anything. We get back to LOM, where I check on the room for tomorrow's guests. The room looks lovely. I'm tired, so I go to bed. Jai messages. I want to sleep and be alone.

I don't think he likes to see me angry and upset. But I cannot pretend or hide how I feel. I'm not a robot; I'm a human with flawed human emotions.

It was nice to sleep alone and get a proper night's sleep. I wake up and go to Arabian Waters for breakfast. I just want tea and toast. I need to go to the bank. I'll ask Jalan to take me. As I am coming out of my room, the painters and Clive are loitering in the stairwell. Clive starts talking about the painters getting paid. I snap and tell him to leave it, adding that he should mind his own business—it's not his concern. I don't think he was expecting it. And I don't see him for the rest of the morning. Who the hell does he think he is?! I'm sick of people telling me what to do. The painters are shocked as well. Jai is still in his room but probably heard all the shouting.

While we're on the way to the ATM on the scooter, Jalan starts talking about not trusting anyone, not even Jai. I'm surprised by this as I thought they were close. He says his father, the landlord, said that he should tell me this. He said not to trust Harry and not to trust Jai. I feel numb! I ask Jalan if Jai is a bad man. He says yes! I really don't know what to make of all this.

Jalan is a really sweet young man. He's about twenty-five, but a very young twenty-five, with a cheeky, smiley face. He's originally from Bangladesh and was an orphan who was adopted by the landlord. I don't have any cause to doubt him. He doesn't seem to have any ulterior motives for telling me all these things.

At the ATM I withdraw two lots of ten thousand rupees, and then I go into the ICICI Bank to enquire about opening an account. After I answer a couple of questions about nationality and origin, as in a person of Indian origin, the branch manager says it's possible to open an account.

Jalan and I head back to LOM, and I enquire some more. Jalan tells me that Jai is from a rich background, but his father doesn't like what he does. I know all this, so it's not a surprise. And to be honest, it's why I like Jai: he's his own man and doesn't want to follow the family line of business.

Back at LOM, the painters are talking to the landlord. I go join them, and we talk about how the painters need to leave to go to another job but are waiting on the last payment. One of them will remain to do the tidying up. The landlord explains that it's not me causing the delay; it's the international banking system. They seem placated. I'm not trying to swindle them, but they've had their fingers burnt before with Harry not paying them for four months.

The one remaining asks about the work in the restaurant. I tell him, "I will not pay for work in the restaurant. The restaurant isn't mine yet." He's fine with that.

Jai appears and sees us all talking. He asks me if everything is OK. I say yes. He asks if I have the money for the painters, and I say yes. He says, "Let me deal with them." He'll take them out and make the payment. Alarm bells are ringing! I go to my room. He follows me upstairs. The painters' door is open (their room is next to mine). Jai says something to them abruptly in their local dialect.

He tells me that he needs to go to the bank with the landlord, and then he'll return.

My head is battered already and it's not even 1 p.m. I'm starving, so I go to Arabian Waters for lunch. Jalan says takeout would take too long. I have lentil dhal and roti and then sit out on the beach with headphones on. I need to chill. There are some locals building a bridge over the backwater stream.

Jai messages me on my UK mobile and asks where I am. I'd left my Indian mobile in my room to charge. So, I head back. He messages, saying that if I still have an angry face, he will leave. (I don't want him to leave.)

The landlord is talking to Jai about Clive smoking ganja on the balcony, asking Jai to tell Clive to stop.

Jai and I sit on my balcony, and I try not to have an angry face. He is going to Hansari to get cash from Harry for the landlord. I tell him to take Clive the chef with him. I haven't seen Clive since this morning. Jai is trying to make sure I'm not stressed, but it's not working. I ask him about the receipt for yesterday's lighting. He says he messaged Mango to bring it. He asks if I have checked my account since making the transaction on Saturday. I have checked my account. I had downloaded the HSBC app onto my new mobile, so I thought I'd try it.

I can't find my Internet banking security key for my current account. It's not in my gold purse and not in my laptop bag. I empty everything out. Jai checks also. He quickly drives to the office. My security key is not there. He checks the car; it's not there either. I'm freaking out! I can't do anything without the security key. I empty my whole suitcase out, which I'm still living out off. Nothing. It's lost! It could be anywhere. We've been all over Nimpura, and we went halfway to Unjaan on Saturday.

I break down. I hide in the bathroom and cry.

Jai finds where I am, but I don't let him in. He can hear me. He's saying, "Arey Baba, don't cry," and telling me that he'll sort everything. He has to go to Hansari. He says he'll come back soon. He leaves. I'm still hiding and crying. But it's the release I need, and it clears my head.

The guests who were supposed to arrive today are a no-show, even after I had called them to confirm their arrival.

Jai and Clive have left for Hansari.

I call HSBC to check on the transaction into Jai's account. It's being reviewed as per the standard rules of international systems. Also, I order a new Internet security key, which will be sent to LOM. The woman is also going to send an email with a link to access my account. Sorted!

Jalan knocks on my door and asks if I want a cup of tea. Exactly what I need! He says he knows someone who can get cheaper bed sheets and towels, and takes me around to Nimeesha Spa, just down the main road from LOM. I speak to the woman there, Nimeesha, who owns the place. Her husband is there also. They tell me about the bed sheet guy, saying he supplies the bedding for their resort, which is called Cherish. They talk about Harry and say that he is not a good man. They tell me not to trust him and Jai. They are not from here (but neither am I). Jalan says he will take me to Cherish. The whole not trusting Jai thing is playing on my mind.

I have spent virtually every day with him. He's a bit too eager to spend my money, and it's not all accounted for, but I don't think he's conning me. If he and Harry are in it together, they are masters of deception.

In the evening Jalan take me to Cherish. The place is beautiful. The huts are not luxurious, but they have so much character. The beds are each raised on a concrete platform with steps leading up and a gorgeous mosquito net curtain. Antique furniture is used for storage. There are twenty-odd huts in total in rows of ten or so facing each other with a block-paving pathway.

The restaurant is a huge beach-style hut right on the beach. The whole place is amazing.

Nimeesha comes and sits with me, and we talk about our backgrounds. She was married at sixteen. Her father chose her husband. They have two children, a daughter who is fifteen and a son who is six. It's so nice to have some female company. There's no underlying pressure, and women have an unspoken understanding. It's the universal sisterhood! Nimeesha is so supportive, and that's what I need right now, especially with everyone saying not to trust Harry and Jai. She says, "Don't worry, it will all work out." I tell her I have faith and believe God will look out for me, which I truly believe.

I have dinner and relax for a while, then I give Nimeesha a hug before heading back to LOM. Jalan is my chauffeur.

I get back to my room, and it's nice and peaceful. No Clive, no Jai. The painters are chilling in their room.

Jai messages to see how I am. He says Harry is talking his usual shit at Hansari.

Sleep!

It's Wednesday, 5 October, I wake up and go to Arabian Waters for breakfast. Jai messages saying he had a fight with Harry and is heading back to Shakthar. I say, "OK, I'll see you later."

Jalan and I had arranged to go to see Uncle Timmi, the contact Nimeesha had given me for bedding and towels. I shower earlier than usual and put on something a bit smarter than usual, a white kurta-style top and khaki shorts. I want to make a professional impression, even if nobody else does.

I'm just sitting on my bed when Jai arrives. He looks sweaty and flustered. He says Mango had picked him up in Hansari and brought him back.

Half an hour later Harry and Clive turn up. Jai is now nowhere to be seen. I pop my head out of the doorway, and Harry asks where Jai is. I tell him I don't know, which I don't.

I don't want to hang around, so Jalan and I leave to do chores. I need to go to the clinic as the eczema on my foot is playing up. Also, I need to get cash from Western Union. And then we are going to see Uncle Timmi. We just tell everyone I'm going to the clinic about my foot.

We reach Thairi and stop to call Timmi. There's a message from Jai to call him immediately. I call him, and he tells me that Clive has told Harry everything that we had discussed about kicking Harry out. I am furious at Clive. Why the fuck would he do that?! The back-stabbing fucker! I tell Jai that Harry arrived at LOM and was asking for him. I tell him I will see him later.

This place is beyond crazy.

Jalan and I manage to find Timmi's Bedding Shop. We

see some bed sheet samples, and both Timmi and Anna, his Russian wife are lovely. We are treated with traditional Indian hospitality and are served drinks and ice cream, which we could not decline. Their three-year-old daughter Katia, the cutest little thing, makes friends with Jalan. She hides in the mountain of sheets and towels and speaks in Hindi. She is more European-looking than Indian-looking. I love the fact that things like this totally break with convention. Anna speaks pretty fluent Hindi too. It is lovely to have met them all.

Arriving back at LOM, I find that it's quiet. Harry is asleep. Clive is in his room. The calm before the storm.

I get a message from Jai saying, "Whatever they say, I did not cheat you."

I reply, "Will they say this?"

Harry wakes up, and we go to one of the spare rooms. He starts taking about the painters and how much I paid them. I tell him that they have the full ninety thousand. He says that's too much and reminds me that he had asked that I speak to him about their payment. He starts having a proper go. I remain calm and state that it was a mistake on my part. Mistake #1. He phones the lead painter, and they're talking in their own language. This goes on for a while. Harry says that the painters were only paid seventy-five thousand rupees of the ninety thousand that was agreed. He is saying that Jai must have taken the outstanding fifteen thousand as his commission. He starts to call him names and goes on about how he is a bad man, saying that I should not have trusted him. Jai is nowhere to be found. Harry calls Jai but gets no answer. Harry is going ape!

Out of the blue I get a call from Mango. I don't understand what he is saying, but he's asking me for five thousand rupees. He mentions Jai's name. I say, "*No!*" I go back into Harry's room and tell him. The case against Jai is not looking good. I can feel the hurt building inside me, along with disappointment and possible betrayal.

A little while later Mango arrives. We start to tally up the spending on the light fittings, and Mango states it came to fourteen thousand, but I had given Jai twenty-five thousand. I haven't received all the receipts from Jai. And Mango has one of the receipts at his home. To be honest, Mango is not helping. Harry is becoming even more furious. He calls Jai and gets through. They are speaking in their language. It's very heated. Harry is calling him a bastard, a fraudster, and all sorts of other names.

This is upsetting me. I message Jai, saying, "If any of this is true, it will break my heart."

Jai turns up, and we're all sitting in one of the bedrooms. Jai and Harry are going at it, really shouting at each other in their language. The pained expression on Jai's face kills me. I go to my room opposite and shut the door. There's more shouting. Earlier Harry had locked Jai's luggage in another room. I open my door, and they're all in the stairwell. Jai is in the other room, opposite. Jai and I look at each other. I message him and say, "I don't care about the money; my self-respect is more important." I want to cry, but I hold it together. I can't believe this is happening. Harry is still shouting.

I'm sitting on my bed, and Jai comes in and stands in the doorway. He says he is sorry this is happening. I don't know what to say. He says, "Tell me what you want me to do."

I say, "I don't know." It's killing me, his sad, pained eyes. I just want to hug him. But I'm too confused now. I don't know who is lying or why this is happening.

Mango and Clive are still milling around in the background.

Jai is still standing in my room. All I want to know is if what is between us is real and not some sort of hoax or game to get my affections onside and con me out of money. All I care about is that the feelings between us are real. I don't care about the money.

I ask him, "If this is a game, was our personal relationship real?" He doesn't say anything. His sad eyes are killing me.

We look at each other, trying to understand what is happening, not just with Harry but also between us. It is as if looking into each other's eyes will allow us to find the answer. I don't know what I see except for his sad eyes. They are killing me. I ask him if there is someone else. He says no. He mentions a girl in Hindavi but says they are just friends now. He stays with her when he is there. He says he has mentioned her before, but I do not remember.

Harry is still ranting in the hallway. He shouts, "Come, Sabbie. We'll go to Arabian Waters."

I say, "I will be there in ten minutes."

Jai and I sit on my balcony, trying to decipher what has happened and determine what we will do. He says he did not cheat me and that every cent was used to help me with LOM. I want to believe him so much. We talk in circles for a little while, and then Mango comes and sits on the balcony floor with us. We talk about the various bills. I ask Mango if I can trust Jai. He says yes, 100 per cent. But they are the best of buddies, so of course he would say that. Mango leaves. I say to Jai that my gut instinct is telling me he's a good guy. We smoke cigarettes and look into each other's eyes. I don't understand how we have gotten here. I don't even understand how we have gotten this close or what it all means. But I do know I don't want to lose him.

He talks about the place in Obrah and how he is going to fund it. He tells me what the landlord has agreed to. He says he doesn't want to live off his father's money. I love that he wants to be his own man! I only half listen. My mind is still whirling with the craziness of this evening.

He asks, "Do you want to continue the relationship?" I nod. I don't want to lose whatever this is or whatever it will be. This doesn't happen to me, like, ever! He says he's fine with the relationship and adds that once I commit, I'm committed. I just want to hold him and kiss him. His sad eyes are still killing me.

He leaves, and I go to Arabian Waters.

At Arabian Waters, Harry and Clive are still discussing the situation with the restaurant. I try to mediate, as it has now been confirmed that Clive doesn't have two pennies to rub together to fund the restaurant. We discuss various options, including the one I had proposed to take over the restaurant. Clive says he has had another offer from a previous place. He goes away for ten minutes to think about it, and when he comes back, he says he is going to take the other offer. I state that we cannot make him stay if that's what he wants. Harry says he will fund the purchase of the oven that Clive needs for his dishes. Clive says OK.

Harry plans out the next steps for opening the restaurant, including all the jobs that need doing. I make a mental note. Harry starts going on about Jai again. I say something to the effect of, "I thought I could trust him. I thought he was my friend." But my heart is still with Jai.

It's late now. We all retire to our respective rooms.

The next day I get up early and go to Arabian Waters for breakfast by myself. I need some space away from everyone. When I get back, Harry calls me into his room, and we talk again about the restaurant. He says that Clive is a good guy. He just has a drinking problem. But he is a great chef, and his skills will be beneficial for LOM. He says he and Clive agreed that Clive would get a percentage of the restaurant business, rather than be paid a salary, and that the split would be 50 per cent for Clive, 25 per cent for Harry, and 25 per cent for me, but Harry will give an extra 10 per cent of his share to Clive. Still, he would need an additional investment from me. I'm reluctant to invest any more money where Harry is involved.

I really don't understand why Harry is adamant about keeping Clive. Even though my opinion of Clive has changed since the first meeting, I'm not sure how this relationship would work. But I leave it for now.

Harry again starts to go on about Jai and the painters. He calls the painters again and talks in his local dialect. He hands me the phone, but I can't understand what the painter is saying. Harry then phones Jai. I say, "Why you are calling him again? It was sorted last night." I go onto the balcony. He follows me out. He yells, "Why are you on his side? Are you two having relations?"

I just reply, "No," saying that I thought the matter was closed.

He says, "It's personal between me and Jai." I leave it and go to my room. I don't want to lose my rag and get upset again. He's shouting at Jai, calling him a motherfucker and a bastard. I'm disgusted at Harry.

I get a message from Jai saying, "What's wrong with you people? This was sorted last night." He is angry.

I tell him, "I'm sorry. Harry's not letting this go."

Jalan and I mill around in the restaurant. He says Sofia's babies are hiding. I ask what he means. Sofia is the resident cat in Hansari, and she had kittens a few weeks ago. Harry had brought the kittens to Shakthar and just dumped them in the restaurant. The poor things have been abandoned without their mother. What a horrible thing to do. One is a tabby, and the other is a completely black kitten, so each has a different dad. Naughty Sofia, ha ha!

Jalan retrieves the frightened, hissing kittens and puts them in the basket they came in. They are the cutest little things ever. It's love at first sight for me.

We take them to my room and release them. They immediately run under the wardrobe, and they hiss at us when we approach them. Jalan collectively calls them "Sophie Mama". Ha ha! We decide to get them some fish, as all they have had is a bit of milk. The poor things must be starving.

Later Harry gets ready to leave for Hansari. We again go through what needs to be done to the restaurant. Jalan and I go to Anjaru to go to Western Union. Cheryl's transfer of £300 goes through. Then we go to the fish market for food for Sophie Mama.

On the way back, we spot Harry's car parked up. We do a

U-turn to see if we can find him. We don't see him, so we return. I suspect he is in the bank.

At the fish market, we bumped into Kamu Chef. I had met him a couple of weeks ago. Jai had arranged a meeting with him in Nimpura to discuss potentially working at LOM. We all had gone for lunch. I liked Kamu Chef straightaway. He strode across the road to get into the car. A tall guy with scars on his face from a recent road accident, he just seemed to have a calming, kind aura about him.

At the fish market, we briefly talked about the whole Harry situation, and then we discussed setting up and running a restaurant. We didn't go into any specifics. I asked him if Jai was OK. He had spoken to him. Kamu Chef and Jai worked together at Glamour and became very close.

I think to myself that you should judge a person not only on his or her own but also on the company he or she keeps. If I am to believe and trust in Jai, the fact that Kamu Chef is a close friend is a good sign.

Jalan and I get back to LOM and take a couple of fish up to Sophie Mama. They drag the fishes under the wardrobe.

It's been nearly a week since all the events between Harry turning up and Jai leaving. It's been pretty hectic, so I haven't been able to do any updates. Work is continuing on the LOM rooms and restaurant.

Jalan had organised cleaners to come and clean the exterior of the building and part of the restaurant. The cleaners did lots of running around to get hosepipes and cleaning products. They did a pretty crap job, to be honest.

I have met up with Jai most nights for dinner. he has been furious with Harry, and he has been planning and setting up his own place in Obrah. He says he hadn't planned to do this, but it's happened. One night while out in Anjaru, he says he didn't expect to even think about a girlfriend. I am pretty sure he was referring to me. A few times he has really done my head in by calling me dumb. I get in a strop, and he apologises for having made me upset. It's like he can read me like a book.

One night he was asking to read some of the novel I'd sent him an extract of when he was in my room during the shitstorm episode, when his sad eyes were killing me. I purposely sent him the portion that refers to him directly and that mentions how his actions made me feel. He initially said, "No, no, no, no, you cannot put this in." I told him to chill, saying it was just for me. I asked if he liked it. He said, "Every little bit of it." He said it pierced his heart, the way I write. This man makes me feel so many things all at the same time. I still don't know where this will go. I decide to take it one day at a time.

The kittens are doing well, and I am now their surrogate Mama. They are very lively and have kept me awake at night by jumping about on the bed while I'm trying to sleep. Once they have worn themselves out, they snuggle up against me and fall asleep. The black one is a male and is quite feisty. He's a bit of a biter when playing. I am not sure how to discourage this. The tabby, a female, gets a little bullied by the black one. But she gives as good as she gets. That's my girl! ☺ She is really sweet and a bit needy, but still adorable. One night they were too feisty, and I had to put them in the bottom drawer of the wardrobe. They actually liked it and slept there the next day.

However, as I don't have proper facilities at the moment, the room is beginning to stink. They have been eating fish and weeing on the floor as I have no litter tray. The smell is horrendous. I asked Jalan to clean it up, but the odour stayed. I have now moved out into a little house. More on that shortly.

Regarding Clive the chef, he has been milling about, making himself not very useful. I have asked him on numerous occasions to move out of the top room. It was a mistake on my part to have put him up there, but little did I know that he was going to be a completely unreasonable human being. He hasn't lifted a finger to help out in cleaning the kitchen. If he was any sort of decent chef, he would be taking pride in his kitchen and making it his own. He's just been sitting up in his room not doing very much. I have remained civil to him, although I did lose my temper one day when I asked him to help move some kitchen items from the ground-floor room into the kitchen. He looked at me blankly and just walked away and went to speak to Jalan. I had to collar Clive about it and ask if there was a problem. He shouted back that he was waiting for Jalan. Bloody hell, he's a grown man waiting for Jalan the housekeeping boy. The items were still there three days later.

Clive the chef has now left, much to my relief. I could not have worked with that man!

The restaurant is still as it was; nothing has happened. Harry's been giving the necessary lip service on how to get it ready. He's gathering his troops from Hindavi to come and do some work.

Last Monday, 3 October, one of Harry cheques bounced. The restaurant's blue plastic covers were still down, covering the entrance, but everyone congregated and hung out there. Jalan, the landlord, the landlord's brother (I now know that his nickname is Fruity, which is a name Jai gave him—don't ask why), Clive, and I were just milling about. I was trying to understand how to get things cleaned up. The place was a mess.

A short while later the landlord reappeared and said that Harry's cheque had not cleared and had bounced. I could see he was trying to remain calm, but underneath he was seething. I, on the other hand, felt calm on the inside, which I projected on the outside. My first thought was that it was Jai who had sorted the cheque. Was he involved in this? I called him and had a quick chat. I just wanted to hear his voice for some reassurance. I was reassured. I was still a little paranoid from the shitstorm evening.

So, we all formulated a plan to drive to Hansari and confront Harry face-to-face—the landlord, the landlord's brother (Fruity), Clive, and I. Clive left his watch in Harry's house and wanted to get it back. We set off on the three-hour drive to Hansari.

In my mind I constructed a script of what I would say to Harry about using my money for his own purposes and how he was a lowlife con man and a cheat. I was calm and was determined to put him in his place.

I messaged Jai, "Karma is a bitch, and her name is Sabbie," which he found highly amusing.

After we set off, the car was deadly silent. No one spoke. Even the radio was turned off. We reached Unjaan in complete silence. The traffic had come to a standstill. Complete mayhem—no one was moving. Scooters were trying to manoeuvre into the tiniest of spaces. All the vehicles—cars trucks, bikes, and scooters—were beeping their horns. I really didn't see the point in this, as there was nowhere to move. But they continued to beep!

It'd now been a couple of hours since we set out from Shakthar. The traffic was not moving, and the morning teas and coffees were taking their toll on our bladders. I debated with myself whether to say anything or hang fire until we got to Hansari, but there were still at least two hours left of the journey—and that's without the gridlock. God knew when the traffic would move. Then the landlord tried to manoeuvre the car onto a dirt parking area. I was hoping there were toilet facilities nearby, but alas, he pulled over and ran into an overgrown area to relieve himself. We all got out of the car, and I asked Clive if there were any washrooms. He said, "No. This is not a place for women to use." I harrumphed. We all piled back into the car, and the landlord inched back into the traffic carnage.

Two hours later we finally got through the traffic, and the landlord floored it. I said, "Can we stop somewhere for a toilet?" Not long afterwards, we pulled up outside a standard-looking restaurant. I, Clive, and Fruity queued up to use the grim washroom facilities. They were not great, but I didn't care. I hovered to pee! I didn't want to touch any surface.

It really pisses me off that whichever restaurant you go to, the toilets are always disgusting. Even if the restaurant is nice, the toilets are always disgusting. Now at every opportunity when I am out with Jai, I moan and express my disgust about bad toilets. On one occasion he got the staff to clean the toilet for me. He really is a sweetheart.

We arrived at Hansari five hours later. We wanted to confront Harry face-to-face without any of his cronies around. It was now approximately 4 p.m., and Clive stated that he'd be in his room resting. We headed to his room without anyone from Light of Moon seeing us. I said to the landlord, Fruity, and Clive, "Everyone remain calm, and let Harry speak first before saying anything." They all agreed.

We got to Harry's room, and it was locked from the outside. He was not home. We headed back to Light of Moon. Harry was not there either. Ravi, Harry's cashier guy who actually monitors the cash flow to pay off any outstanding credit balance, was at the till. He welcomed us, and we all sat. We were brought tea, but the landlord and Fruity declined. Clive and I accepted and ordered a bottle of water. We were all exhausted from the five-hour journey. The wind in my sails had totally deflated, and I didn't have the energy to even talk to anyone.

After about half an hour Harry arrived with Karan. I couldn't make out his blank facial expression, but he greeted me and Clive. The landlord and Fruity had gone out and were loitering with intent on the street outside. Harry offered me his hand to shake. I had mosquito repellent on, so I declined. Karan and I fist bumped instead. They both joined me at the table. Clive was sitting at a separate table. No idea why.

The landlord and Fruity came and joined us, and they started to discuss the cheque situation. Fruity called someone at the bank, and it transpired the bank had been trying to call him to authorise the payment. Harry hadn't been answering his phone. After a short discussion, with Harry translating back to me, we find that it's the same system that international banking uses, meaning that a large amount of cash being transferred requires approval. The landlord and Fruity seemed satisfied.

I still had doubts, but hopefully the fact that we all turned up unexpectedly gave Harry a little shock.

Clive went with Harry to pick up his watch, then we all got back in the car to head back. The whole trip could have been avoided if Harry had answered his phone. We mostly sat in silence on the way back.

We arrived back in Shakthar about 9 p.m., all of us exhausted and hungry.

Jai was stressed. I was stressed. The evening provided a respite from the daily challenges and events. We sought comfort in each other's company. We hugged and slept.

The next morning, I awake and go for breakfast at Arabian Waters. I leave Jai sleeping in my room.

I really need a new smartphone to manage bookings and marketing and just to keep in contact with everyone so that I don't have to rely on places with Wi-Fi. Today is "Get Sabbie Madam a new phone day". I need to pay with my UK debit card. Hardly any places take cards here. Jai, Clive, and I head towards Nimpura, stopping at various places. He negotiates prices for me. I love it when he is all manly and masterful. It makes me feel protected. We head towards Unjaan to a mall. We find a place on the way where I like the look and feel of a Vivo phone. (It's a bit on the expensive side, though I never have liked the cheap stuff.) We go to another shop but end up going back to get the Vivo. Yay! I have a shiny new toy to play with. I'm so happy! Not that I'm materialistic or anything.

We go to lunch at a tapas place called Home. The food is nice, and it's a cute little place. Clive has pasta, and Jai has chicken with mash, but it is swimming in oil. He's not keen. My mushroom on bruschetta and eggplant dish is nice.

There are some pretty young things at the next table. I wonder if Jai has checked them out. I really must curb the green-eyed monster. It's not good for me!

After arriving back at LOM, we all retreat to our rooms for

an afternoon chill. It's been a good day so far. Jai has been smoking all my ciggies. The lad still has "tension in the head". :D

In the evening, after much debate about dinner and going clubbing, we decide to go to Anjaru. We're all getting along, and even Clive has redeemed himself with me. He has the weirdest accent. He speaks Hindi with a sort of Chinese accent.

I wear my camo pencil skirt and a black T. My tummy is going down with the weird eating habits. I feel good about myself.

We arrive in Anjaru and sit at beach table at Angel. After walking up the beach, Jai points out the place where Jasmine used to hang out—Something Pyramid.

We order drinks and food. Jai's black dude friend turns up, and they skin up. I don't have any, as I don't like smoking in public places and with people I don't know. Clive the chef is fucked in the head already. :D Jai and I laugh at him. We message even though we're sitting next to each other. I love it! We can't be openly affectionate, but it still feels intimate.

Food arrives, and a beach dog comes and sits in between me and Clive. Jai is on my right. The dog is looking all pitiful. I ask it, "What are you looking at?" I say this a few times. Clive is calling the dog "Miss Hindustan" or something. Jai thinks Clive and I are talking to each other. He doesn't see the dog. :D Clive is mashed. It's my and Jai's entertainment for the evening. It feels good to laugh and joke. We all need it.

Jai and I promise Clive that we won't leave him and drive off like we did the first night they arrived.

When we get back, Clive goes to bed, and Jai comes to my room for a smoke. Well, I smoke a joint and he watches, and we talk about the evening and also the New Zealand woman who will turn up at some point—another one of Harry's acquired acquaintances. Jai talks about his plans and what he wants to create at the place we saw yesterday. I love his ambition. It's a turn-on!

Jai stays back, and we laugh and joke and roll around until the early hours.

Chapter 4

IT'S BUSINESS!

It's now been a couple of weeks since the end of the events of the last chapter, and things are progressing slowly but surely.

Even though it's only been a couple of weeks, it seems like the days somehow stretch into eons. But at the same time all the days roll into one. The concept of time is distorted. Trying to get anything done here requires multiple calls to people who say they will arrive at a specific time but then don't turn up. This is a whole new level of *mañana*. I'm finding this really frustrating, but I suppose I have to adjust to it.

So, for this chapter, I've not written in a chronological fashion but as blocks of events relating to the same subject that may have occurred during the last couple of weeks. It's been difficult to find the time to sit down and write; therefore, I have summarised each event to the best of my memory.

My Little House and the Kittens

Firstly, I now have my own little house that I am renting for the season. I've paid for two months up front. It's about five-minute walk away from LOM, but Jalan comes and picks me up in the mornings and drops me off in the evenings.

It's a detached house with a little veranda, having one room with a bed and wardrobe. It has a nice-sized kitchen off the main room with a gas cylinder stove and a fridge. It's pretty much fully functioning without all the modern gadgets. I bought myself a little kettle and a toaster so at least I can have tea and toast in the mornings.

There is a decent-sized shower room with hot water. The kittens' litter tray lives there, and the kittens get banished to the bathroom when they are wreaking havoc while I'm trying to sleep.

The house is pretty private even though it's on one of the main roads leading to LOM. There's a river a few feet away, but it's only a few inches deep. I imagine it turns into a torrent during the monsoon months. I won't be here at that time.

I like my little house. It gives me some privacy from LOM—my little retreat from everyone and their dramas. I've been in the house for two weeks now, and I'm used to spending time here.

The kittens have adjusted well too, and they run around like loons most of the time. They have discovered how to climb the bars on the windows and the curtains. They can easily jump up and down from the kitchen counter.

They are approximately four months old now, and Jalan and I have taken them to the vet to get them checked out as they were doing runny poos. The vet gave them a clean bill of health and said it may have had to do with a change in food. I am feeding them Whiskers kitten food, as it's not always possible to get fresh fish all the time. Plus, fish stink the place out.

The black boy kitten I've named Brutus Maximus Beans. He beats up his sister and is basically a greedy-guts. He also is a mama's boy and loves getting cuddles. He's still a bit of a biter, but less so now than when we first found him.

The girl kitten is smaller than the boy and eats less food. She is a bit braver though and is the first to venture out. She only comes in if I get Brutus in first. I call her Lollipop Honey.

She likes cuddles too, but not as much as Brutus. Brutus, who gets jealous when I'm cuddling Lollipop, gets in between us. They are the cutest, and I love having them here running around, chasing each other, and just being mad kittens. It's the first time I've had kittens, and OMG, they are so cute. I still miss my Lizzie though, my beautiful furry Queen. I wonder what she would make of Lollipop and Brutus. Hopefully as a big sister she would take them under her wing, but who knows.

The vet says the kittens will need to be spayed and neutered soon; otherwise, I might have more kittens on my hands. I was like, even though they are brother and sister and he says "Yes!" it does look like Brutus tries to mount Lollipop sometimes. But I think he's just playing. I will need to keep an eye on him.

I keep them mostly in the house as they are still babies, but they are itching to get outside. The other day I let them out, and they went to the back of the house, which is essentially a mini jungle. I couldn't find them to get them back in, so I just went to LOM as usual. When I got back, there was no sign of them. Even Jalan couldn't see them. He said they would be back at night when they were hungry, but a dog had been hanging around earlier, and I was starting to worry.

I messaged Jai saying the kittens had run away and that I was a bad mama for having left them. I was upset. He said he would be here in half an hour. As soon as I sent the messages, I heard a faint meowing. I opened the door, and Brutus was sitting waiting to be let in, but I didn't see Lollipop. But then I heard more faint meowing, this time from the back of the house. I went around and saw that she was perched on top of a pile of wood. I grabbed her and brought her back in. I was so relieved. I'd been having visions of a crow or something carrying them away.

Anyway, I haven't let them out since, even though they still want to. I realise they are Goan cats and I can't keep them looked up, but they are still my little fur babies. I will chaperone them and ensure I'm here when they are out. I will let them out by themselves eventually.

They are now due for the next vet's visit. I will get Jalan to take me.

Light of Moon Rooms

The rooms at LOM are pretty much completed. Just the middle- and ground-floor do not have curtains. I'm waiting on the same material for the upstairs curtains to be ordered and then the curtains to be made.

The painters had returned to clean up the mess they had made, but they only stayed a day and half. They promptly left as I wouldn't give them money for food. FFS, I had paid them ninety thousand rupees for a shitty job, and then they went off in a strop. People keep saying here that you give someone a finger and they'll take your hand. So fricking true! I swear, the people of this country are like children. Considering that India is one of the most ancient civilisations in the world with some of the most enlightened minds, the general populous still act like immature teenagers. Seriously, this place is mental!

I have had some bookings for the rooms. Yay! A lovely older but young-at-heart English couple booked to stay for three nights but ended up staying for five. They were touring India on a beautiful black Harley-Davidson. They loved the place and said the shower was the best they'd had in India. It was great to speak to English people without having to water down or simplify my English. This is one of the reasons why I wanted to do this, to meet new people and make friends. They haven't sent a Facebook friend request just yet, but the Internet connection is notoriously bad here.

Another young couple, Austrian, stayed for a couple of nights, and then a young Israeli couple stayed who were lovely. They didn't even mind that the restaurant wasn't up and running.

An Indian couple stayed for one night, but as there was no restaurant, they checked out and went somewhere else. This was a referral from Harry. They had phoned Harry and said they were leaving. The fucker made it out to be my fault because I had booked the ground-floor room for them, but they were paying double. As soon as I confirmed the rate from my email on my laptop, I said I would upgrade them. Harry went on with himself as usual, saying that it was a bad first impression and that the first impression is what counts. He said that I need to listen to him because he's the big businessman! They left because there wasn't a restaurant, not because of the room rate. I know how he works now. He tries to blame other people for his mistakes.

In addition, one of the Kovvi guys, Mohammed, came to take photos for the place so that I could update all the online platforms with images of the redecorated rooms. It was lovely to see him, and he did a good job with the photos. But it transpired that he basically charged me double the going rate, or the rate that the website guy's friend would have charged me. However, I had only given him a 50 per cent advance. I don't know when I will see him to give him the rest.

The website is in the process of being updated. It's been done, but it's offline. Anup the website guy says there isn't any Internet at the moment. We will see how long this takes. Some workers had cut the electrical cables while cutting trees. Seriously, I can't comprehend the inadequacies of these people. But don't get me wrong, the majority are hard-working people making a simple living.

Bookings.com has been updated with the new photos and room rates. As soon as the photos went up, I received four bookings. Yay again! But I'd uploaded the photos before I had a chance to update the rates, so some of the bookings are at the old rates. I will see how the new rates go down.

I created the Facebook and Instagram pages too. The page got lots of likes, numerous comments, and a few shares on

Facebook, and the Instagram page also got a good response. I need to boost the profiles, but that will cost—not a lot, but it will cost nonetheless. I think I will do that. It will be worth it.

I need to start to promote locally too, with taxi drivers and other places in the area.

It has been a week or so since the Bookings.com update, and reservations are coming in thick and fast. I have had a couple of no-shows, but there's a place nearby that has had overbookings, and I am getting their referrals. I'm linked in with a lovely young woman at Serenity Retreat. She's tiny and very sweet. She's been getting harassed by the guests who are being referred to me.

So, in the first time in the history of Light of Moon, the rooms have been fully booked. To celebrate the momentous occasion, I bought some Indian sweets and shared them with the landlord, the guys in the restaurant (which is now up and running), and few people from the local community. I am so chuffed that things are working out. The hard work and stress at the beginning is paying off.

Jalan told me that Fruity said I was like the Hindu goddess Lakshmi. She is the goddess of money and good luck. I'll fricking take that! :D

If Harry thinks he can drive me out of the business, he has another thing coming. No way in hell could he have done what I have done! He's being extra nice to me since the whole episode about the reception when he told me, "You are greedy." I still keep him at arm's length and only really speak to him when I need to or just to keep him a little bit sweet. I think he knows not to fuck with me.

I am keeping all the cash from the rooms and will not be distributing it until at least a month has passed, and that will be only after all the expenses have been paid.

But it's not just about getting the bookings in; it's about engaging with the guests on a human level and ensuring that they are made to feel welcome. I'm enjoying meeting all these different people, especially guests from the UK. There's been a group of young people staying, and one of the guys is from London (Rochdale to be precise). I had a nice chat with another of the guys, who is super fit, about living the dream. That's why I'm doing this, to get out into the world and meet as many new people as I can. And one day, that one special person will come into my life who will make everything beyond perfect. Jai is pretty damn close, but he's a lot younger than I. More on that topic later.

The Restaurant

So, the restaurant has still been a contentious subject. Nothing had happened since my last update in the previous chapter.

A week ago, Harry was at Shakthar, and he made a big deal about how nothing was yet happening with the restaurant. He formally declared that he could get the restaurant up and running in four days. I said to myself, "Let's see what happens."

He had brought three guys with him to help set up the restaurant: Ali the carpenter, an old guy who is a plumber (I didn't get his name), and a young lad called Amit. They proceeded to knock down the restaurant washroom to make the reception area, and part of the balcony to create an entrance to the rooms from the other side of the building.

This caused another ruckus with the landlord, who is very protective of his building, which he has worked hard to build with his fishing business. I can totally understand this! Harry had previously explained his plans and seemed to have gained permission to do this work, but seeing the work actually happening did not sit well with the landlord.

Four days came and went, and the job was left. The reception area was half knocked down. Harry had left instructions with Ali and Jalan to get some "Gwandees" (labourers) to finish the work, i.e. concreting the step down from reception and the steps leading up to the balcony and tidying up the reception area.

Meanwhile, a couple of day before Harry left for Hansari, we were sitting around the big dining table in the restaurant and he stated that he was not interested in running the restaurant, saying that if I wanted to run it, I could. All it would require was "a little investment" as all the kitchen and bar equipment is there and he has already spent seven lakh buying all this equipment. However, Jalan had previously told me that all the equipment had been purchased by Ravi, who ran the restaurant the previous season. So, more porkies from Harry.

Harry explained that all he wants is one lakh from the restaurant takings for the season. I just say OK.

So, I am seriously considering running the restaurant. At least I would have full control over what happens with it. However, my main concern is ensuring that the kitchen is up and running so that I can provide breakfast to my guests.

During the conversation, I said very little and told him I would think about it as it's a big commitment. I also mentioned that I do not have experience with running a restaurant.

The majority of the people here are telling me not to run the restaurant, including Jalan, the landlord, and Jai.

While I was talking with Harry, another one of his guys turned up, a Nepalese-looking guy called Satish. Harry explained how experienced he is and said that he is a good guy, adding that I should talk to him.

Once Harry left, Satish came and joined me at my end of the table. I asked about his job history, which is extensive. He knows a lot of people in North Goa, including a lot of the regular tourists. He explained that he speaks Russian and that he can pull a lot of customers in from the street to eat.

We also discussed the financial side of setting things up: the initial costs of stocking the restaurant and bar; the cost of the salaries for the main chef, the tandoori chef, the second chef, the assistants, and the dishwashers; and his salary. He wants one and a half lakhs, which can be split over the course of the season. This seemed excessive to me considering Harry only wants one lakh.

We looked at the possible income the restaurant can bring in and the spending patterns of English and Russian customers. Russians spend double the amount of what English guests spend. It looks to be a little gold mine, this restaurant.

Anyway, we had a good chat, and I told him to come back on Sunday to discuss things further.

Once Satish left, I had a general chat with Jalan, mentioning that Satish could pull in a lot of customers and that we could make a lot of money.

Later that evening, Jai messaged me and said to get ready because a taxi was coming to pick me up. "It's a surprise." I was intrigued to say the least. Will it be a romantic dinner for two? A special dinner date?

This now brings us up to date.

The taxi comes, and Jagu the taxi driver takes me to a place on the way to Anjaru. I ask him, "Shall I pay?"

He says, "No, I'm coming in too. Everyone is already there." I'm confused.

I am greeted by Jai, the landlord, Madhav, and Jalan. Jagu and I join them.

I sit opposite Jai, and he gives me a loving look. I melt a little inside.

I tell Jai what I want to drink, and he relays the information to the waiter also ordering some veg food for me and some nonveg food for the others. They are all talking, and the landlord and Jai are thick as thieves. Jai translates some of the conversation for me. The landlord is saying that he has no problem with me running the rooms, as Harry had previously explained this to him. But Harry has not mentioned me running the restaurant, and this is a problem.

The landlord and I have a good relationship now (after all the shopping trips). I don't want to jeopardise the relationship.

I am still of two minds about the restaurant.

We all eat, and I am mostly checking my Facebook on my phone. Jai messages from across the table to see if I'm am angry. I say, "No, just checking FB." I love it when he does that. Our relationship is still a secret from everyone. He still calls me boss, Sabbie Boss, or Lady Boss. ☺

To be honest, I did feel a little ambushed when I first arrived. I don't mind so much that it is all the lads and just me. I can cope with that. But it's that everyone seems to have an opinion. I know they are all looking out for me, but it still feels as if I am being controlled and manipulated, not just by everyone at the table but also by Harry.

After dinner we all head back to LOM. Jagu drops everyone off, then drops me off at my house. Jai comes around a few minutes after I arrive. He asks me if I still want to run the restaurant, and I say I don't know. He runs though some more in-depth figures for me. I would need in excess of three lakhs to set everything up, including advance salaries for all the staff. And that's before the restaurant even starts running. I know Jai well enough now to know that his numbers are sometimes inflated, but seeing it in black and white (well, on my phone calculator), I am a bit freaked out. It would mean a further investment of approximately £3,000 to £4,000.

I know Jai doesn't want me to run the restaurant. I ask him why he thinks Harry asked me when I previously offered, Jai said it hurt Harry's heart and that I was greedy. Jai's reply is that he thinks Harry would be able to cheat me, seeing as I don't know how to run a restaurant. This insults me, but he has a point.

I'm still mega confused about the restaurant, but I think I would become too stressed running the restaurant, including managing the staff and purchasing all the stock. And I also want to have a personal life while I'm out here. I don't want the extra headache. I want to be able to go out with my friends, spend time with Jai, and generally have an easier life. In addition, the extra investment could seriously impact my finances at home. I think the restaurant could be a money pit. I don't want to bankrupt myself just to gain control of things.

And if I were to run the restaurant, Harry would still be on my case, perhaps even more so than now, when I am just running the rooms.

I silently make up my mind that I don't want to run the restaurant.

The next day, I phone Harry and tell him. I say I would help out with partly decorating it, but I don't want to take on the extra pressure and responsibility. He says OK. So that is that!

The next couple of days, I become preoccupied with the reception area, which remains in the same condition as it was when the painters left. I decide that I shouldn't be paying for it as I am not running the restaurant.

This information gets back to Harry via Ali. I can't remember if it was me who called Harry or vice versa, but I get a mouthful from him, saying he knows best and that guests complained that they had to walk past the family home to get to the room. He also said that booking companies have asked for a picture of reception for their sites. Whether this is true or not I don't know. But he starts calling me greedy and selfish, saying that I only think about myself, and that he is the businessman and he knows about these things. He says he tells people to their faces what he thinks of something, whether it's good or bad. I listen, and then I state that I do not appreciate being called selfish. I'm dumbfounded and in shock. I'm pissed off and I can't be arsed, so I walk back to my house.

To add to the frustration, Harry has left these three guys on their own and has and only given them five hundred rupees for supplies and to feed themselves. For the next few days it's muggins here giving them money to ensure that they are fed.

The next day I arrive early at LOM. I sit and explain what

Harry had said to Ali, who is actually a good guy. I, Jalan, Ali, and Amit, who is now called Baby because of his age, form a kind of friendship. Neither Ali nor Baby speaks any English, but we all seem to communicate and take the piss out of Baby. He is a Jain (a type of Hindu) with very strict eating and cleanliness rituals. He doesn't eat any meat products, garlic, or onions (Jai says it's because the bulbs grow underground!). He wants to work in the restaurant business but won't wash anyone's dishes if he is to be a kitchen hand. And he won't clean toilets if he is to work in housekeeping. We all try to explain to him that he won't get far if he restricts himself. But he's only seventeen; he has time to grow. He tries to be all "Yes, Madam." He's a sweet lad, if on the lazy side.

Surprisingly, Ali is on my side too. He's a little guy in his late thirties, I'm guessing. And he has worked in Saudi Arabia, amongst other places. His catchphrase is "Very bad man", which he uses at every opportunity. We all sit round the big table and have a fun timepass. :D Baby and Ali argue from sunrise until sunset. They are a comedy duo and entertain me and Jalan no end.

It's nice to have some comedic entertainment with these guys as when Harry is around it's all very serious. It's just "The Harry Show" when he's around: "Sweet sugar this, sweet sugar that." He is so full of shit that it's seeping out of every pore. The stench is nauseating.

Anyways, Ali and Jalan try to locate some Gwandees for the reception area. I decide I will pay, but I will get my money back from the rooms. I know I have been manipulated! And I will get back what I am owed! At least I know. Ali says that if Harry phones, I should tell him it will cost five thousand rupees for the reception area.

It turns out later that Ali and Jalan couldn't locate Gwandees, so Jalan suggests asking Vikram (Nimeesha's husband) if he can supply contractors from his place, Cherish.

I speak to Vikram, and he gets one of his guys to come

around to quote a price: five thousand rupees including materials.

The contractor says he will come the following day with materials (which turns out to be same day they start to work). So, the reception area is starting to take shape. The top has been concreted to make a flat surface, and the step has been created leading up to the new entrance.

The next day, we somehow have working Wi-Fi, and I'm in the process of uploading pictures to the various online booking sites. At around 4 p.m. Harry turns up in his car with another bunch of blokes. It's stereotypical; the car is packed with twenty people, and it's only a little Maruti Swift (OK, a slight exaggeration, but still!).

So, all these guys pile out, and I recognise one of them from LOM Hansari. Harry says hi, and I say hi back. But I don't respond otherwise. The guys all disperse and make themselves busy. Harry sits and explains that he has brought the chef and the team for the restaurant.

I continue to upload pics and update rates on Bookings.com.

The next couple of days are taken up with the guys setting up the kitchen and some of the outside restaurant. I am impressed. They are working, and the kitchen actually starts to look like a working kitchen, as opposed to a dumping ground.

The guys consist of one of Harry's chefs from Hansari, Dev Singh, a guy called Satish, and a few others I don't know. They don't talk much, but they seem to be friendly enough. I don't talk to them much either. I think this is Harry's plan to bring his own people in.

A couple of days later, I'm out with Jalan getting some food for my house. He says that Harry has basically brought these people in and that it's his plan to isolate me and make me leave LOM. That will never happen. I will fight to keep my place there.

However, later on in the evening, I am sitting with Satish, a cute young guy. He's the only one of Harry's workers who is able to speak goodish English. We talk briefly about the breakfast situation—how it will be set up and what will be included in the inclusive breakfast. I then ask him what his experience is and what he has done before.

He tells me the places he's worked in Hansari, Manali, and Kovvi. I ask him if he knows the Square Box guys, i.e. Lucky and Bally. He replies yes, adding that he is good friends with them. I tell him I know them from a couple of years ago. Satish says he thought he recognised me. He asks, "So you are a good friend of Lucky?" I say yes. I think he was implying more, but I don't give anything a way. He asks if I have talked to Lucky. I reply no, saying he is probably busy. Satish says that they are setting up two different places in Kovvi now.

I say, "I know."

Its amazes me that Goa is such a small community, especially in the hospitality industry. Anyway, as we are both friends with Lucky, Satish now considers me as a friend of his. This is good news for me. Harry thinks he can oust me, but everyone loves me in the end! ☺

A couple of days pass, and Harry leaves. Satish and even Dev Singh, now Dev Chef, are more talkative. They all say "Good morning, madam" when I arrive in the mornings. Dev Chef is a fellow Punjabi, which immediately forms a bond between us. The comments made by Jalan are soon water under the bridge, and the restaurant guys express their real opinions of Harry. They are not as big a fan as was first implied.

The days pass, and more work is going on. It's slow progress, but the restaurant is moving in the right direction. The guys have fitted the lights, put the fencing up, painted the floor red, and put up nice white material to cover the restaurant ceiling.

A new bamboo sign has been created to put over the driveway, and it actually looks good. I had my doubts at first, but once you come around the corner, it definitely catches your eye.

Staff food is being cooked, and I sometimes eat with them, although it's always the same thing, dhal and rice. On the odd occasion I eat there in the evenings. Mistry, another of the chefs, makes a delicious aloo gobi and roti, so nice and fresh.

Satish and Dev Chef discuss the menu, and I help them to type it up on my laptop. This takes approximately three days as the menu is extensive with all the usual cuisine types: Indian (obvs) Chinese, Continental, Thai, and tandoori. It's not the route I would have taken for a menu, but it's not my call as I'm not running the restaurant. Over the past three days, we have all gotten to know each other better. These are all good guys, not so much "Harry's people" as I'd first thought.

The bar is coming along too with some beers now in stock.

The day to open the restaurant has been announced as Monday, 7 November.

I think we'll all work well together. I want to learn from these guys too. I'm looking forward to the restaurant being open.

Jai

Oh Jai, Jai, nearly perfect Jai.

Since my move into my little house, we have pretty much spent every night together. He comes over once we have both finished our work. Sometimes he brings me dinner if I haven't eaten already, and we stand in the kitchen eating and chatting about the day.

Most of the time we're both exhausted and just cuddle and sleep, which is lovely. Other times, if we've had a drink, we roll around and talk into the early hours of the morning, just generally talking shite to each other.

He is still in the process of setting up his new place in Obrah, Creation Valley, and is under a lot of pressure to get things ready for the opening night on 9 or 10 November. I am so impressed with how much he has done over the last eight weeks. He has pretty much set things up from scratch in that time, and here we can't even get an existing restaurant to open.

I am actually proud of him and what he has achieved so far. I haven't told him this, but I say he is amazing in a message.

However, there are still doubts in my mind about the relationship—and it is a relationship, not just casual fling. We briefly discussed this late one night before my head became mashed and I needed a cigarette, but we didn't have any, so we just went to sleep. Neither of us are great about expressing our feelings, not face-to-face anyway.

So, the two points of contention are his age and money.

One night we went to dinner with Timmi and Anna. I had introduced them as a contact for getting bedding for Jai's place. Timmi took an immediate liking to Jai, I think he saw rupee signs as soon as he saw what Creation Valley was going to be like.

So, we both were invited out. During dinner Timmi and Anna were getting a bit lovey-dovey. More it was one way, with Timmi mooning over Anna for most of the night, which she mostly dismissed. She and I went out for cigarettes, and I learnt that she is a really interesting person. Jai wasn't too impressed with her. I don't know if that was for my benefit. Anna is a very attractive woman.

During one of the mooning sessions, Timmi asked Jai if he had ever "romanced" (I am not sure what he meant). Jai said no. Timmi, exasperated, asked Jai how old he is. Jai, I felt reluctantly, told him twenty-five. I didn't say anything. Jai had said to me at Charlie's at the very beginning that he was going to be thirty next year. I was inwardly shocked, but I didn't react. We had had a little smoke at Timmi and Anna's place before we'd left, so I just kept calm. Also, Timmi and Anna were not aware that we are seeing each other. And I'm not the type of person to cause a drama in public.

The rest of the evening I tried to create some distance between me and Jai. Both Anna and I would go out to smoke and leave the boys at the table. When the boys came out for a smoke, we would go back to the table.

I'm freaked out that Jai is so young. It's essentially a twenty-year age gap. However, I have lied to Jai too. I told him I was thirty-six on our first road trip to Hansari. Little did I know at that point what would happen between us. I didn't in a million years think we would become so close, so quick.

When we get back to my house later, we're sitting on my veranda having a cigarette. I try not to be close to him. I know he can feel that something is wrong, but he doesn't say anything. I say to him that I'm tired and he should go home, but as we continue talking, I don't want him to leave. I just say, "Come inside," and we go to bed.

He says something to the effect of, "Have you been following your heart or your head?"

I say, "It sure wasn't my head." I realise my heart is an idiot!

We do not mention the subject of age again. But it's playing on my mind still.

The few days later whilst at my house, Yatu messages and he asks, "How's the love life?" I tell him, "Fine," but then I tell him about the age difference.

The thing that is bugging me is that if I let my feelings go completely, then one day Jai will have to tow the family line and get married to someone more "appropriate". And what will happen to me then? I'll be even older and left with a broken heart.

Yatu says not to break up with him. Cheryl had said the same thing when I messaged her.

I think to myself, *People will have an issue with my age, but maybe I'm the one with the issue.* I don't know what to do.

The other issue I have is that I have lent Jai money for his place. He is getting money from the landlord, who has offered a loan, but that money has not yet come through. So work will have to stop on his place.

One afternoon, I was at my house and Jai popped in. He seemed distracted. He said he wanted to talk and asked me to promise not to get angry. So, immediately I was on high alert.

He asked if the landlord had talked to me about lending him fifty thousand rupees. I didn't understand what he meant, but the bottom line was that Jai needs more money to continue with the work at his place. And he wanted the landlord to be a guarantor for him, ensuring that I would get the money back. He was essentially asking for more money.

I was really pissed off that he would ask me again. I had already lent him fifty thousand rupees.

I told him that it just puts doubt in my mind about him and makes me wonder why he is in a relationship with me. I was seriously pissed off, and I told him so.

He explained that the chequebook for his account into which I had made the transfer hadn't yet arrived, so he could not pay the labourers. The debit card has a limit on it from what I gather.

I felt like I was put under a lot of pressure and being emotionally blackmailed. Everything was so great between us, and then he did this (again). It seriously made me doubt everything. He said that he is not misusing the money. He promised not to break my trust and said that it will not affect our relationship. I think he was telling the truth. But what am I supposed to think? He said he will give me the money back on Monday, when the money has cleared his account.

It just makes me think. Harry is supposed to be the bad guy in all of this, and if it is actually Jai, then that would make him a million times worse. Harry has never tried to seduce me to gain my trust and ask for money outright. If this is what Jai has done, it would seriously kill me, and I would never be able to trust another human being again.

You hear about men who seduce women to get money. Could I really be that gullible to fall for that type of scam? Have I really been taken in to the depths of manipulation and deceit? It would seriously turn my world upside down.

Just writing this down, I realise that I am being a complete fool, but I did lend Jai the money (again). I know I am being an absolute fucking idiot! But my gut instinct tells me I can trust him and urges me to be patient. *Trust* is a big word to be bandied about, and he tells me to trust him. We will see in a few days, on opening night, if it's all been worth it.

I know what you're thinking: *Fucking stupid woman!* I would be too!

Other than the two aforementioned mind fucks, everything has been going great. Prior to the second loan, Jai and I would just hang out, enjoying each other's company. On the odd occasion when we would go out to dinner and generally talk about various subjects, he continued to take the piss, but two are now playing that game.

Most times we just hang out at my house. He torments the kittens, and I try to stop him. He is really growing to like the kittens' company. He even took a selfie with Lollipop, and he talks to them both. At night, the kittens snuggle up between us, or we wake up to find that the kittens have bookended us. Sometimes it feels like a little family. No way in hell would I say that to him, though. God! I'd freak out to high heaven if he said that to me! But it feels nice nonetheless.

We have even had quite deep and challenging conversations, about God and religion. Just recently (a couple of nights ago, so it is still fresh in my mind) we even ventured onto the subject of love.

We have determined that we are more than just friends with benefits; it's something deeper than that. Neither of us ever imagined this happening. Jai said he initially came to Goa for only a month to help Harry out. He asked if I ever expected to be sleeping with a man this soon. I said, "Never in a million years." He said he thought he would meet a European woman and maybe have a bit of a casual fling. I told him I thought I would meet some European guy while sitting in the restaurant. I tell him that no matter what happens in the future, I always want to be his friend.

He said that for the next couple of months he needs to work hard, and then he'll become a free man. I didn't understand this.

He said that until January, he cannot say "I love you." He needs not to be committed.

But I can feel his feelings. He does care for me, and I care for him too.

But, still, I tell him that in a few months I will be back in the UK anyway.

I tell him that in the beginning I didn't even see him in a romantic way. I'd thought, *Why would he like me anyway?* And because of that, I didn't need to be anything other than myself, including the angry me. The next day he messaged and said that he never thought why I would like him. I said I couldn't remember what made me like him; it seems like years ago now.

I told him I'm not the marrying and kids kind of person, but I believe in love and want a lifelong commitment with someone. He asked if I have found that person. I said, "No, not yet!"

Fuck, my head was battered at this point. I hadn't expected this conversation! I realised we're both crap at expressing emotions. This was familiar ground. I should have just said how I was feeling. At this point, I was very confused.

Red flags seemed to be raising everywhere!

But again, this was familiar ground: when the road gets a bit rocky, I run a mile. I block myself off emotionally and self-sabotage. It's good I am able to recognise it though. That's progress for me.

Maybe this relationship is an experiment in real-life therapy. If that's the case, it's important to see it through to the end.

Up to Date, and What Now?!

So now we're pretty much up to date. Harry is in Shakthar setting up the last bits of the restaurant. The reception area is still a pile of rubble. I've been dealing with bookings and ungrateful guests. I've learnt that Indians are very demanding and have high expectations for cheap prices. Russians are cheap AF and are very much like Indians. All the UK people who have stayed have been lovely.

I still need to grow a pair of balls though, but they are coming along nicely. By the end of the season I will have this nailed, and global domination will be fully under way.

Today I have done a lot of chilling, which I've needed. Jai has been busy with his place, so it's nice to have some me time. Even though I miss him, it's good to get some space and perspective on things. Writing (typing) generally helps to clear the mind. I have missed this too.

So, what's next? Carry on with the bookings? Hopefully the money will continue to roll in, but it's not always about the money. I need to go out more and meet new people. I also must make time to catch up with Anna; I'm missing female company. Nimeesha is around the corner, so I will pop in more.

Jai's place is going to open in a few days, so I will probably be seeing less of him now anyway as we'll have conflicting schedules. I will let that fizzle out naturally if that is to be, rather than forcing any situation. I will still make attempts at getting my money back and hopefully will get some back tomorrow. We'll see.

Chapter 5

BLACK MONEY

It's been a couple of weeks since the end of the last chapter. Finding time to keep a daily account of events is too tedious now, so now my approach has changed. I'll do a summary of the past two weeks' events. The risk of this approach is that I may miss some vital information and details. However, the last two weeks have been dominated by one big event that no one could have foreseen, and which was beyond the control of anyone at LOM, including me and all the people who have been involved in the previous chapters.

This one event has changed everything on a national, if not international scale, and has impacted the whole of India, including all who live here and all who visit.

Monday evening, 7 November, two weeks ago, I was in bed scrolling through Facebook as I do on a nightly basis. It was the US presidential election with Trump and Clinton and I was monitoring the outcome of the election. While I was scrolling, an item appeared on the *Times of India* newsfeed. It stated that as of tomorrow, President Modi has declared that the RS500 and RS1,000 bills would no longer be legal currency in India. This was to be a "surgical strike" carried out in order to curb the black money market and to stop the funding of terrorist activity across the global. Firstly, I thought this was a joke article; surely it couldn't be true. I shared the article on Facebook to check if any of my Indian friends knew anything about it, but no one responded.

The next morning, I arrived at LOM. Jalan and the landlord were standing outside his house. I asked them if the news was true, and they replied yes. My immediate thought was, *WTF? And what am I to do with all the hard cash I have received from room rent?* I had nearly two lakhs in my safe in my house, mostly all in RS500 and RS1,000 notes.

More news followed. I learnt that everyone had until the 30 December to deposit old notes into bank accounts or exchange them at any bank or post office. That was one consolation.

At the time, I was in process of setting up my own bank account with ICICI Bank. It was pretty much set up, so I started to deposit money into that account, my first deposit being forty thousand, followed by another forty thousand the next couple of days. I was still reluctant to deposit money into Harry's account as there was the risk that it would just disappear, and then nothing would be left for my share or even to pay the bills.

However, the impact on everyone was instantaneous, not only the locals but also tourists who had just arrived and exchanged their money for rupees, again mainly RS500 and RS1,000 notes. Both locals and tourists queued outside banks to exchange their money, but the limit to exchange was only two thousand rupees at a time, and ATMs were only issuing a maximum of two thousand rupees at a time also. The bureaucratic process meant that the serial number of each note to be exchanged had to be noted on a form. It was complete madness.

All loans and large money transactions have been suspended. And people are feeling the pinch, especially where credit is concerned. People are giving credit in good faith, but as businesses can't access to their money, credit is not being paid. Jai is feeling this hugely with setting up his place. The guy is super stressed, and the project has been delayed by weeks. More on this later.

The thing with India is that the majority of people do not have bank accounts, especially in rural areas. Transactions are done with hard cash, even large sums of money. I read a story that a woman committed suicide the day after completing a land sale with hard cash. People have died while queueing to exchange money. Queues have been literally going on for miles, and money to exchange has been running out at banks. Just imagine queuing in the Indian midday heat, and then the banks closing their doors. I'm surprised there haven't been riots. The whole process has not been thought out. And now there is a shortage of smaller-denomination notes, i.e. RS100 and RS50 notes.

The impact on LOM's business has been huge. People are cancelling bookings or are just not showing up. There were four no-shows in two days. A group of European women had booked, turned up, and seen the rooms (deluxe rooms, which they liked), but then they decided the cost was too high as they couldn't pay in cash. So, they just left. That was a forty-thousand-rupee booking! There was no point in me asking for at least the money for the first night, as they didn't have it. I saw them having breakfast the following day in a cheaper place around the corner.

Also, LOM doesn't have a card machine, so Western people can't even pay with card. One benefit is that Russians exchange their currency into dollars, and the dollar is a highly valued currency. So, we have started to take dollars, but I cannot exchange foreign currency just yet. Dollars are safe for now. Further, I've had to borrow Nimeesha's card machine, which has helped, but as it's a small business, the money going into their account is being taxed. So, I asked Vijay at Serenity Retreat, who has been more than helpful.

Anyway, business is slower, but I'm still getting bookings in. We are just being flexible with payments. I'm trying to sort out a card machine, but it needs to be linked to a bank account. The landlord said he would help. We'll see how that goes.

I've had to start to deposit money into Harry's account as one of the new rules is that I now need a PAN card to deposit any additional cash into my account. A PAN card is like a national insurance number, which I also need to set up a PayPal account for LOM. The whole payment process has been a real pain to arrange and sort out. I am still not set up, but Harry is threatening me with a card machine, which would mean the money would go into his account. Again, I am reluctant to do that.

Later I discovered that a PAN card is only required for deposits over fifty thousand rupees.

However, Jai advised me I don't need a PAN card to deposit cheques, which I confirmed with one of the Bank tellers at ICICI Bank. I can deposit the cheque from Nimeesha into my account.

I am just hoping the situation settles before we hit December and then the Christmas and New Year period, and that by then we have a card machine sorted.

The thing with all of this is that part of my plan was to make some off-grid money by coming to India, and now that part of my plan is completely ruined. The legality involved is twice as difficult for me as I'm not an Indian national, but an NRI (non-resident Indian). Opening a back account has been a lot of rigmarole, and now I have to potentially pay tax on the LOM room rent.

Modi is ensuring each Indian national is tied into the banking system and, in turn, the global banking infrastructure. The guise is to stop the black money market, but the rich have ways of securing their finances, while the poor pay the price. It's always the person in the street, the little person, who pays the price.

So, I'm having to become a semi-legit businesswoman, but if I'm to do this properly and build a real future for myself, I need to be legit. I am not just doing this for the entertainment. We'll see what happens in the next couple of months.

I just have to mention something about Donald Trump winning the US election. Seriously. What. The. Actual. Fuck! What is happening with the world that some idiot imbecile can win the most powerful position on the planet? The comparisons with Brexit are obvious, but it's the rise of the alt-right, and the ideology of racism, separation, sexism, and blatant hate, that is scaring the shit out of me.

Maybe I'm better off staying in India for the foreseeable future. The West is going down the tubes. Let's see what Trump does for the world!

Well, that's enough about global politics and economics. Back to business!

The restaurant is fully up and running, and I've got to say the Restaurant team are doing a really good job. The atmosphere during the day is nice and chill. I mostly work from one of the tables in the restaurant. I get coffee on demand/request, and I get food made for me if I feel like it. I enjoy general chit-chat and banter with the restaurant guys, and with guests when they check in and check out, and with Jalan and the Landlord.

In the evening, the restaurant is low-lit with candles and nice round lantern things randomly hung. The music is varied but is mostly Indian "wedding" music. Sometimes they'll play some pop dance stuff. I played my tunes from my phone last night, and I think they were a hit, if I do say so myself. #smugface

The food is actually quite delicious, from the plain masala omelette to the Laffa wrap, which is super yummy. But one downside: it's super rich and very greasy sometimes, so I tend to limit when I eat there. Cocktails are good, although they could be better and more imaginative. It's the usual cosmopolitan, Martini, mojitos, etc. The Bahama Mama is nice though.

If I go to the restaurant at night, there's always a bit of customer relations going on too.

A couple of times I've sat and chatted with single male

guests. I can feel the staff's beady little eyes on me, ha ha, much to my amusement. A couple of them have been quite nice.

Also, I have been getting on better with the restaurant team. Satish is a sweet lad with a smidge of a lazy eye. But he's nice enough, and as he knows Lucky and Bally from Kovvi, interestingly, I get a bit of juicy gossip on Lucky. Satish said that at one-point Lucky had about nine or ten girlfriends at the same time. These would most likely have been holiday romances, where the young woman was swept off her feet by the romance of Goa. Little do these women know it's all a game. Anyway, Satish went on to say on one occasion, Lucky was juggling two sets of women in the same restaurant but at different tables. And then in walked a third, who pounced on Lucky. He did a runner and left the women fighting over him.

I think I had a lucky escape there (pun intended), or was my inner voice right to leave that well enough alone? I should listen to it more often. But do I know my own soul? Someone recently said that I don't! Again, more on that later.

There's also Dev Chef, Joe the barman, Satish's *mama/ mamu* (meaning maternal uncle), Patal the tandoori chef, and Mistry (the other chef), who is very strange and starey. He creeps me out sometimes. There's also Amit, who nearly had a fatal accident but just ended up with a smashed big toe. Very lucky escape for him. Lucky kid! And there are a few others whom I don't really associate with.

Also, there's Jalan, who's still doing a grand job. Jai is trying to poach him for his own place, but I'm not having it. Jalan is staying with me. Who else is going to give me all the gossip about everyone?! There's Jagu, who is Fruity' s son. He has been helping Jalan out with the rooms and helping with the check-in of the guests when neither I nor Jalan is there.

The landlord still hangs out sometimes but generally keeps to his own business, at least as much as these people can. The blokes are worse than the women at gossiping.

The room bookings are doing really well, even after the black money surgical strike.

It's nice meeting new and different people. Most of the time they are fine and reasonable people. On the odd occasion, there is no pleasing them. When that happens, I just let them go. I don't want unhappy guests at my place. But most everyone is happy with the place.

Harry sticks his oar in a few times a week. Fair enough. He is my "business partner", but I'm the one doing the hard graft. And it seems it's the same in Veenram too.

I had a really good chat with Karan a week or so ago. He was feeling rather despondent, and I suppose I was a sounding board. He's basically going through what I went through when I first got here (and still do sometimes). He's feeling isolated and feels like Harry is not supporting him. He has the added disadvantage of being completely foreign, and in Goa it's very much who you know rather than what you know. At least I look Indian.

It's very difficult for foreigners to make something of themselves if they don't have local support. In that way I have been lucky. Once you have that local support network, things are a lot easier. But Karan hasn't felt supported, not even by Harry.

Of course, in Harry's eyes it's a very different story. Everything is going well. Although he did admit just today that business in Hansari has really suffered because of the currency situation. I think he is trying.

He also enquired about Jai, asking if I had seen him. I said, "Yes. We are friends, and we go for dinner and drinks sometimes." He said that one of his "contacts" sees me with Jai in Tarana nearly every day. Which is not true! Harry started going on about the petrol cap going missing on his car again, which he blames Jai for. I told him if he holds onto anger, he is only hurting himself.

He went on about putting money into his account and

how he now needs to register all his income for tax purposes. He says that all guests must be invoiced and "officialised" or something to that effect.

That is all possible, but again the bottom line is whether or not I can trust him. Later that evening, I relayed the conversation to Satish. He looked worried and said the same thing. But if it were to come to the crunch, he and the rest of the restaurant could walk away. Could I walk away at this late stage?

My answer is no. I'm not going to get beaten. I will do this one way or another.

The Landlord has already hinted about giving me the next place when they build it. I need to get this season done before I commit myself to anything longish term. The next season is more than likely, though.

So, business-wise the restaurant is going well, apart from the odd interference from Harry or annoying and demanding guests.

It's now juicy gossip time. I know you have been waiting patiently for it.

I've continued seeing Jai, still very much in secret. He's got a nice place in Tarana, where I stayed over three or four times. We sit on the balcony chatting shit generally. Sometimes we have a smoke; other times we just have a drink and some food.

One night we played My Tune, Your Tune and had a couple of shots of vodka. The fucker tricked me. He poured one for each of us, but when we went to down it, he didn't take his. I made sure he took the next one! I think he likes the wild woman side of me. I need to let my hair down a little. I am still very reserved with people in terms of letting them get to know the full me, especially the wild side.

Jai has seen it a couple of times.

But with LOM taking up most of my headspace and my time, and with Jai still in the process of setting up Creation Valley (that's the official name now), including the holiday cottages and the on-site restaurant, Amun Ra Café (also the official name), he's been majorly stressed. Money is still tight. At times I cannot tell if it's just stress or something else. He doesn't always reveal his feelings verbally. I'm finding this a little off-putting, and then I just create space between us.

However, we spend most nights together, usually at my place.

As much as I totally enjoy being with him, there has been a number of red flags that have been popping up.

These aren't in any specific order, but these things did seem to happen in quick succession and have been building up in my mind:

1. He's been taking the piss out of my weight. A couple of times, he's put his hand on my tummy and asked, "How many months?" He says it's not serious and that I'm too serious. Damn straight I'm serious. He really shows his immaturity sometimes.

   Also, he has been telling me what to wear. We went to this reggae event thing, and I wore my camouflage pencil skirt and a black T-shirt. He had advised that a one-piece would have been more appropriate. Fuck that! When does anyone ever wear a proper dress to a reggae night? He said didn't like the skirt, but I wore it anyway.

2. Speaking of immaturity, the age this has really been bugging me. I know he's twenty-six, twenty-seven in January. I still haven't told him what my age is.

   One evening we were sitting and chatting in my kitchen. We have to sit on the countertops as there are no chairs in my place. We got onto the subject of marriage. He said he is getting pressure from his family to get married. He is the eldest boy and is still not married. His cousins are now starting to settle down, and he is getting the obvious emotional blackmail tossed at him, like "Think about your grandfather."

I told him I know what it's like to be emotionally blackmailed. I have been there.

He continued, saying that everything is set up in his home town for when he gets married: the house, money I suppose, and the beautiful, highly educated, adoring, and subservient wife. He said he wouldn't get married until he was at least thirty and has made something of himself. At the moment, he can't commit to anything or anyone. And that means me too. He said it wouldn't be until January before he knows what will happen. At that point he will know if the business is a success or not. If it isn't a success, then he will have to leave me behind, as he can't take me with him.

However, a couple of weeks ago he wanted to take me to his parents' as a "friend" while he attended a family wedding. I'm not sure if I was to attend the wedding or not, but I couldn't put myself in that situation in any case. Fuck, no way. Imaging sitting with your young lover's parents, who might possibly be the same age as you, and pretending to be just friends and making polite chit-chat. I should have done it just for the total bizarreness of the situation and laughed to myself. Anyway, I don't think it would have happened. Jai never did end up going to Gandabaan for the wedding.

Anyway, I listened to him. What the fuck am I meant to say? "Ah, ah. There, there, it'll be all right! Don't worry. I'm here to support you and comfort you while the stink of possible heartbreak is looming over me." So, this is another major red flag that popped up.

3. Flag number three: late night phone calls from women, or one particular woman as far as I am aware. One time we were at his place, and he took quite a long call on

the balcony, speaking in soft tones. He said it was his cousin who had had a loving marriage, but it went pear-shaped, and they were now divorcing. Fair enough, if that was the case.

I'm learning that Jai has a lot of female friends. This I don't have a problem with. I think he is quite a sensitive guy underneath. But it's the blatant lies that bother me. Prime example: we were lying in bed watching Emmanuella videos on YouTube on his phone. (OMG, I fricking love Emmanuella, the most talented little girl I've seen in a long time. She is funny as fuck!) We were laughing away, and a phone call came in from Anisha. Jai swiped to cut the call. She called again. He took the call in the kitchen. I was wide awake and could hear everything even though he was speaking in a whisper.

She must have asked him where he was because he replied, "At home, sleeping." Clearly not! Then came another reply of, "You can't ask me that, but I can't tell you." The call ended. He came back to bed, and we fell asleep with only a "Goodnight, boss." I didn't even want to turn around for a kiss. We fell asleep with the heavy silence between us.

However, and very ironically, at approximately 1.30 in the morning, my phone rang under my pillow. I sleepily answered it. I didn't know who it was. It turned out to be a guest I had been talking to the evening before, which Jai had seen when he was visiting the landlord outside LOM. I hadn't seen him at all. But I had asked if the guest would come and have a smoke with us in Tarana. The guest respectfully declined the invite as he'd realised I was talking to a guy. Was it the way I spoke?

After I recognised the guest's voice, I asked the guest if everything was all right. He said yes. He asked me if there was anywhere he could get alcohol at this hour. I said I didn't know, maybe try the restaurant guys.

He went on to ask me if I wanted to have a smoke. I let out a soft little laugh and said no. It was late. The call ended, and I went back to sleep, feeling the distance between me and Jai more so, but also feeling a little bit pleased with myself.

The next morning, we awoke. He went to his place, and I left for LOM. I don't think many words were spoken.

4. Moving on to red flag number 4. Now it's been nearly three months since Jai and I have been seeing each other, and this has all been very much cloak-and-dagger—more so since the restaurant guys arrived.

   It's beginning to take its toll on me, all this sneaking around. We're both grown adults, and if we want to have a relationship, we should be able to conduct it without judgement.

   But it's all very complicated, the biggest point being that Jai and Harry are ultimate frenemies. I'm stuck in the middle of all this shit.

   When coming back from Tarana one morning, we passed Bhanu, the landlord's youngest brother, in his Tempo (a little van thing), and on another occasion Peri (the landlord's daughter) was outside her workplace. And Jai's car has been spotted outside my house by the landlord and Jalan. Jalan told me that the landlord asked why Jai's car would be outside my house, and he replied that Jai sometimes brings me food.

   I'm really getting to the end of my tether here, feeling so frustrated at the childishness of it all.

5. And lastly is the big albatross in the room—money! I still haven't gotten any of my money back. It's like a big black cloud that is constantly hanging over our heads.

   And then came another downpour. I had already lent Jai money to pay off some legal claim against him, which cost ten thousand rupees. And now he was asking for more, twenty-seven thousand rupees to be exact (I checked the messages). I absolutely blew my top at him via WhatsApp. I couldn't even talk to him. He asked if I was angry. What do you think, Sherlock? He said he knows I am angry. And I got the usual spiel of him. I told him that he's worse than Harry because he has made me care for him, and it does my head in and makes me doubt why he is with me. He told me to chill and relax. What the fuck! I told him that I've nearly reached my limit, and I listed the foregoing items as my reasons. I ignored messages after that and hid in High Life to have a cold coffee.

Seriously, this guy makes me so angry that I could break something.

Anyway, I didn't lend him the twenty-seven thousand rupees. Now I can't remember if it's the same night or the night after. I have been in an emotional fog of late. But I've decided I've had enough of this.

I asked him to come around, and I'm not even sure how the conversation started, but we were sitting on the kitchen counter. I started to tell him that things are stressing me out, all the money stuff, the sneaking around, and the late-night phone calls. I mentioned that he makes me feel shit when he says stuff about my weight.

After a long while, I mustered the courage and mentioned my age, telling him that I am much older than what I'd initially said. He said he didn't think about the age difference. I said that in the end he will probably marry someone more suitable. And if we were to continue the way we've been going at thing, then my feelings would grow and then I would be left broken-hearted.

Before I realised what I was saying, it seemed like the only solution was to finish things with him. I said it would probably be the best option and that we would save each other a lot of heartache before things got more serious. He didn't say much but asked if that is what I really want. I said yes. I said, "It's for the best for both of us." We sat for a little while longer, and he said he'll leave. I said, "OK."

I walked him to the door and closed the door, immediately realising, *Shit, what have I done?* I felt like I'd lost everything!

Then an hour of messaging ensued. I said, "I'm so sorry that I have hurt you." He hates me now, and that kills me. I know I've made a big mistake.

He said, "You were there from the start, and now you have walked away just when things are getting started." He says he was with me for the support and that it was not just about money and sex, adding that he has plenty of options for that. He's not even fighting for me. He said, "Why should I?" I made the decision to end it without even talking to him. I made the decision, so why should he tell me how he's feeling? I can sense his anger at me and his hurt. But he remains calm.

He is killing me! I'm distraught. But I cut my losses and say, "Good luck. I know you will be amazing." He says the same and concludes that we'll leave each other alone.

Gutted is an absolute understatement. I know I have lost my best friend. I truly will be alone out here. I message Cheryl and tell her what's happened. She provides a rational perspective and says that I panicked about the whole series of red flags. She adds that I shouldn't be focusing on the future, suggesting that Jai may be embarrassed about the whole money situation.

Yes, I have panicked. I recently read an article about the shadow self, a primitive part of the brain that controls the fight or flight response when a person senses fear. It talked about how the shadow self can make us do crazy things, make us loose it, and basically override the higher, more conscious brain. Obviously this a very general summary of the shadow self idea, but it resonated with me. I must buy the book to read it in full. What can I say, I'm only human, and I get angry and do stupid things out of fear and self-preservation.

> The Shadow Effect of the Shadow Self states as humans we have a dual existence, in that without dark there is no light, without lies, there is no truth. It's this duality that we deny ourselves, and when we deny this dualistic element of being human, then that's when the Shadow Effect of the Shadow self takes over and controls us into making judgements, and we act out of fear. It's the fear of who we are and what we want to be.[1]

The shadow self theory says that to overcome the shadow effect, we must acknowledge it. If we do this, then we embrace the dark side of the dualistic existence (sorry, *Star Wars* fans. I may have some of this wrong, but I have referenced the book so you can read it too).

Anyway, back to this crazy reality of mine! So, after messaging Cheryl and deciding to cut my losses with Jai, no matter how hard it's going to be, he messages me to ask if I have had dinner.

What the fuck?! I don't get what's happening here. I tell him that I'm too upset and feel too sick to eat. He says he wants to meet one last time.

He comes over, and we talk more. I ask him why he has come over. He says he's being a good friend. We're lying in bed, and again he says that he cannot commit until he is a success. He has his principles. I burst into tears and turn away from him. I say he is doing my fucking head in.

---

[1] Deepak Chopra, Debbie Ford, and Marianne Williamson, *The Shadow Effect: Illuminating the Hidden Power of Your True Self* (New York, 2009).

Eventually we fall asleep as if it's the most normal thing to do after a three-hour break-up, if that's what you call it—even if I don't think this is a proper relationship. I don't know what this is. Friends with benefits?

The next day, we basically resume as normal. But I'm still filled with doubts and concerns.

The days at LOM are starting to become mundane. But the day is getting into a sort of rhythm. I generally walk to LOM and arrive by 9.30 a.m. The restaurant guys always offer me a black coffee and cold milk on the side. I cannot function without this!

Guests check out, and new guests arrive in the afternoon. I actually quite enjoy this, meeting new people. Mostly they are couples, young nubile things doing their yoga retreat or classes. I have a general catch-up with Jalan and tell him about the booking schedule. I've started to write down the comings and goings for the restaurant guys, as the dimwits couldn't understand my Excel schedule. Sometimes I have lunch at the restaurant, and other times I go home to check on Brutus and Lollipop. They are getting big, especially Brutus. He's a bit of a meathead now. I now let them out in the mornings, and they do their poohs and wees outside. Then I head back to LOM for an hour or so, or if need be I make a trip somewhere.

I then return to my house and rest and refresh, and then head back to LOM for dinner and catch-up with guests if they stay for dinner. I return to my house around 10 p.m. at the latest.

Jai comes over when he has finished at the site. We watch Emmanuella vids on YouTube for a bit of a timepass, and then we fall asleep.

It's Creation Valley's and Amun Ra Café's opening night soon.

Chapter 6

STATE OF PARANOIA

Even though things are moving along at a bit of a mundane pace, there's always that underlying distrust with pretty much everyone.

The rationale behind the three-hour break-up was still lingering. The ever-present annoyance of Harry and the cautious friendships with the restaurant guys have also been taking a bit of an emotional toll.

Furthermore, it doesn't help that Jalan (with all the best intentions) lets me in on the restaurant gossip.

One saving grace has been the check-in of Samantha and Ryan, who in a very short time have pretty much have become my agony aunt and uncle. We hit it off pretty much immediately.

At the time it was Jai's opening night on the following Monday, so I asked them if they would like to go. They said yes. Fab! Something to look forward to.

The next day Jalan and I went out on the hunt for kitten food. We did a big round trip to Thairi—a big roundabout or circle as the Indians call it. He started telling me that the restaurant guys still don't know where I live but are curious. They know the general vicinity but not the exact place.

He started talking about what they have been saying

about me, the usual "madam this, madam that". Most of it is speculation about what I do in the evenings after I leave the restaurant. I'm not too concerned. But he says that both Dev Chef and Satish are basically spying on me for Harry—or words to that effect. He said that Satish is a dangerous man. This upset me as I thought Satish and I were getting along. It irked me somewhat. He said that sometimes when he drops me off, he does a bit of a round trip to make it seem like I live farther away than I actually do. And when I ask him to pick me up in the evenings, he says he's busy so that the guys do not follow him. A couple of times I've had to walk in the dark back to LOM (I'm determined to get a car now). We left it at that, and after an unsuccessful kitten food hunt, we headed back.

On the way back via Tarana and Obrah, Jai drove past us, heading towards Thairi. I didn't have time to respond. I think Jai beeped his horn at us though.

Over the course of the same few days, I see Jai in the evenings. He's stressed about the run-up to opening night. The Monday opening has been delayed due to various issues, but mainly because there is no electrical supply to his place.

He's stressed but seems to be acting a bit shady. One evening he told me that Anna was helping to set up the opening night and that she was now his events manager. I was a bit taken aback by this, as he had previous expressed an annoyance with Anna and Timmi. I didn't say anything, but again I had an uncomfortable feeling about it. He said she was helping with DJs and Russian translations for the flyer. They had spent four hours at Kandar Printers designing the flyer.

I like Anna, and I do not have an issue with Jai working with her, and that's the God honest truth. What I am concerned about is why he hadn't mentioned it before. Why the secrecy? It just seemed to come from out of the blue.

The following night, again back at my house, he was telling me about the opening night. We were standing in the kitchen, and I noticed a sparkle of glitter on his eyelid. He rubbed his eyes, and I went over and firmly moved his head to see clearly, but the glitter was gone! Again, I didn't say anything, but I was furious inside. Later, after smoking a joint, he was lying on my bed, and I was sitting on the edge. I didn't want to be near him. He was saying he needed his new venture to work and that he was committed to Anna and the Russians. Now this really got under my skin. I didn't say anything again, but I thought to myself, *You spend nearly every night with me, and you're more committed to the Russians and Anna than you are to me.* The anger was brewing—I could feel it—but I tried to hold it together. I just said to him, "You have to do what you have to do!" I was feeling restless, so I went into the kitchen to finish the joint, leaving him on the bed. I paced from the kitchen to the bathroom. My head was mashed.

We were both stoned, and I felt like there was a massive rift between us. I'm sure he felt it too.

We went to bed. He put his arm around me, but I kept my distance. My mind was spinning from everything. In the morning he left, saying, "Bye, boss," from the door. I just waved at him. He asked if I was angry.

I was still annoyed from the night before, but I just said, "I've just woken up." Fuck, man, he seems to know everything that I feel, sometimes even before I do.

The day passed without event. I spoke to Ryan and Samantha, telling them that the opening night was delayed, but asked if they still wanted to go out somewhere. They said yes. Thank goodness. I had briefly explained to them about the whole Jai versus Harry situation. I felt like I needed to share that to lift the burden somewhat, and because they are completely impartial to the situation.

That evening I headed back to LOM. I saw Ali by the taxi stand outside LOM and realised Harry had arrived. I greeted Ali, saying, "Hello, my friend," and shook his hand. I like him. He is a good guy even though he is one of Harry's goons. But he's got a good heart.

I walked over to the bar and greeted Harry and shook his hand. I was dressed up to go out with Ryan and Samantha. I wasn't sure what he made of this. The restaurant was busy, which is a good thing.

I asked how he was. He said, "Good." I told him I was going out with guests. He just said OK. Hanu and his goon friend were at a table too. I said hi to him. Ryan and Samantha were having dinner. I left them to eat in piece. While I had something to eat, Harry was in the restaurant with Dev Chef and the other kitchen staff.

After a while, I arranged a taxi to take the three of us to Charlie's in Laksara. Haroon, one of the drivers, took us, and we chatted in the taxi. Jai called while we were on our way. I told him I was going to Charlie's and said I would call him back.

Haroon asked what we wanted to do about getting back. He asked how long we would be. I said probably a couple of hours, until twelve o'clock. He said he would wait for us.

We arrived at Charlie's, and it was busy, but we got a table on the terrace. We ordered drinks. I took a couple of minutes' leave to call Jai back. We checked in, each asking how the other was. I told him I was with guests and at Charlie's. He said, "OK. Have fun. And good night." It felt nice just to check in, but still I was plagued by insecurities from the previous night.

The three of us chatted, and I went into a bit more detail about the whole Jai versus Harry situation, but not too much. They said that when we were in the restaurant there was a guy shouting into the phone about a deposit, and they realised it was Harry. His reputation precedes him. Ryan coined the phrase "It's like Hollyoaks, but Goanoaks," which is quite apt given all the dramas. I also explained about Jai being a lot younger than I and the whole Indian marriage scenario. But I tried not to dwell on the negatives, and we talked about general stuff too. They told me about themselves and how long they've been together since they were sixteen. They mentioned how they used to bomb around on a scooter. They told me that all their friends were having babies and settling down, but they didn't want that just yet, so they'd decided to have a "breakaway" tour. They are my kind of people. We had a laugh, which is what I needed. However, the best part was speaking to fellow English people. I didn't have to adjust my speech for the locals to understand.

Before we knew it, it was twelve o'clock. We headed back to the cab. All of us really liked Charlie's, which I was so pleased about.

I got dropped off at my house. I decided not to message Jai and just go to sleep.

It is now the next morning. When I arrive at LOM, Harry is sitting at the big table with Rana (Jai's chef, whom he has sacked. I think there was a clash of personalities, and Rana had been gossiping about Jai's business). I look around and say, "Well, this is interesting!" with a smirk on my face. However, inside I am in a state of panic about what is going on.

Harry starts going on with himself and saying how Jai owes Rana thirty thousand rupees. I really don't know what this refers to. Harry then starts with his usual slating of Jai and mentions the crockery and money he has "cheated" me out of.

I keep quiet for now, but I watch the proceedings.

Samantha and Ryan come down for breakfast. Seeing all of us around the table, they sheepishly say good morning and then sit down.

You can cut the atmosphere with a knife!

Then Harry starts to target me, saying how he doesn't like to ask all the time and how he needs to see the accounts and the guest inventory. I say, "Yes, we can look at it now."

He says, "OK. After breakfast."

I don't have cigarettes, so I take the opportunity to go to the shop and call Jai. I'm still paranoid about the money I have lent Jai and how that is creating a deficit in my accounts. I'm starting to lose it with him as he keeps saying he will give me the cheque tomorrow, and then tomorrow never comes.

I call him and ask when I will get the cheque. He promises

that he'll give it to me later. He says he can't talk now as he is with friends. It's 10 a.m.! I ask him where he is. He says Thairi. I completely lose it! I am angry now. I shout at him: "Who are you with? I don't give a fuck about anything else; I just want my money!" I tell him I want the cheque today.

The poor guy puts up with so much of my shit!

After buying cigarettes, I head back to LOM. Harry and I spend a good hour going through the inventory, the expenses, and the total amount that has been received so far. He starts going on about how his "accountant" has told him about paying taxes and getting a TIN and a Light of Moon billing book with individual numbers, and how guests need to get a bill when they check out.

This is all sounding practical, but the reality is that we are (or more to the point, I am) just winging it at the moment. The reception hasn't even been finished, and it stinks of toilet as the sewage pipe is still there.

After the interrogation, I make my way home to pick up a cheque which Vijay from Serenity Retreat had given me for their overbookings. I also call Jai and ask him to meet me.

As I arrive at my house, Jai arrives a minute after. He looks worried. I express to him that I'm freaking out because of the money and how he keeps failing to deliver on his word to give me the cheque. He tries to explain the reasons, but it just sounds so lame. He says that when I shout at him it upsets him, and that this morning he went to pick up friends from Gandabaan.

Harry is calling me. Jai leaves. I walk back to LOM.

I have calmed myself a little, but I still have to go and face Harry. I collect the cheque from the safe in my wardrobe at house. Halfway, whilst walking back to LOM, Dev Chef goes by on a scooter in the opposite direction, and he stops to chat. I know that Harry has sent him to check on me. Luckily, I am way past my house. Jai left in the opposite direction, away from LOM.

I ask Dev Chef where he's going. He says he is going to see the BBQ guy. There's nothing at the top of my road! (Later I discover that there is an ironmonger at the top of my road who previously built a BBQ.)

I arrive back at LOM and hand Harry the cheque for forty-five thousand rupees (approximately). At first, he is reluctant to take it, but that doesn't last long. He takes the cheque and pockets it. I knew that would placate him, the money-grubbing son of a bitch.

He had said that he wanted a copy of the guest inventory and expenses, so I put a copy on my pen drive to take to the print shop later.

We sit down for lunch, Harry, one of his goons, Ali, and I. Harry starts to waffle on with himself again. Previously he had had a shouted at Amit, telling him that he needs to go back home as he is not performing as he should, with Harry saying that he isn't running an ashram but a business.

Now, during lunch he starts to go on about how I was adamant about keeping Amit. I respond that I said nothing of the sort. He adds that we were both sitting at the table when we had the conversation. I tell him that conversation was about Jalan, not Amit. He goes, "No, no, no." I remember the conversation clearly. He is basically saying that Jalan has to go because he talks to the landlord about what happens at LOM. I refuse to agree with him and say Jalan is not going anywhere.

This is a prime example of Harry trying to twist a situation and fuck with my mind. This time it doesn't work, as I know exactly how that conversation went.

He then starts to go on about my friendship with Jai, saying that multiple people are saying that I have invested money in his place, adding that I spend every day with him in Tarana. People have seen me with him. He goes on again about the whole business of Jai cheating.

I say to him, "I haven't got time to spend every day in

Tarana. And my personal life is separate from LOM. I'm here to do a job."

I know he's trying to fuck with my mind, but it's working. I keep a calm exterior, but inside I am seething with anger and paranoia. I say over lunch that I don't understand why people just make things up for no reason.

He says that if one person says something, he doesn't believe them, but if five people say the same thing, he has to believe what he is hearing. He also says that he has contacts who tell him things, some of them telling him that they have seen Jai had with an Indian woman who is English Punjabi. How the hell would anyone even know that I was English without speaking to me?

My response is something to the effect of, "Well, that's up to you. And if people want to make a deal about seeing me with Jai, then that's their problem. And, yes, I meet him for drinks and dinner sometimes, but saying I am with him every day is ridiculous."

The only person who would have seen me with Jai is Raja (Jai's sacked chef). One evening, I had asked him to sit with me in LOM for a conversation, just to see what the guy was about as he had been randomly popping in to see Dev Chef. He looked petrified as he sat down. He didn't really have much to say for himself apart from relaying his work history. He knew Jai and Harry from their Glamour and Palm Tree Vista days. Also, I wanted to find out if he had invested in Jai's place, as someone (maybe Jalan) had mentioned that he was a partner. He had not invested but was waiting on his salary for the month when work had not yet started.

Why the frick had Jai gotten involved with this guy? I have no idea. Jai pretends to be the big man, a one-man show, but he also needs his back covered. I have his back!

Anyway, we finish lunch, and Harry goes to his room to sleep.

In the meantime, all the restaurant staff, along with Jalan,

Ali, and I, mill about, joking about how Harry had told Ali about flying to Hindavi. After much debating, Ali and the other goon decide to leave. They take their belongings on their heads with them to the bus stop to make their own way back to Hindavi.

Jalan and I go to the print shop in Shakthar Market to get the inventory and expenses printed.

Jalan drops me off at home afterwards.

On my return to LOM in the evening, I find that Harry has left, much to my relief.

I chat with Sam and Ryan for a while after my dinner. They ask how things are going, and I say, "Another eventful day in Goanoaks."

Jai phones to see what I am doing and asks if I want to go to Charlie's with him and a couple of his friends. I say yes, and when I head back home, they all come and pick me up.

Jai's friends are a young Indian couple. Jai knows the guy from his college days. I can't remember their names, but they seem really nice.

On our arrival at Laksara, the men walk ahead, and I talk to the women. She is really sweet and tells me that they have only just gotten married, and it was a love marriage (as opposed to an arranged marriage). She is Christian, and he is Hindu. I admire her for this. Slowly things are changing in India. The acceptance of love marriages is slowly becoming the norm.

At Charlie's we all sit and chat. I mainly listen. The guy and his girl take the piss out of Jai and laugh about his escapades during his college days. They also talk about the women he dated back then and what he was like as a student.

It has been a pleasant evening, but it is getting late. We head back to Shakthar.

On the way back, both the girl and the guy fall asleep in the back of the car.

The music is on. Jai turns to me and says, "What happened this morning?" He says he doesn't like Anna, adding that he doesn't have time to mess around. I look at him. Part of me is embarrassed by the way I reacted, but all the sentiments are still true. Still, my delivery needed to have some impact, otherwise he wouldn't have "heard" me. One thing which is not true is that I only give a fuck about the money. So not true. There's only one thing that I really give a fuck about, and he is sitting next to me.

Earlier in the day he had messaged me after the afternoon meeting with Harry. He said I had a problem with trust. He said he was already having a bad day; he'd accidently ran over a dog. I told him, "That's terrible."

Back in the car, I say that he's right about the trust thing. He just says, "You don't trust me." We just look at each other. I don't remember the rest of the journey home, apart from dropping Jai's friends at his place in Tarana, and then getting back to my house. I also don't remember what happened next apart from just going to sleep. I was feeling emotionally exhausted.

All this anger and paranoia is actually physically exhausting too.

In the morning we wake up. It's later than normal, and I'm running a little late. We're lying close in bed, and he says I need to be more dedicated. Fuck, that is low! Fucking pissing me off as soon as I wake up. I turn around, burst into tears, and get up. I don't need this shit first thing in the fucking morning. He says, "What happened? I was only joking!" Whether this is true or not, it seems to be the pattern: he says something, and if I get upset, he says it's a joke! To me in my emotional state, this is like a kick in the stomach. And I had only just awakened. Talk about timing.

I'm standing in the kitchen, trying to pull myself together but failing. He follows me in. I've surprised myself with the way my feelings are just bubbling under a thin layer of skin, and I'm shocked at the sheer audacity of his remarks.

If he were as intuitive as he says he is, he would have realised that I am feeling fragile. Sometimes I think he does it on purpose to get a reaction out of me. Well, he got one! He tries to feebly hug me. I half surrender to it.

He leaves, and I try to figure out what the hell is going on with me. Never have I just burst into tears over a remark, whether it was intended to hurt or not. I realise I need to do something.

Now I can't remember if I had prearranged this with Valerie or not, but I actually do some yoga. It feels so good. Val had asked if there was a specific type of yoga that I would like to do, so we do some de-stressing yoga.

Just to interject, and to backtrack slightly, while all the above has been happening, another bone of contention has arisen between me and Jai: that he borrowed the fridge from my house. One of the fridges at his place had broken, and I had reluctantly lent him mine. I was concerned because the fridge actually belongs to the house owner. And if something were to happen to it, I would be liable. However, after a few days of "I'll give it back tomorrow" and tomorrow never coming, today it finally comes. While Val and I are doing yoga, Madhav turns up with the fridge. So, one less thing to worry about.

After yoga I ask Val if she wants to come to the opening night of Creation Valley and Amun Ra Café. She says yes (yay!) and says she will bring her friend along with her. I had met Val's friend when they both stayed at LOM. And they now live in the blue house opposite mine, but I haven't seen much of them. I did bump into Val once since.

Anyway, after yoga, and feeling good about myself, I start to half get ready. I don't put on dress on I am wearing for opening night. The guys at LOM would have a heart attack. I reserve my full, how shall I say, feminine allure for only certain people, Jai being one of them.

I walk to LOM and arrange for a taxi with Jagu. He's a good guy, and I know (or at least I hope) I can trust him. After dinner I will get Jalan to drop me at my house. Then once I have changed, Jagu will come and pick up Val and her friend, and we will all go to Amun Ra Café together.

So, the plan works, and we arrive at Amun Ra. The place has a few people in it, but not loads. Anna, Timmi, and their daughter are there. I go say hi to them and then go give Jai a side hug. Full contact would give the game away. I get seated with Val and her friend (realising I don't remember a lot of people's names). We order drinks. The place looks cool. The bulb idea works really well with all the pine and the bar counter. And he's painted one of the walls black so people can write their comments and feedback.

I feel so proud of Jai and what he has achieved from literally nothing. He is what has driven this project following his vision of what he wanted to create. At this time, I'm not even thinking about the money. My "contribution" was nothing compared to what the end figure must be, never mind how he got it.

Part of me will always love him just for creating this place.

The DJ is playing disco house-type tunes. I, Val, and her friend try to have a conversation. Val and I are fine with English, but the friend doesn't speak English, so Val has to translate.

I pop over to see Anna again and have a brief conversation with her. I do like her, but I can see a crazy (not in a good way) side to her. We chat a little, and I ask Katia (the daughter) about her tattoo.

Earlier in the day I had bought Jai a little good-luck gift. I wanted to get one of those Chinese lucky cats as he used to have one at his business in Hindavi. But I couldn't get one (but I didn't even try, to be honest), so I bought this little bronze metal cat. I go over to him and give it to him. He chuckles and puts it to the side.

Subsequently, the cat is on the drink display behind the bar in a prime location. I am very happy about that.

The night progresses. The three of us women get complimentary cocktails. It helps to always know the barman. :D I ask the DJ to play Jai's favourite tune on my phone, the one he always asks for, “Nasty” on the deep house mix. I watch his reaction, and a cheeky smile appears on his face. This also makes me very happy. Val and her friend decide to leave, but I’m not ready yet. So, I ask Jagu to come pick them up, saying I’ll settle the bill with him in the morning. I say bye to Val and her friend.

I go and sit with Anna, Timmi, and Timmi’s cousin or brother or someone. Katia is asleep in one of the chairs. Poor kid!

I have a tequila with Anna and get into the tunes. The music is a bit funkier now. I don’t really talk much with Anna after that. They are smoking weed. I decline a few offers. I don’t want to have a “whitey” in front of people. That would have to be an instant death moment. Nah, no way I’ll risk it.

Around 1.30 I decide to leave. I go to the bar and try to get Jai’s attention and ask if I can get a cab. He says he will drop me off. He asks if I had had a good time. I say, “Yes, I needed it.”

He drops me off and says he’ll come back to my house after closing.

I must have fallen asleep coz I don’t remember Jai coming back or even sleeping.

Chapter 7

NEW FRIENDS, OLD FRIENDS

We wake up slowly, and I feel like a weight has been lifted off my shoulders. I needed a night out, and having a couple of tequilas and beers, and the music, really helped to get me out of my head (not off my head, out of my head).

I have decided that the money Jai owes me and the deficit in my accounts can easily be solved by transferring money from the UK. I will be transferring money for my house and car anyway. I have decided I need a car. I am sick and tired of having to rely on other people to get me places.

I've test-driven one car, but it was too new and a bit on the large side. So, I opt for a smaller, automatic car, which I am actually really enjoying driving.

The money transfer will also help lessen the pressure on me to account for everything and increase the pressure on Jai to pay me back. I won't have to hassle him all the time. I am sick and tired of feeling like shit all the time.

As well as improving my money situation, I've decided to have more of a positive outlook and not let the negatives get to me.

I arrive at LOM, and already things seem lighter and brighter. I have the usual coffee and masala omelette for breakfast. It even tastes better today.

Guests check out, and I catch up on the bookings schedule.

The next couple of days seem to pass without any great drama.

On Saturday is Jai's second event. He asks if I'm coming down. I say probably.

I go on my own. I sit at the bar with a beer and watch Jai do his thing, the one-man show. It's getting busy, and people are waiting to be served. But Jai seems to handle it, roughly.

As I'm sitting, a tall guy comes to the bar, and we start talking. He seems interesting. He's German. I can't remember his name but will call him Gerard for the sake of ease.

He says he's in Goa making a film/documentary with his friends. He points to a chubby Indian guy with messy shoulder-length hair and round glasses sitting at the end table. He asks, "Where are your people?"

I point to Jai and a couple of the waiter guys, and say, "Those are my people." We chat some more about the global political situation, Brexit, and the state of each other's countries. His English isn't great, but we manage to communicate. He talks about the price of Jägermeister in India and how cheap it is, also telling me that it's used medicinally in Germany.

Gerard is tall, cute enough in a geeky kind of way, and interesting, so I join him and his friends at their table. He introduces me to his other German friend, Alex (I remember his name!). We talk about general stuff. I tell them about LOM, and I give them my business card. They don't seem that interested, which is fine.

After a while, Jai comes over and asks me for a cigarette, which he takes from the packet on the table. I loosely introduce him to my new friends.

I'm not sure what Jai is making of this, the fact that I've just sat down with a bunch of random guys. Maybe the coming to ask for a cigarette is a way of acknowledging that I am at a table of guys, and he wants them to know I know him. I really don't know. The intention wasn't to make him jealous; it was just a case of I was there on my own, and I wanted to talk to people and not sit at the bar looking like a Billy No-Mates.

After a little while I go for a little wander and am standing by one of the bamboo posts watching people freaky dancing. The DJ is good, playing the trademark deep house Jai has adopted as his style. Jai comes over and asks if I will take some pics and takes another cigarette. I'm not sure if he's keeping an eye on me or just asking to take pics. I mill around for a bit, take some pics, and have a little dance.

Gerard and Alex join me for a dance. Gerard asks if he can dance with me, I say yes, but his intentions are different; he puts his arm around my lower back. I turn and say politely, "I only mean dancing." He says that in Germany when a guy is interested, he always asks to dance first, and then even if he wants to kiss the girl, he always asks. I say, "That is good, but we can only dance and nothing else."

We dance for a while, but I'm getting a little bored. I don't have any of my friends here. I don't mind being on my own, but in social situations, it can be a bit lonely. I can't rely on Jai as he's working the one-man show.

So, I take some more pics, go to the loo, get another beer, and sit back down where Gerard and the group were sitting.

I sit and watch the proceedings, enjoying the music. Later Gerard comes and joins me. We chat for a while, and he says that most of the women in the place are trashy/tarty, but he can tell I'm not like that. I am the only nice girl in the place; that's why he likes me. He seems to be sincere, and I take the compliment. He asks if I am with someone. I say I have feelings for someone and that I cannot go with another person just like that. He asks if it is the guy at the bar. I smile and say yes. I ask, How could you tell?" He says it's the way I look at Jai. I didn't realise my expression gives my emotions away so easily.

Gerard says some more pleasantries, gives me a hug, says, "Good luck with everything," and goes to join his friends.

Earlier on, Ashok, one of the landlord's taxi drivers, was

sitting at the bar. I suppose he had come to support Jai and hoped to get a free drink or two. I go and join him. I ask him if he could drop me at home. He says he is on his scooter and it is fine. He is half cut, but for some reason, these people seem to manage to drive just as well when drunk as when sober. It's beyond me how they do it.

He's a nice guy, Ashok. He's older, about fifty maybe, a family man. While standing at the bar, he says he loves to listen to music and have a drink. This amuses me as it's pretty much deep house/techno playing. But music is music. It's what makes you feel that counts.

We decide to leave. I get Jai's attention from the other side of the bar. I want to hug him, but we manage a firm handhold. Not a handshake but a handhold! Fuck, I'm feeling too much for this guy. He says he'll call me tomorrow, which he does.

Over the next couple of weeks, I meet some of the people who have become urban myths to me since I have been here. They have been talked about since day one, and they too have a past and history which originates at LOM. I suppose if this diary were written by the actual hotel, these people would be in Series 1 to 3. Then I would have first appeared in Series 4. So, they are as much a part of this story, but they were involved before I had actually arrived on the scene.

I also met some lovely South African Indian women. They have become a much-needed source of female companionship. They are here on holiday and happened to book at LOM at the last minute. They came to look at one of the rooms but ended up staying at Queen's Resort, which is literally opposite Creation Valley and Amun Ra Café.

We seemed to hit it off immediately, and swapped numbers. We said we'd go for dinner sometime.

In addition, I want to do something special for New Year, and I had seen a post on Anjaru Events on Facebook about a woman who does Bollywood dancing. I had spoken to her briefly over the phone and decided to meet to discuss plans for New Year.

She comes to LOM, and we chat for a while about the event and how it will be planned. Her name is Ishwari. She is such a lovely, warm, kind-hearted woman, and she's all about female energy and empowerment. We hit it off from the outset. She seems to get me and my creative side. Again, another source of female friendship.

To give a timeline, I'd say this all happened during the second week of December, and the urban myths have become reality for me.

So, we'll start with Ravi!

Just to recap, Ravi ran LOM a couple of seasons ago, I think it was. And he is one of Jai's closest friends. They know each other from Hindavi, where they both lived. They go way back and were part of the original party crew, which included Harry, Jasmine, and Ramesh, Harry's brother.

Jalan had mentioned a couple of days previous that Ravi was coming to Goa. Jalan and I were going to Nimpura in my car, and while driving past Amun Ra Café, Jalan said that he saw Ravi. I pulled over quickly, and we both jumped out of the car to go to say hi. I wasn't going to miss this opportunity. We introduced ourselves and exchanged pleasantries. It's weird seeing someone whom you seem to know so much about, although you don't know them intimately. I had previously only spoken to Ravi briefly while on back of a scooter. I suppose upon the first meeting you cannot really size anyone up. To be honest, maybe I was a little star-struck. He has always been hailed as a good guy, honest and hard-working.

Anyway, it was a brief meeting, only a few minutes, and I invited him to come over to LOM sometime for a drink and a chat. Then Jalan and I got back on our way to Nimpura and the mall. We were going to the pet store and to get Jalan some new clothes.

We gossiped a bit about nothing of note that I can remember.

We arrived at the City Mall and went to the pet store on the same block to get pet food for the kittens (who by now are big, especially Brutus. Lollipop is still a dainty little thing).

OMG, the fluffiest kitten in the world was at the pet store. I picked it up, and it let me. Jalan looked so smiley (more than usual). We bought the pet food, and I bought a stick with feathers at the end of it for the kittens to play with. On the way out, we played with the kitten with the stick. It jumped up and fell on its side. It was the cutest thing ever! Jalan loved it! It was so nice to see actual genuine joy on someone's face. We reluctantly left the pet shop—well, I reluctantly left the pet shop.

At the mall, Jalan bought himself some smart clothes. I bought myself a couple of black vests and some nail varnish. I went to look for some new sandals for myself. Jalan waited outside.

I wasn't in the shoe shop a minute when Jalan came in and said, "Madam, there's an emergency at the hotel." For fuck's sake! Just as I was getting into the mental shoe-buying zone, I got very rudely pulled back into reality. That was the biggest, quickest comedown in all of history.

So, we got in the car and headed back to LOM.

The emergency was that a pipe to fill the tank on the roof had broken loose, and water was coming down the side of the building. Meanwhile, the landlord was ranting about something—the hot water and the switch for the solar heater. As usual Amit got the blame. I'm beginning to feel sorry for the kid, but he's his own worst enemy. He just doesn't know when to shut up.

The plumber was called, who was on a standing on a ledge on the outside of the building without any harness or anything to attach himself to while fixing the pipe.

A crowd had already gathered by this time. Each event like this is always accompanied by a throng: the landlord's entire family, including children of various ages and sizes, the grandparents, and several hangers-on. There's always some sort of drama.

On the other side of the building the sewage tank was beginning to overflow behind and outside the kitchen.

Jesus! If it doesn't rain, it pours.

While this was going on, Ravi appeared at LOM. He came over to where we all were standing, greeted the landlord and a few others, then headed back to the restaurant. I told him to wait for me.

After a short time, Ravi and I sit at my table by the wall. We talk generally about LOM, Jai, and obviously Harry. He tells me of his experience working with him, including how he had bought the fridges and various other pieces of equipment and how he had cleared all the credit that was outstanding when he left. He says he wasn't the type of person to leave things unfinished.

He says that the restaurant was a source of great headaches, and eventually he had had enough and left LOM and went back to Hindavi.

He really does seem to be a good guy. I warm to him. He's soft-spoken and has a somewhat cute baby face. He is also from Bangladesh. He and Jalan have a great relationship as Jalan is from Bangladesh too. They are brothers from other mothers.

We talk more about Harry and how I have found him to be. Without actually slagging Harry off completely, we come to an unspoken understanding. I am basically going through what Ravi had gone through with Harry.

Because of the mad day, I haven't even been back home to shower. I have dinner while talking with Ravi, and it's now getting late. The water issue seems to be fixed, and there is nothing we can do about the sewage tank at the moment. I take my leave and head home. I'm done in!

So, my first proper encounter with Ravi was a pleasant one, and he plans to stick around for the next couple of weeks to help Jai out over Christmas and New Year. No doubt I will be seeing more of him.

Now let's move onto Jasmine and Hakim the baby.

The arrival of Jasmine has been greatly anticipated by everyone, least of all me. I have only briefly talked to her over Skype prior to her coming to Goa, and then she'd sent a few messages on WhatsApp asking for "nice" rates for her friends to stay at LOM, which I accommodated as much as I could considering I am the one running the business.

She arrives at LOM on the evening of 18th December. I am standing outside the landlord's house, and Jasmine and Harry walk in to LOM. We see each other, and I go to greet her. We hug, and I say, "Welcome to Goa" (or something to that effect). The vibe I get from her is warm and friendly. I don't sense an atmosphere or any negativity, which I am pleased about. Hakim the baby is super cute.

Over the next couple of days, Jasmine and I talk and get to know each other better, in between me doing all the room scheduling and dealing with check-ins and checkouts.

Harry is in the background, milling around. I don't speak to him or look at him much—not if I can help it anyway.

Jasmine is friendly. Over lunch one day she expresses how impressed she is with how I am running LOM. She is full of praise. I am friendly but am still cautious around her. She is Harry's wife after all. But overall it has been a positive experience meeting Jasmine.

In the evenings, I usually have dinner on my own or am sorting shit out regarding the hotel. One evening Neil is my guest. Another night I am host to Jag from High Life, and he keeps me company.

So new friends are introduced to old friends. Now back the craziness of Goa. I won't give any spoilers, but I will say that it gets fucking seriously dark and all hell does break loose.

Chapter 8

BITTERSWEET

It's approaching Christmas, but it doesn't feel like it. Jalan and I have been to Nimpura to get Christmas decorations and a Christmas tree, in the hope that I will get into the festive spirit. Maybe it's the hot weather or that I've just been too busy to even contemplate Christmas celebrations. Also, being away from family and friends is not helping. Back at home I would be buying gifts for the family and getting ready to go home to London. Obviously, that is not happening this year.

Some of the local businesses have put decorations up, but I'm just not getting the feeling.

Later that same week, Jalan, Amit, Satish, and I go to Unjaan to look for Christmas lights. Satish doesn't know what Christmas entails, as he is Hindu, so I explain to him what Christmas is all about—the religious meaning and significance and the whole putting up of decorations. I act as a consultant on what decorations to choose, and then back at LOM I show him how to decorate a Christmas tree. There are two Christmas-type trees at the entrance to the restaurant. Amit and Satish decorate one while I do the other.

I think Satish likes the decoration side of Christmas. He gets proper stuck in.

Jalan is putting plastic stars and tinsel on the entrance to the hotel. It looks pretty shitty, but it's better than nothing.

As well as preparing for Christmas, I am organising the poster for the New Year's Eve Bollywood Extravaganza. I have been to Kandar Printers to design a poster. I have downloaded some of Ishwari's previous pictures and incorporated them into a Bollywood-style poster, and I do say that it looks pretty amazing. I am getting some posters and postcards made. It feels great to create something out of nothing. My creative juices are flowing.

It's Christmas Eve. I have kept in touch with Zayirah and Aleema, the South African Indian women. We arrange to go for dinner at Amun Ra Café as they are staying opposite at Queen's Resort. I have told them that Jai the barman makes excellent cocktails.

I get there first, and Ravi is sitting with some of the waiters. Madhav is around somewhere. Jai is not in the restaurant when I arrive.

I greet Ravi and sit down with a beer. I have dressed up for dinner, and I think I look nice. I have worn a black and white dress I had picked up from Lamuella. The last time Ravi saw me, I was a sweaty mess.

Zayirah and Aleema arrive. We are the only guests there for dinner. The place is quiet and has a completely different feeling from the previous party nights. I like that we have the place to ourselves.

We order food and chat while we wait. They are both in their early forties. Zayirah is in the medical profession, and Aleema is in IT sales, I think. They are both intelligent, funny women. We talk about our backgrounds. They are both from Muslim families, but they don't subscribe to Islam in an orthodox way. They are very liberal, and Zayirah explains that she takes from all religions what she needs spiritually. These are my kind of enlightened modern women. I explain my Christian background, saying I do not follow Christianity as such. My values lie more in humanism and broader spirituality.

The conversation turns to romance and partners. They are both single. Zayirah tells me about an older guy she was dating, but then it all went wrong and the guy went all weird on her, basically distancing himself from her. I tell her all men are children really, and they don't seem to be able to open up and have a conversation. Aleema and I tell her she's better off without him.

Jai has arrived, and I introduce him to the women. He goes and sits with Ravi and the others on the opposite side.

Aleema and Zayirah tell me they are best friends and that they have been coming to Goa for years. They have many friends here, and this time they have come to visit their god-daughter.

They invite me to come to a party tomorrow (Christmas Day) at place called Flash in Thairi. It's a club, and they're having a charity event. I accept the invitation!

Then Aleema opens Tinder on her phone, and we have a laugh over the availability (or lack thereof) of dating prospects. They tell me I should go on Tinder; maybe I will meet someone while I'm out here. I don't tell them that I am seeing Jai. I tell them that my friends in the UK made me go on Tinder, and the first lot of messages I received were obscene. I tell them, "Please don't make me go on Tinder," in an overly dramatic way.

I ask if they want cocktails. Aleema says yes. Zayirah doesn't drink. Jai makes us two cosmopolitans.

Jai messages from across the restaurant, asking if I want to go to a party afterwards. I say yes.

It's about 10.30, and my two friends decide to call it a night. It was so nice to spend time with intelligent, funny women. It was exactly what I needed.

I hang back to wait for Jai. There seems to be some sort of mothers' meeting going on with some of the Goan contingency, including Madhav, Bhanu (the landlord's brother), and a couple of other faces.

Jai and I get into his car. He's on the phone and turns to me to ask if it's OK if Ravi joins us. I agree straightaway. Ravi jumps into the back seat.

We first head to a new place in Tarana. It's the opening night, and Jai's DJ friend is playing there. I suppose we're going to show support and boost numbers.

We get to the place after driving a few minutes down a dirt road, where a lot of these places are, sandwiched in between the main road and the beach side. There are nice-looking multicoloured beach huts along a paved walkway with lighting on either side.

Jai had picked up a few posters and a bunch of flyers. It seems it's not quite a party but PR activity. Ravi and I sit at a table, Jai asks what we want and then heads to the bar. Ravi is not drinking. I have a vodka and Red Bull. After bringing our drinks, Jai goes off with a handful of flyers.

The place is pretty empty. What looks like a Goan family are sitting on a raised chill-out area. Four people are sitting at the table next to ours. The other side is occupied by young hip Indian types.

Techno is blaring (totally out of place), and it's hard for me to hold a conversation with Ravi. We both revert to checking our phones. Jai mills around, chatting with various people.

I'm not sure I like this. I was told I was going to a party, not a PR stunt.

After about twenty minutes we leave and head towards Anjaru. On the way, Jai drops off flyers at the premier Russian bar in Obrah.

In Anjaru we head towards a place which Jai says they used to frequent back in the day. I don't remember the name. It's on the right-hand side of the beach. We enter an enclosed area with a big tent-type structure. It's reggae this time. I like it. We find seats and order drinks. Jai doesn't have money, so he calls Madhav to bring some. He goes off to collect the money. The drinks arrive. Ravi goes for a wander.

I debate with myself whether to show Jai the poster I have created for the New Year's Extravaganza. I decide to show him. I just say, "Look at this!" He takes a look and starts to say something about Harry and his sluttish ways. I tell him that it's nothing to do with Harry, saying that it's my idea and asking why he always has to be so negative. I sarcastically say, "Thanks for the support." He does a U-turn and says if it's something I've done, then he fully supports it.

It's too late. I'm wounded, and he knows it!

We walk over to the edge of the dance floor. There is all sorts of freaky dancing happening. Ravi rejoins us. A few minutes later Neil walks over, and we all greet him. I give him a half hug.

We then go to a place on the other side of Anjaru beach. It has an enclosed entrance. They are playing progressive techno, which is the lowest common denominator of techno—no depth, just pure repetitive beats. So basic! We get drinks, Jai drops off some flyers somewhere, and the three of us try on my silver-sequined Santa hat which I've worn for the festive season.

We chat for a little while. I ask Ravi about his kids and wife. We take a couple of selfies and then leave. Jai wants to go back to the first place. So, we head back to Tarana but drop Ravi off at Jai's apartment on the way. We arrive back at the first place but do not enter. The crowd is leaving.

JJ, Jai's DJ friend, is outside. Jai does the "bro" thing for a short time, and random people say bye to me as if they know me. I wait by the side of the car, smoking a cigarette. I'm a little tipsy at this point. I can't handle the booze these days. I only had a couple of vodka Red Bulls and a couple of beers.

After we leave the techno place, we decide we are hungry, so we get a fried rice parcel to take away. While we wait and chat about nothing in general, for some reason Jai wants to arm-wrestle me. I put my elbow on the table in readiness, but he declines. I tell him in my mild drunken state not to dare me to wrestle. I will wrestle him now in front of everyone in the takeout place. I don't think he knows if I'm serious or not, but I would have jumped him if I were even more drunk. Luckily for both of us, I wasn't.

By the time we get back to my house, it's 3.30 in the morning. We eat fried rice and go to sleep.

Well, it's now Christmas Day. Jai whispers "Happy Christmas" as I awake. I mumble the same back, and we have a little cuddle. He leaves soon after. It's the big party tonight at Amun Ra from 2 p.m. to 6 a.m.—dawn to dusk as the flyer says.

I get ready and head to LOM. It still feels like a normal day. I feel melancholy as I'm not with my family and friends at home. There are a few check-ins and check-outs in the morning, which I deal with, and then the late afternoon is quiet. I speak to my brother in the afternoon and then to Mum later on. I send a few "Merry Christmas" messages.

The Aunties (Aleema and Zayirah), as Jai has nicknamed them, which I don't approve of, message to confirm details for that evening. I will pick them up on the way in a taxi, which I arrange with Jagu.

After a slow day I go home to get ready for the night out with "the Aunties". I can't decide what to wear, as the plan for me is to go back to Amun Ra after Flash. Aleema and Zayirah say they're only be going for a couple of hours. I end up wearing a long black shirt dress, denim cut-offs underneath for decency's sake, and gladiator sandals.

I call Jagu to come get me, and then we go pick the aunties up from Obrah. Jagu parks up, and I go into Queen's to collect the aunties. I see Jai across the street outside Amun Ra and shout him over. We say a quick hello, and I say I will see him later on.

With the Aunties picked up, we head to Flash in Thairi. Jagu knows where it is. On the way a little frog drops onto the car windscreen. We all have a laugh over how determined the little fucker is to stick to the glass. Probably holding on for dear life. To Jagu's credit, he doesn't swipe the little frog with the wipers.

After arranging for Jagu to come pick us up around midnight, we enter Flash. I am suitably impressed. It's a wide-open space maybe half the size of a football pitch with a large white bar island in the middle. Flash is on the waterfront, and the water is lit blue. Aleema takes me over to show me. There are comfy seating platforms around the edge of the space and dining tables near the restaurant. The decor is mostly white and modern, but as with all things Indian, it's a little rough around the edges. The palm trees are hanging over as a natural leafy ceiling.

The DJ stage is at the far end, and the light show is impressive. Lasers are shooting out from behind the DJ stage. I do love a good laser show. The music is funky dance music, more my thing than the music at the places Jai had taken me and Ravi to the previous night.

The three of us sit at one of the restaurant tables. Zayirah orders a chicken roll thing. I order a small kingfisher. Aleema is sick and wants to order a tea. She has had some Ayurvedic treatment to clear her sinuses. The waiters are terrible and don't seem to know if any sort of tea is available.

We chat, and after a short while after we are joined by Riaz, a really good friend of the aunties. They had told me a little about him the previous night. He is half Jewish, half Muslim. What a split personality combination. He's a nice guy, and he and Aleema flirt like crazy, but it seems all harmless banter, not anything serious. He asks Aleema to help at the entrance with collecting ticket money. He says he is surrounded by idiots. We all laugh. Both Aleema and Riaz leave, and Zayirah and I chat. She mentions the older guy from the previous night. And then proceeds to tell me that, Riaz has organised the event as that's his job. He runs a promotional events company called Third Eye Events. He seems like a really cool modern Indian kind of guy.

As the night progresses, we are re-joined by Aleema and an eclectic bunch of other people. Firstly, there's an older

American Indian guy called Roy. Then there's a French guy called Phillipe, who we have been told is a gigolo. I'd never met a gigolo before, ha ha! There is a modern hippy kind of woman who proceeds to roll a joint with cannabis oil. I do not partake in the passing of the joint. God knows how strong this stuff is, even though I know it's meant to be super medicinal and is now known to have many healing properties, including the ability to kill cancer. Aleema has a toke to help with her cold and sinuses. There's also another random Indian woman who is completely off her head with eyes as wide as saucers and pitch-black, wide-open pupils. She's doing some freaky dancing which fascinates me as it's all weird leg movements. She can't sit still. It's highly amusing.

I don't really participate in any of the conversation, but I do listen intently. Roy is from Manhattan, New York, and has basically disowned his family back home because he has decided to pursue a more enlightened existence. He lives in the jungle interior of Goa, and it sounds awesome. His housekeeper grows cannabis plants on the land. He talks about the manifestation of abundance. He's interesting, but he doesn't engage in conversation with me directly. Everyone is chatting, having a giggle.

I turn to Zayirah, and we discuss the antics of a gigolo. Phillipe does seem to have a certain sexual allure, but he also looks like he needs a good wash. He's attractive in a dishevelled kind of way. Maybe he's just too exhausted from all the gigolo-ing to contemplate the benefits of a good hot shower and a shave. He goes off to talk to some women, maybe clients or potential clients.

After a while we all get up to dance. We stay close to our table. The DJ is good. It's funky house/techno music, and I'm loving the lasers. It's impressive. I let the lasers wash over me. I record some videos to show to Jai later on.

It's now 12.30, the time we had agreed that Jagu would come get us. Also, Jai has messaged asking when I will be getting to Amun Ra. I tell him, "Soon." He says to bring the Aunties too. I'm not sure how things are going back at Amun Ra. I say I will try to persuade them.

After some more throwing of shapes; taking a walk-around, trying to locate Riaz; and saying a fond farewell, I manage to get through to Haroon, and not Jagu, who will come pick us up. We make our way to the exit. Haroon says he will be fifteen minutes and tells us to start to walk to the big white church at the Thairi crossroad.

We start to walk. It's getting late now, maybe one o'clock in the morning. We are passed by groups on scooters and in cars. Ten minutes into the walk and we are scared shitless by barking dogs on the road. One, it seems, is trying to attack us but is probably trying to protect its patch. But we're all pretty unnerved by it. Other dogs start barking in the night, and we try to act cool. Another ten minutes pass, and it seems we're nowhere near the big white church. I try to call Haroon, but there is no signal. We walk for what seems an eternity and stand by an entrance to a resort, it seems like, for our own safety. I call again and get through to Haroon. He says he's on Thairi Bridge. We all screech and say, "That's miles away!" Zayirah takes the phone and speaks Hindi to Haroon and gives him a good telling-off. We tell him we will wait by the resort entrance. We don't want to walk farther in the pitch-black with rabid dogs on the loose, baiting for our blood.

After about five minutes, Haroon grinds to a halt at the entrance, and we pile in. I tell him we're all going to Obrah. As we had walked most of the way down from Flash, we tell him that we're only giving him 400 rupees, as opposed to the 450 we had initially agreed on. He can't say no with three angry women with him.

We get to Obrah. I ask Aleema and Zayirah if they want to come to Amun Ra for a little while. They decline but walk me to the bar. Jai is there, and he greets us all, saying "Happy Christmas" to the Aunties. I hug the Aunties goodnight and thank them for inviting me to Flash, and they leave. I don't think they will get much sleep as the Christmas party at Amun Ra is planned to go on till 6 a.m.

By the time we arrived at Amun Ra, it was past 1.30 a.m., so I am now pretty tired. I get myself a beer and sit at the far end of the restaurant. A DJ stage dance floor has been set up in the parking/driveway area. There are a few people dancing, twenty at most, a mixture of young Russian yoga types, some of them dressed in a neo-punk way with neon hot pants. Some older men are there too, a mixture of nationalities.

The tables in the restaurant are not full, but enough people are milling around.

The music is deep house. But to me it lacks any depth and frankly is monotonous and basic. But there are a few funky beats to keep me entertained for a while.

Ravi and Madhav are behind the bar. Jai is milling around, making sure the proceedings are going well.

After a short time, he comes and sits with me and asks if I'm hungry. I say, "A little bit." He shouts something over to one of the waiters, and a few minutes later a plate of veg fingers arrives. I casually eat them while telling him about Flash. I show him the vid of the lasers but can't tell if he's impressed or not.

At one point while he is sitting next to me, we both look at each other. It's a deep intense stare without any words being spoken. I don't know what to make of this.

We engage in small talk for a little while, and then he suddenly gets up and rushes over to the dance area, where he speaks to an older Indian man and then ushers him away into the restaurant. He returns to me, and I ask him what happened. He says the Indian man was harassing a white woman who was dancing. I suppose this is his job now, to make sure the guests are not uncomfortable and Amun Ra doesn't get a bad reputation.

Then all of a sudden, the power goes off and the music stops. The generator or something has blown a fuse (I don't actually know what happened, to be honest). A few bods run over to the side of the DJ booth and fiddle with some equipment, and the music returns. Cheers rise from the freaky dancers. However, after ten minutes the power goes out again. The freaky dancers are not happy. Again, the music comes back on after a few minutes. I take this as a sign that I should leave.

I ask Jai to call me a taxi. He says he will take me home. I'm tired by now. We make small talk on the way to my house. He looks tired too. I think to myself, *How is he going to stay up until 6 a.m. to finish out the night?*

We arrive at my house. I give him a hug and a peck on the neck while still seated in the passenger seat. He lets out a little moan and says, "See you later." I go inside and give the kitties a little fuss. Then I wash and get to bed. I sleep like a log.

The next day, Boxing Day, I receive a message from Jai asking if I'm still awake. The message was sent at 4.30 a.m. I decide to reply later when I get to LOM.

I arrive at LOM and am still tired. It's quiet, though, considering it's Christmas. Only half the rooms are booked, but I'm a little relieved as it has been hectic over the last few weeks. New Year's Eve and New Year's Day are fully booked.

I check and update the booking schedule, sharing all the updates with Jalan and the restaurant guys.

I reply to Jai's message from last night, telling him I was asleep. No doubt he's still asleep after last night's party. Later we speak on the phone, and he tells me that they closed the party at 3.30 a.m. The 6 a.m. finish didn't go as planned. I had thought to myself that it was a bit ambitious.

The day proceeds without great event. Jasmine and Harry arrive later on, and at 3pm-ish I go home for rest and a nap. I come back to LOM later in the evening and have dinner with Jag from High Life. When he leaves, I join Jasmine and Harry, the latter of whom makes us a strawberry daiquiri. He's on his best behaviour, it seems to me. I finish my drink and then I head home. Jai comes around once he has finished at Amun Ra Café.

Over the next couple of days it seems world has been turned upside down. The events that proceed change everything in terms of me and Jai, Amun Ra Café—everything! I won't give any spoilers, but never in my wildest dreams had any of us envisaged the most despicable act of betrayal that ensued.

The day starts off as normal. I head into LOM. I do the usual updates and check out payments, and then around lunchtime I get ready to leave to go to Kandar Printers in Nimpura to pick up the flyers and posters for the New Year's Eve Bollywood Extravaganza. I ask the restaurant guys if they want anything from Nimpura. Satish requests some more Christmas stars. I say, "OK, no problem."

I go on my own. It's nice to have some time to myself, especially while driving. It clears my head as I need to focus on actual driving, including dodging other cars, cyclists, dogs, cows, and a multitude of other hazards, and therefore I'm not thinking about the daily dramas that surround LOM.

I arrive at Kandar Printers and speak to the young woman who helped me put the design together using the graphics software. She is sweet, and I think she enjoyed creating the design with me. She says she clicked the poster on her phone. The posters look really good, and I am very happy with the results. I pay up and collect the posters and flyers.

I don't want to head into Nimpura Market as parking will be a nightmare, so I buy some rather plain but nice-looking plastic stars from the shop downstairs from Kandar Printers. Mission accomplished, so I head back.

On the way back, I spot Jai's car parked outside his apartment building in Tarana. I contemplate stopping and calling him, but I don't. I have things to do. However, as I reach Obrah on the drive back, I look over to Amun Ra as I slow down to manoeuvre the speed bump, and I see Anna and Timmi. I quickly turn into Amun Ra's driveway to say hi. The DJ stage is still there. I park up and go into Amun Ra to greet Anna. She is very happy to see me. We hug. I go say hi to Ravi too, who is sitting at the table at the far end.

Anna and Timmi are in their usual state of intoxication already. They offer me a drink. I decline, but they insist on getting me a beer. I relent and have a small glass of beer just to wash down the cigarette flavour. They offer me a joint, which I definitely decline.

They ask if I have seen Jai. I say no, but I mention that his car is parked outside his building. They say they have been trying to contact him and then proceed to rattle on about the money he owes them. I tell them (again) that it's nothing to do with me. They go on about how I have always paid my bills, saying that I have been the best business person they have had the pleasure of working with. I graciously say, "Thank you."

Anna then goes off on a mad tangent and starts talking about conspiracy theories, asking if I have heard of the illuminati. I say yes, adding that I have done a lot of research, and she says that she'd only just recently read about them, having spent the last three days glued to her computer, researching. She waffles on about a friend of theirs in London who has a big business and a lot of power. She says she emailed him to ask him about the illuminati, but he hasn't replied. If he is one of the illuminati, he is hardly going to tell her, is he?! I like Anna, but she is one random chick—probably why I like her.

After a short time, I go to properly say hi to Ravi. He asks about Jai. I say I saw his car outside his apartment. He says people are asking where he is and waiting for him, including Anna and Timmi. I call Jai, but there is no answer. Ravi seems a bit on edge. There are various people milling around the parking area, including Madhav, who seems to be at the core of the group. I ask what is going on. Ravi says he thinks people are playing games. I ask him who. He says he doesn't know yet. We walk to the side of the restaurant and behind the blue sheeting which is hiding the construction area where the first lot of cottages are going to be built. I ask again what's going on. He says, "No one is able to contact Jai, and all the creditors are here asking for money."

I think to myself, *No wonder Jai doesn't want to be found.*

Ravi says that he has told Jai to focus on the restaurant and to make that work, rather than the parties. Ravi is a sensible guy. I can feel his concern for Jai and Amun Ra.

Behind us are the beginnings of the cottages that are due to be constructed. The concrete foundation pillars are in place, but that's about it. It really looks like a bomb has hit the place. There are various debris lying around with pinewood piled up on one side. No work has been done for a number of weeks. I believe Jai's plan was to start making money with the parties and then to start to phase in the construction of the cottages, which seems reasonable. However, from what I can assume from the brewing mob, and from Timmi and Anna, the vultures are circling for their outstanding credit payments, including the pinewood guy whom Timmi is connected with.

Ravi and I go through the restaurant. I am starting to feel the tension and decide I'd better leave before I get dragged into the ensuing mob. I say "bye" to Ravi and ask him to ask Jai to phone me when he speaks to him. I also leave a few flyers with Ravi at the bar and give one to Anna, who seems uber-excited about the idea of Bollywood delights.

I decided to pop home, as it is on the way, to check on the kittens and just have a moment to myself. Randomly I receive a phone call from Madhav. He's asking if I have the paperwork that Jai had given me to look after. I ask, "Which paperwork?"

He replies, "The contract with his landlord." I lie and say I don't have it, adding that Jai needs to speak to me. I tell him to tell Jai to call me. I hang up. I call Jai again, but again there is no answer. I'm getting perturbed. Even if he is busy, he normally answers to say he is busy and to tell me he will call me back. It is even stranger that Madhav is calling me.

It's now late afternoon, and I head back to LOM with the printed posters and flyers for New Year's Eve Bollywood

Extravaganza. I have a cup of chai to chill and call Jai again, but still no answer. The scenes at Amun Ra and Madhav's call are playing on my mind. But instead of dwelling on that, I focus on my work and chat with the restaurant guys about the poster.

Satish and I decide to go along the street to put up some posters and flyers. He staples a poster outside the entrance, and I go along to the shops on the strip and hand out some flyers to the proprietors there. We end up going all the way down to Serenity Retreat at the bottom of Vida Road, and then all the way along to the top to the main road via the backstreet places. We pretty much cover most of Vida Road with Bollywood Extravaganza posters.

Jai calls and says he will see me tonight and explain what's been happening. I tell him that Madhav has called about the paperwork, and I tell him that I said I didn't have it. However, at this point I am distracted with the poster posting, and Satish is waiting, so I say, "OK, see you later."

By the time we finish posting flyers, it is dark. I am hungry and sweaty from the day. I decide to have dinner before I head home. After dinner, and once I make sure everything is OK, I leave and drive home.

On the way, as I turn onto the main road, I slow to take the corner. Jai and Ravi drive past on a scooter. Jai signals for me to stop, which I do. This is very strange! Jai gets off the scooter, gets his jumper from Ravi, and gets in the car. I'm surprised, to say the least, and I ask him what's happening. He says he had a fight with Madhav, saying that he hit him. I'm in complete shock now. I continue to drive back home through Shakthar Market. Jai explains that Madhav had brought the whole mob I had seen earlier to Amun Ra to demand the money they were owed and said he was going to take over the Amun Ra. I'm dumbstruck. How can this be happening?

We get to my house. Jai is visibly shocked. We talk more about what has been happening. Madhav had paid some local Goan heavies to basically threaten Jai because of the credit he owed. He had paid a local don-type character called Albert to use sticks to beat Jai. "Fuckin' hell" is all I can say. Jai basically punched Madhav in the face and then left Amun Ra with Ravi in tow. Jai left his belongings in Amun Ra, including his phone and car keys.

Madhav basically stabbed Jai in the back and successfully orchestrated a coup. I can't believe what I am hearing. Madhav has turned out to be the biggest snake in Obrah and Shakthar. Jai had completely trusted him. It was Madhav who handled all the money. He's been Jai's right-hand man throughout the whole process. Fucking evil snake! It seems that he saw the money coming in from the parties, and the greed monster took over. He wants the place for himself, the ex-alcoholic, with his only credentials being selling fish. How the hell is he going to run a bar and restaurant?!

Jai is devastated, and I can see he is scared and angry, but there is very little he can do at this point. He doesn't have a support network in Goa, and Madhav has taken advantage of that. Jai is on his own. Apart from me and now Ravi, he has nothing—no money, no clothes except what he is wearing, no phone, no car. He has lost all his savings that he put into the business to get it started, and that includes the loans that I had given him. At this point, this is the least of my concerns.

I just can't believe something like this could happen. If anything, after all the things I had heard about Harry over the months, I would have thought Harry would turn out to be a problem. I did not expect something like this to happen to Jai. Madhav the evil snake!

We discuss what should happen next. We don't know. Jai stays at my house as usual. We decide to sleep on it. I still can't believe this is happening. I tell him I will be with him and support him with whatever he needs. I also tell him that he needs to phone his mum and dad, at least to get some advice. He says, "We'll see." Eventually we fall asleep, hugging each other tight.

I awake in the morning, and Jai doesn't make an attempt to

get up. He says he is going to stay until things calm down, and then he'll go and talk to the Amun Ra landlord. I don't want to leave him, but I decide to go to LOM as usual. I have to keep up the pretence of normality. Jai calls Ravi from my phone. I leave a key to my door in a matchbox outside my house so Ravi can get in.

I say I will be back as soon as I can. Then I lock the door behind me, leaving Jai at my place to hide out without even a phone so I can call or message him.

At LOM the day starts off in the usual manner. I carry on with the pretence as if nothing has happened. Maybe the news from last night hasn't filtered along the grapevine. I look for signs of any chit-chat amongst Jalan, the landlord, and the restaurant staff. All is quiet.

I focus on work. It's still quiet on the bookings front, but I do the usual updates and inform Jalan and the restaurant guys of today's check-ins. There is only one guest to check in today. I see no sign of Jasmine and Harry at this point, which I'm grateful for. I don't need their prying eyes watching my every move. I'm still unsure about Jasmine or how to take her, but time will tell. Ultimately, she is Harry's wife, and obviously her loyalties lie with him. She doesn't know me. As far as she is concerned, I am running the hotel.

I notice that there aren't any Bollywood Extravaganza flyers on the tables, so I speak to Satish, and he asks for more New Year's posters and flyers as they have used all the ones I'd had printed. I make the call to Kandar Printers and place the order. Plus, it's always a good excuse to go to Nimpura and have some time to myself.

In the afternoon I make my excuses and head back to my house to make sure Jai is OK. Jai has called from Ravi's number. He says he has given him his SIM and asks for the code to my old Samsung Galaxy S4, which is still on the table in my house. I give him the PIN, and he messages me once Ravi's SIM is in my S4, so now at least he is able to contact me.

When I get back to my house, his face is still full of anxiety and hurt. I ask what's happening. He says he needs to get out of Shakthar for a while and needs to book a ticket to Gandabaan. I say, "OK, but how?" He says he's not sure yet, but there is a bus from Nimpura at 5 p.m.

But he cannot be seen, so it will be a task to get him out of my house and out of Shakthar. Shakthar is such a small place, and Jai is known by many of the locals.

He says he has arranged with Ravi to bring some of his clothing from his apartment, along with any other items he can get hold of.

So, after a short while, we decide to leave for Nimpura. I feel like we're both running on adrenalin. The thought of being caught is mind-numbing with an actual real threat to Jai's physical well-being. I don't want to sound overdramatic, but the situation is potentially life-threatening. My heart is aching with the thought of what might happen, the thought that someone could purposely bring bodily harm to Jai.

We get ready to leave, and we hug. As he hugs me, he says, "I love you, Sabbie Boss." I'm not sure what he's said, and he repeats the words I have been waiting to hear.

My heart is filled, and I reply, "I love you too, Jai." He pulls away, and his eyes are filled with tears. He says he didn't want to say it until he was settled, but it may be too late for that, so that's why he said it. My heart aches at the bittersweet moment. The words I'd been longing to hear for the last few months come at the moment when we are about to be separated for God knows how long.

But we pull ourselves together and head out to my car, which I had parked outside my house instead at the top of the empty lot. Jai gets into the driver's seat. We head to Nimpura. We meet Ravi with Jai's bag. I give Jai some money. We hug again, and I turn to leave to return to Shakthar and LOM.

My heart is breaking and overflowing with love.

Chapter 9

HIDE-AND-SEEK

I leave Jai and Ravi in Nimpura to get their respective buses. I'm not sure if Ravi will be going to Gandabaan or directly to Hindavi. My heart is aching at the thought of Jai having to leave under these horrendous circumstances and with the knowledge that I won't see him every day.

I head back to Shakthar and go straight to my house.

I receive a message from Jai, saying, "Thank you for everything," telling me how much he really loves me, and saying that he's never felt so much for another woman in his life—the others had all flirted with him and left. He will come back to Goa not for himself but for me. He really loves me. And I was the reason he stayed back in Goa.

I am overwhelmed with his words. This is all a woman ever wants to hear all her life, and the man who is saying it to this woman is running for his life halfway across this vast country. Conflicting emotions are running through me. The feeling of being loved by this man fills me with a joy I have never felt before. It's almost like the universe is in perfect balance, but at the same time, he is moving physically farther away from me, albeit not by his own choice. The irony of the situation is numbing.

I reply, saying I love him too and that we will be together again soon. Never did I imagine I would meet someone like him in Goa. I tell him I know it's not been easy between us, but I love him for the fact that he's had to deal with my temper tantrums (whether justified or not). I tell him that if it wasn't for him, I would have left Goa. I tell him everything will be OK.

All I want to do is hug him, kiss him, and be with him to soothe his anguish.

It's getting late, and I'd arranged to meet the Aunties for dinner as it's their last night. I get ready and go to LOM to show my face, make sure everything is OK, and try to keep the pretence of normality. All seems as it should be. Harry and Jasmine are there, chilling in the restaurant. Harry has been more present at LOM since Jasmine arrived. We have generally kept our distance from each other. He has been playing the nice guy in front of Jasmine. I casually let them know I'm going to the Parisian for dinner with friends, the Parisian being one of the places which is renowned for its French cuisine.

I meet the aunties at Queen's, in their room. I had parked the car outside Amun Ra, which is deserted. I can't bear to look inside; it's breaking my heart to have to block out what has happened.

Henry and his mother are there. I met them a couple of nights ago at Beach Street Restaurant. They are from South Africa too. Henry's ex-wife and their daughter Kimmie were there too. They are also joining us tonight.

We decide to walk along the beach to the Parisian, which is in Tarana, the next resort after Obrah. Zayirah and I walk ahead of the others, and I briefly tell her what has happened. She is sympathetic, but I think I might be bringing the mood down.

We arrive at the Parisian, but there is a disco happening at the Ibiza resort next door. We can hardly hear each other. After much debating, we decide to leave and head back to Obrah to find another restaurant.

We are joined by another couple, an older Indian woman

and her English husband. Balindar and John, I think their names are—nice people.

We reach the main road in Tarana to get taxis, but after a few minutes' negotiation we end up walking back to Obrah. The road is poorly lit, so we use our mobiles to light the way. A random dog accompanies us back to Obrah. After much deliberation about where to eat, taking into consideration Henry's dietary requirements, we end up at Napoli, an Italian restaurant.

I'm distracted and I'm not feeling particularly sociable, but I make the most of the situation. Furthermore, it's refreshing to be out in the evening instead of sitting in LOM's restaurant. All I can think about is Jai and his having to escape this den of treachery. He messages saying he's waiting for his bus. He says it's the worst day of his life, and he has lost everything. I try to ease his pain by saying it will be OK once he gets home and sleeps.

Everyone is jolly and taking photos of each other. I'm sitting at one end with Balindar and John. They're originally from London but have now settled in Hindavi, running some sort of consultancy business for foreigners relocating to India.

It is a pleasant evening, and we have a nice dinner. I end up giving Henry and his mum a lift back to Shakthar.

I get back home and call Jai. He is still on the bus, so I say I am just calling to see if he is OK given the circumstances.

I fall asleep without my big guy next to me and with the thought of him travelling on his own to his home town after five years away. I wonder what will be waiting for him. The kittens provide me with much-needed comfort on this loneliest of nights.

The next day, the pretence continues. I arrive at LOM, update the schedule, and share it with the restaurant and room guys. A few guests are checking in and out today, so I must hang around, which is fine.

The atmosphere is calm and relaxed, which is a marked

contrast to what I am feeling inside. Outwardly I try to act my usual "authoritative" self.

It's the day before New Year's Eve, so there are still some preparations that need to be done. I still need to collect the additional flyers I had ordered for the New Year's Eve Bollywood Extravaganza. Around lunchtime I make a quick visit to Kandar Printers, where I pick up the flyers and then return to LOM.

I check in with Ishwari about the performance tomorrow. She's all good. The day passes without event, and I head back home for the afternoon. I have a little joint to relax. I message Jai to see if he is OK. He has arrived at home but is despondent. He didn't receive the most welcoming of responses from his parents. He says that he has returned as a beggar and that they are annoyed that he has not contributed anything to the family for the last five years and has now returned penniless.

My heart goes out to him. I am annoyed at his parents for rejecting their son in his hour of need. But I don't know his parents. I can only assume that they are typical Indian parents, meaning that the concern is always what the community will think and whether or not their name will be tarnished. I try to console Jai and tell him I will be there for him.

After a while, and with thoughts of Jai running through my head and with the joint taking effect, I sleep until the evening.

While I am sitting and having dinner in LOM that evening, Jalan comes over and mentions Jai. He asks if I know what happened. I reply, "No," adding that Jai hasn't been replying to my messages. Jalan starts to talk about what he has heard, that Madhav had thrown Jai out of Amun Ra Café and had paid some local gangsters to beat Jai.

I act shocked at what he's just said to me. I say, "I can't believe what you're saying." He continues, saying that all of Jai's creditors had gone to Jai's place to find that Jai had run away. No one knows where he is. He said that Madhav had planned this, that he had seen the money coming in and wanted the money for himself. Jalan says that he and the landlord had told Jai not to trust Madhav, but Jai did not listen. He called Madhav a fraudster.

Jalan says that Jai had been stabbed, but no one knows where he is. I am shocked at this, firstly that the rumour mill has already started, and secondly that someone could actually think that it's OK to stab someone.

He says that Madhav will find out soon and ask what will happen to Jai, saying that all the money he owes will hang over his head. He says that a police case has been raised against Jai, but Madhav will also be investigated.

This goes on for a while, and I listen and ask the odd question. He asks if I know where Jai is. I say no but add that I am worried about him, especially if he has been stabbed.

It is getting late. I just want to go home. I hang around for a little while so as not to be too suspicious by leaving early. I speak to Jasmine for a while as Harry has left for Hansari. But I just want to get home.

I get home around 10 p.m. and call Jai to tell him what Jalan said. He is still angry and hurt about what has happened. He wants to take revenge on Madhav and also on Harry. But what can he do?

He tells me his parents are bugging him and that they are not going to support him. They think he will take their money and run away again.

We talk sweetly to each other. He tells me he loves me, and I tell him I love him too. I miss him in my bed, just having his warmth against me and his arm around me while we sleep. The kittens snuggle up to me in his absence. I'm missing him so much.

The next day, New Year's Eve, is the big New Year's Extravaganza! The day starts off as usual. LOM is fully booked with only a couple of rooms checking in today.

The day goes by in a blur. I had arranged to pick up Ishwari around 7.30 p.m. I go home first to get ready, and then I drive to Anjaru. I said I'd pick her up at the chai wallah's stand. The traffic is horrendous along Anjaru Market road. I call Ishwari and ask her to walk towards the main street. I drive down it slowly, but I do not see her. She is phoning to say she is still walking. I had turned around at the car park junction, but I am being nudged along by other drivers who are beeping their horns continuously.

Ishwari phones again. She is by Casablanca and Rendezvous, which are in the other direction. We have been going in opposite directions. I turn the car around, and I slowly make my way down the market street. Eventually I see her, and she is in her outfit. She looks stunning. She has a friend with her, Christina, who is going to help with outfit changes.

They both get in the car, and we greet each other. Feeling relieved but running late, I turn the car around and eventually make it out of the market street onto the main road. I absolutely bomb it back to Shakthar, rivalling any of the local drivers with my speed and precision in avoiding oncoming traffic. On the way I call Satish to have some food ready for us before the performance.

We arrive at LOM, and all the restaurants guys' heads turn to see Ishwari. She really does look stunning in her white sari-type outfit with silver embroidery, immaculate make-up, and jewellery.

We have dinner. Ishwari sets up the laptop with the playlist. Jalan decides to be the music master.

So, it's now time for the New Year's Eve Bollywood Extravaganza. I do a brief awkward introduction, and Ishwari comes out and gets into place.

The restaurant is full, and the neighbours have pulled up chairs outside to watch the performance. I am a little nervous for her, but she is a consummate professional.

The music starts, and off she goes in a whirl of white sari, arms swaying and feet tapping. The music is typical Bollywood. The guests are taking photos and videos. A crowd of locals have gathered at the end of the restaurant.

I video her on my phone, but my position is behind her, so I get most of the video from behind. The photos are blurry as she is moving so fast.

At one point the music stops mid-flow. I run over to the speaker and plug the connector in, but Ishwari continues without missing a beat.

At the end of the first performance, the guests and the crowd clap enthusiastically.

The second performance is funkier and livelier. Ishwari gets some of the crowd to join in the dancing. I cajole some of the little kids, including Peri, one of the landlord's daughters.

As the performances continue, the crowd seem to be waning, and the applause at the end of each performance decreases. After five performances, we decide to call it a night. By now Ishwari has been dancing for nearly two hours.

I thank her, and we hang around. Some of the guests have their picture taken with Ishwari, as does Jasmine.

Harry hasn't turned up. In between performances, Jasmine has been going ape on the phone with him.

In between performances, I have been messaging Jai with updates.

Jag from High Life also made an appearance during the performance. He had invited the LOM team to High Life for bringing in the New Year.

The New Year's Eve Bollywood Extravaganza has come to an end. I am hoping it was a success and that it leaves a lasting legacy at LOM.

Once Ishwari leaves, Jalan and I walk along the beach to High Life. Fireworks are going off, and the lights at High Life look lovely and inviting.

I'm still feeling sad that Jai is not here. He had planned to come to see the performance from the side-lines only a couple of days ago.

Jalan and I get to High Life. Jai phones, but I cannot hear him over the music. Jalan and I walk over to the bar. On our way there, some random guy approaches me and says hi, mentioning that he is the owner. I reply, "Really?!" And I go to the bar instead.

Jag comes to sit with me for a while, and we chat about Ishwari. He says he had seen her a couple of times at Casablanca, but only from afar. He is taken with her. He leaves to manage the restaurant. I ask Jalan to take some photos of me, but I end up doing selfies instead.

Later the restaurant guys join us, and we head to the dance floor. We are enjoying the music and laughing at Mistry's dancing. He is the freakiest dancer. Who would have guessed the quietest one of the lot would be the funkiest dancer? Ha ha!

A short while later, the guy who said he was the owner comes and stands by us, just watching and shaking his head. He tells Mistry and one of the others to get out. I intervene and say, "What's the problem?" He replies that I am the only one with class and that the others need to get out. I just turn to my guys and say, "We're leaving."

As we walk down the beach, we're all slating him. I'm shouting, "Fuck them. Fuck the lot of them," speaking not just about the High Life owner but also about everyone who has wronged Jai and me.

We end up at Arabian Waters, and there's a decent crowd. All the guys are dancing now. I stand by the bar, chatting to a white couple. Everyone is happy and smiling. I am too on the outside. Inside, one thing is missing: my big guy!

It's now approaching one o'clock, and I just want to go home. Jalan and I go back to LOM. I go for a wee, and then he drops me off at my house.

I get inside and call Jai. I wish him a happy New Year and chat about the performance and the night in general. He has been to his uncle's restaurant but is back promptly. I fall asleep as I'm a little drunk.

Happy New Year 2017! My big guy is not here. He's had to run for his life away from Goa and from me!

Over the next couple of days, the news of Amun Ra and Jai filters out. I get the odd question asked of me. Dev Chef asks what's happened with Jai. I tell him I don't know. Harry has a field day. The smug look on his face is disgusting to me. A couple of evenings after Jai left, we are sitting at LOM for dinner. Both Jasmine and he are there. He sits opposite me and starts gloating, saying that he knew Jai was a cheat and con man, which is why he threw him out when he had the chance. He says that Jai can't be trusted, adding that he has left without paying his creditors and that he has taken the money with him. I sit and listen without saying a word. Harry tells me that he had tried to warn me about Jai. He asks me how much money I have given him. I say, "Only a little." He adds that people are saying that I gave him fifteen lakhs. Fifteen lakhs (nearly ten thousand pounds in English money)! I laugh in his face, asking how I could have given Jai fifteen lakhs. At most I had given him £2,000. Harry is going on about how he knows everything that goes on, how he has eyes and ears everywhere, adding that people respect him.

Bloody Jasmine pipes up, saying that she knew Jai was a bad man from the moment she saw him. (Wait a couple of days and see what she says when Harry is not here.) She mentions that she does not trust him, going on to say, "Baby, you the man," to Harry. I am sick to my stomach hearing this.

Harry goes on about how Madhav is the biggest cheat, saying that he had given him the responsibility to look after LOM during the off-season, but he had not secured the building.

This goes on for a while. I just want to smack his smug, ugly face. He's not actually ugly, but his inner ugliness seeps through his pores like poisonous smog creeping in from the ocean.

I just keep quiet. I will not get riled by Harry. That's what he wants to see, a reaction, and to prove to himself what a good guy he is.

I go home and call Jai and tell him what's been going on.

He is fuming and wants to seek revenge against all the people who have hurt him. I don't blame him, and I back him up.

Over the next few days the news is spreading. I don't say anything to anyone. Inside my heart is breaking, but I try not to let it show. Whether that's working or not I don't know.

Jai and I talk every night before we go to sleep. He talks of revenge, but I try to calm his extreme thoughts. He is also battling with his parents. They don't seem to understand what has happened, or else they don't care. I don't understand how parents can refuse to support their child in his hour of need.

Jai is having trouble sleeping, he tells me. Everything is running around in his head, which is completely understandable. He is going to have to start his life from scratch. He has no money or savings; everything was put into Creation Valley and Amun Ra Café. He hardly has any clothes. He literally has nothing and no support apart from me. I will be with him no matter what. I will do whatever I can to help him.

He tells me his lifestyle is different in Gandabaan. He says he feels ashamed. All his friends are settled, whereas he ran a business for two months and then left. He wants to get his identity papers and wants to come to London to work. I tell him he can stay, but he needs official paperwork to work in London.

We talk about mundane things and chit-chat generally. Also, he asks me some of the big questions about my life. He asks why I never got married. I told him I was married before. He says, "Why not again?" I tell him I've never met anyone whom I wanted to get married to and that my life has taken a different, unconventional path.

He asks if my family would accept him. I say, "Of course they will. They just want me to be happy."

We talk about the night we hugged in the UV Bar and how our relationship started from there. We met each other when we were not content or happy with our lives. He says he saw something in me which maybe other people have not seen. He doesn't say what though.

We tell each other how much we are missing each other. My whole being aches for him at these times. He says the day I say, "Jai, come to me," he will be there. I say I just want him to be safe, adding that I can wait. But I don't know long I can wait. I say I will come in March when I have finished at LOM. He says he will come just for me, even though it's a war zone.

He is willing to risk his safety for me.

I tell him I need a holiday, but I can't wait till March when I finish at LOM for the season. He says he will come and take me out.

At this point I am sick and have been coughing a lot. I went to the doctor, and he gave me antibiotics, which have helped somewhat. It doesn't help that the house is dirty. The kittens play outside in the bushes and the "jungle" at the back of the house. I haven't put flea treatment on them yet, and I can see flea dirt on the bed. The house smells, and I don't know where the smell is coming from. I have washed the floor. In addition, smoking joints and cigarettes before bed is not helping. But getting stoned numbs the pain of everything that has happened and helps me forget that Jai isn't there. The stress of LOM is always there too. I don't like to drink, but a cheeky little joint takes the edge off the stress and the strain. But it's difficult to sleep, and my breathing is heavy and makes a clicking sound.

I got myself a separate SIM card to call Jai with. I suppose calling from a separate number provides a level of security and increases the trust between me and Jai.

It's now mid-January. It's been two weeks since Jai's premature departure. LOM has been busy, and there have been issues with hot water supply. Guests have been complaining, especially a few of the Russian guests. Jalan and I have been trying to investigate the root cause of the issue.

The water supply is complicated, not like in the UK, where the water is supplied from the main lines. In India the supply is a tad more complicated. The process starts with rainwater from the monsoons gathering in a well. The water then goes through to a small reservoir/water tank supplying the hotel and neighbouring properties. This is then pumped up to a tank atop the hotel to supply the rooms, and then it goes to the solar tank to heat up the water (note: this is not drinking water). However, the water reaching the tank at the top needs to be pumped with an electric pump. So, to determine where the point of failure is, each process needs to be checked.

However, after investigating the issue, it is determined that the issue is with the way the plumbing and taps have been installed. In some rooms the tap needs to be turned left; in others, it needs to be turned right. Each room seems to differ. The plan was for Jalan to explain the system to each of the guests when they checked in. What a fricking palaver.

Anyway, I gave the complaining guests a reduction on their room rate just to keep them happy as they were inconvenienced by not having hot water as advertised.

There is always something going wrong. The Wi-Fi is still a massive bone of contention. The main restaurant's Wi-Fi, which goes through a main line to the Wi-Fi network, keeps breaking down. The restaurant guys keep changing the password and fucking up the connection with the IP address. The company providing Wi-Fi sends guys out, and they shout at the restaurant guys for messing up the IP configuration.

The Wi-Fi for the rooms is provided by a different network, which I had set up. This is done with a router and a Wi-Fi dongle. The data limit is reached quickly, especially if the hotel is full. To get this fixed, I need to call up the Airtel guy Vijay, who is also getting pissed off at me. However, he does investigate and tells me the data limit has been reached. To resolve this, Jalan and I go to the Airtel branch in Nimpura to pay any outstanding bills and add data to the dongle.

Everything seems to happen at once, and the restaurant guys complain to me, pressuring me to get things fixed. While I am happy to fix the rooms' Wi-Fi, I cannot take complete responsibility for the restaurant. Everything does my head in.

However, they are supportive in other areas. For example, one evening I was at home around 8 p.m. It had been a busy day, so I wasn't planning on going back to LOM. I got a call saying there were ten guests waiting to be checked in. I said I didn't have guests checking in. So, I bombed it back to LOM, and there were ten people sitting round the big table, all with rucksacks, looking exhausted.

I spoke to the main coordinator of the group. They definitely had a booking for five rooms, which they had booked last October. I had no record of the booking. Internally I was in a mild state of panic, but I stayed firm. I told the young woman, Valeria, that I did not have a booking. She was not happy! Which was understandable. So, I made various phone calls to other hotels and resorts to accommodate them. But there weren't rooms available, plus the group wanted to stay together in one place.

So, I was standing with the restaurant guys and discussing the situation with them. They said that as the guests had already arrived, they should take priority. Which made sense—but what about the other two rooms with guests who were due to check in? However, they had not arrived.

I made quick phone calls to the guests booked in for the two rooms. One hung up as soon as I said I was calling from LOM. The other guest picked up and said they had cancelled the booking. There were three rooms available already. So, with these two rooms now cancelled, I was able to accommodate all ten guests who were sitting at the big table. The rooms were not what they had originally booked, but at least they were together in one place. Crisis and tears averted. Thank God!

Jalan and I showed the rooms to the guests, and they seemed to be happy. I said to Valeria that I would give them a concession on the room rates, which she was more than happy about, considering the mild trauma the confusion had caused.

At the end of their stay, they were very happy guests, and Valeria and I had become friends. And the restaurant guys made sure they enjoyed their stay by providing them with excellent service.

Recently Jalan has been getting rather cheeky. He's talking back, and it's beginning to piss me off. One day I get a call from Satish asking about guests checking in and guests complaining about toilet paper and not having clean sheets. I head back to LOM to resolve the issue. I ask Jalan what has been going on, and he says there is no toilet paper. I say, "Just get some from Bhanu's shop [around the corner], and I will get a proper supply the next day." He goes on to say the guest issue is my problem and my fault. So, I tell him I will deal with the guests, but if there is a shortage of supplies, he should just get them.

It isn't so much the issue as it is his attitude now that he is all pally with Harry, who is probably filling his head with ideas above his station. I tell Jalan and Amit that if they have a problem with working at LOM, then the solution is simple. I will not tolerate attitude from them. If guests complain, they should send them to me, but they should think for themselves also. They simply do not listen to me and disregard what I say. I will not put up with this. Amit is slowly coming around as I had told him his days are numbered. But I expected better from Jalan. He's just not bothered any more.

Satish says that they won't listen to anyone. Maybe it's better to put things down on paper for them. So, I create a schedule of jobs for them. The next couple of days I take them aside and explain the schedule to them.

Fuck, man, it feels like I am working with a bunch of imbeciles sometimes. They act like children. But I know this is all Harry's doing, filling Jalan's head with ideas about going abroad, promising trips to Dubai and taking him away from Shakthar and India in general. Jalan, the dim-witted lad wants to escape the clutches of his adopted family, i.e. the landlord, and Harry has provided an imaginary escape route in order to get him on his side.

I go home and vent to Jai. He asks why I am angry. He has

previously said that he doesn't know how to handle my anger when it's directed at him. I tell him it's more frustration than anger at having to deal with idiots.

Later I speak to Jalan more softly, telling him that I cannot be there 24/7 and that I need his support to run the rooms. He seems to take this in, but we'll see what happens.

Over the course of the next couple of evenings, Jai says he wants to come to Goa and talk to me face-to-face. I tell him I am scared of him coming here in case something happens. He says he needs to talk to me. I know what it's about, but I don't say anything. I have already transferred five thousand rupees into his uncle's account just so he can have some spending money.

I am still ill with the cough. He says that when he comes, he will bring magic and all my ills will vanish. God, he has a way with words. It just makes me melt.

So, it's been agreed that he will come back to Goa to see me next week. We talk logistics. He will get the ticket with the money I have sent him. He will take the overnight bus from Gandabaan and will arrive in Goa by Friday morning. I will pick him up from Nimpura before I go to LOM. He will basically hide out in my house for a few days so we can spend time together and talk about what's going to happen in future. I know he will ask me to fund him. He's mentioned it briefly already. I always have a bad feeling when he asks me for money. But I know I am his only choice, his girl.

The next couple of days actually move quite quickly. LOM keeps me busy with guests and the running of the day-to-day tasks. I draw up a list of tasks for Jalan and Amit. In reality, I know it won't work as there is always something urgent that needs to be done, but the task list will add a bit of structure to the day and hopefully stop them from quarrelling amongst themselves.

This was the suggestion of Satish which I took on board. But again, reality is never as straightforward as we might hope. Reality has a random, chaotic mind of its own.

One afternoon, once I had updated the room schedule for the restaurant guys and the room guys, Jasmine arrives with the baby but no Harry. It's a good opportunity for us to chat without the ever-looming presence of Harry.

We sit at one of the tables in the restaurant. Satish and the bar guys are milling around. Hakim, Jasmine and Harry's baby, is being entertained by Jalan. They are the best of friends. Jasmine and I chat about general stuff. I learn about her background, how she lived in London for a good twelve years, that she's originally from the United States, and that her parents are of Middle Eastern heritage—Egyptian, I think.

She tells me how brave I am to do all this, moving to another country all on my own. She also tells me how well I'm doing. I graciously accept all her compliments.

Somehow, we get onto the subject of Jai. She says that when they all used to hang out, he actually looked out for her and was a good friend. I'm surprised that she said this. It's not that I doubt what she says, but when Harry is not there, the confession reveals exactly what I was thinking about their relationship.

I just tell her that Jai has been a very good friend to me. I don't tell her of what Harry had previously accused him of and the drama that ensued. I also don't mention that since that moment, it actually brought me and Jai a lot closer. Call it the Romeo and Juliet effect—star-crossed lovers thrown together because they have a common foe.

It is from this moment that the beginnings of a sort of relationship form.

We continue to chat, smoking ciggies and drinking coffee. We are essentially the two madams of Light of Moon. We have lunch, and then I make my excuses and go about my day.

I head back home after getting supplies from Shakthar Market. I'm glad to get home to the solitude of my one-room. I leave the door open for the cats to run about. They really do keep me sane amidst the madness!

I message Jai and check in with him. I must have fallen asleep, as the next thing I know it's dark already and time to get showered and back to LOM to keep myself entertained somewhat.

The morning of Jai's cloak-and-dagger visit arrives. He got to the bus at Gandabaan the previous evening and was due to arrive around 8 a.m. However, the bus is delayed by three hours. I decide to go to LOM as usual and then return to my house when Jai is near. He's getting a rickshaw from Nimpura straight to my house.

The adrenalin is pumping to say the least. I keep it cool at LOM. It helps being on the laptop, doing schedules and checking out guests.

The countdown has begun. I'm in Unjaan in thirty minutes. I'm in Thairi, five minutes away from Nimpura. I'm in the rickshaw! That's my cue. I make my excuses and head back to my house. Fuck, I feel like I am in the zone, clear-headed and sharp! But at the same time, I am experiencing pangs of nervousness.

I arrive home. Five minutes later I receive the phone call. Jai is outside in the rickshaw. I grab a few hundred rupees to pay the driver. As Jai gets out of the rickshaw, the house landlord's heavily pregnant wife appears from the purple house next door. Standing with her is the house landlord's brother. They are both intently staring at Jai. *We're fucked!*

I give money to Jai for the rickshaw, and we head into my house. We're both freaking out. We were spotted, but at least it was my landlord's heavily pregnant wife. I'm not 100 per cent sure, but I'm confident enough that they won't say anything. Jalan knows them. We calm ourselves down. We hug. It's needed. We chat for a little while. He says he saw at least five faces that could have identified him, including Fruity, the brother of the LOM landlord, who is close to Harry, but none of them saw him.

We briefly discuss moving Jai somewhere else, maybe to

Henry's house, who is a friend of the Aunties. But Jai doesn't want to go. He doesn't want to involve outsiders. I concede, but if anything happens, I don't know how I will protect him.

I need to get back to LOM. But Jai is visibly unnerved by the highly controversial arrival.

There's food in the house, as well as cigarettes and enough supplies to be getting on with. Unfortunately, it's just him and his thoughts, and maybe the cats to keep him entertained.

This is the craziest situation of my life, and there have been a few of them. My runaway young lover, a potential con man and victim of espionage, is literally hiding out in my little house in Goa. You can't make this shit up!

I head back to LOM for a couple of hours. My head is getting battered! Nothing of note happens, not that I would be able to focus on the job in hand. My mind is fixed on Jai at my house.

Some more guests arrive, and I happily check them in.

Jai is messaging all the while. He's panicking. He says he needs to move in case the house landlord tells LOM's landlord that he's seen him. I say they won't say anything. Paranoia is setting in. He messages to ask if I have seen Madhav. I tell him to calm down and take deep breaths.

I tell him I'll be back in an hour, around lunchtime. He messages to request some Coke and Old Monk. I oblige as I drive back home.

We snuggle up on the bed. It feels so nice to have physical contact again, even if it's just me stroking his hair. We kiss. Never before have I felt so close to another human being.

I don't know if it's the heightened senses arising from the intrigue and deception that is exaggerating my other emotions but being with him is like a feeling of homecoming. It's all-encompassing, with no ulterior motives but just a pure sense of oneness. But as with all feelings, it morphs into something else along the line.

By now it's dark. I make sure Jai is calm and comfortable. It's time for me to feign normality. I get ready for LOM.

I have to wait till 8 p.m. as the solar guy is coming; there is still no hot water in the evening. However, as with everyone in Shakthar, who have their own timelines, the solar guy doesn't turn up. I decide not to hang around. I need to get myself and Jai dinner, so I go to a place on the way to Anjaru to order us something to eat.

It's in the opposite direction, but I figure it will be safer. Jai had suggested Palm Tree Vista, but the guys in there know me from when we used to go there when I first arrived.

I arrive at the place. I park up and put my hoodie up. I order and wait. Jai has requested Old Monk again. With the food in hand, I head back the house, on the way getting the Old Monk.

When I get home, I find Jai sitting on the bed in darkness. Poor boy! We eat and talk about the next steps. He can't just stay in the room for four whole days and nights. We decide to go away tomorrow evening to another part of North Goa. I'll look at hotels tomorrow. And on the way back I can drop him off in Unjaan, so he can catch his bus back.

I'm pretty much exhausted, so I lie on the bed. I must have fallen asleep coz I sort of wake up with Jai taking off my glasses for me.

The next day normal duties ensue. I had booked us a hotel room in Chandpurim. It's near enough for me to get back to LOM early the next day, and it's close enough that we'll pass through Unjaan so I can drop Jai off at the bus station.

During the day he is messaging me. He says he can't talk to me face-to-face as my anger scares him. He says he needs money, approximately twenty thousand rupees, to get his identity papers made. I tell him it only makes me angry when he surprises me with things like this. I know I'm the only one who can help him. His parents are not supporting him.

The landlord's pregnant wife is still outside the house, but judging by the sounds of it, she has been there most of the day.

Jai is lying low. He messages that he is actually not scared, saying that he has always wanted to date an underworld don's daughter. He's always wanted adventure and excitement because of a girl. And I am giving that to him. I can't believe the guy; he's enjoying this. But I'd be lying if I said I wasn't also enjoying it.

The day consists of a visit to Lamuella, just for a bit of a mooch to kill some time between duties, and then heading back home. I buy a nice shirt dress and leggings that take my fancy, and also a large leather handbag for the overnight stay away from Shakthar.

There are a couple of check-ins at LOM, but other than that, it is a calm day. The guests arrived early.

The solar engineer came and said the solar is working fine. He ruled out any issues with heating the water. I will see in the evening if the water heats up.

After a day of what seemed like just killing time, I head back to my house. When I arrive, Jai is hiding in the bathroom. He says the landlady has been out there most of the day.

It's now early evening. We both shower and get ready to leave for Chandpurim. I had parked the car outside the house so Jai could just jump in without having to walk up to the car parking spot.

I wear my new clothes, and Jai says I look nice. I make sure there is enough food for the cats. I also make sure they are safely inside the house before we head out. Jai puts on my black hoodie, which is a bit snug on his big frame, but it zips up.

I go out, unlock the car, and put Jai's bag into the boot. It's now dark. Undercover, Jai gets in and lies on the back seat.

After securing the house with the cats inside, I get into the driver's seat and head out of Shakthar. I head towards Thairi, going the opposite route via Obrah and Tarana.

Jai lies low, and we chat most of the way. I say I need to phone Jalan and tell him I'm not coming in that evening and that I have gone out to Anjaru.

I stop just as we pass Chatu and Gohar and make the call.

Jalan just says, "OK. Enjoy." With that weight off my mind, Jai and I continue to chit-chat all the way to Chandpurim.

I tell him more about my past and how I was pressured into marriage, and then I describe my eventual escape. He listens. I tell him how I had basically done everything in my life on my own, from going to university to buying a house and a car. Everything! I suppose in a way I'm telling him this to ease his fears about what his life has become. He has nothing, but my point is that it's not the end and that life can be restarted.

Upon reaching Chandpurim, I see it's pretty much a popular resort. The streets are lined with tatty tourist clothes shops, restaurants, and hotels. it's a bit like an Indian version of Blackpool.

We can't find the hotel. After a couple of phone calls, some of the hotel staff come and meet us on the main strip, and we follow them in the car to the hotel. It is down a narrow side street. I manage to manoeuvre the car safely into a very tight parking spot in front of the hotel.

We check in and take a look at the room, which is sufficient enough. To keep costs down, I book a room that isn't the plushest. It is a grubby little haven for the evening and the night. We ask about breakfast, dump the bag, and head out to get some dinner.

We find a restaurant with a terrace up top, assuming this will be safer than a restaurant on the roadside.

We sit and order drinks, a large vodka and soda for me, a Blenders and Coke for him. As I look around, I see that the restaurant is full of old and middle-aged white people, something you would imagine in Costa del Sol rather than Goa—well, at least to my mind.

There is a guy with a sound system singing live songs. They are a mix of Hindi songs and old white people music. He does Elvis, Roy Orbison, and Abba. I'm just laughing to myself as it could be an English wedding reception. The performer is encouraging people to get up and dance. No one moves. But there is one couple already slow dancing, arm in arm.

It's too loud to have a conversation, but we try to talk. Jai is still paranoid, and I tell him to relax. The vodka and sodas are taking effect, and I can feel my mind and body relaxing. I order another drink when the food arrives. I had wanted Chana Masala, but they didn't have any. We go for the standard chilli mushrooms and palak with roti.

After dinner we decide to walk to the beach. It's at the end of the street. We walk for a bit, just chit-chatting about general stuff. But there's not much to see. We head back to the room.

In the safety of the room, and with a little bit of a buzz on from the drinks, Jai rolls a small joint. We smoke and relax and actually laugh for the first time in a few days.

We lie down and roll around, enjoying each other's closeness. He blows my mind, this one!

In the night he gets up and turns on the air-con. He's naked, and from the low bed he looks so sexy in the night light, tall with broad shoulders and thick thighs. I'm in too deep!

We sleep contentedly with his arm around me.

The next morning, we get up early, order breakfast, and get showered. Over breakfast we discuss the finances a bit more in depth and book his bus back to Gandabaan via Paytm on my phone. The bus doesn't leave until around 6 p.m., so the plan is to drop Jai off at the City Mall. He can watch a movie, and I will come back later to take him to Unjaan.

Basically, he needs twenty thousand rupees to sort out his identity papers to get a job and open a bank account, essentially to get his life back on track to start again. He also wants to get a passport sorted. I am always reluctant to just hand over cash. I feel I need to put up a bit of resistance, but I am too weak in love to resist him. Call me stupid and naive. I have said these things to myself on many occasions now. But I cannot leave him stranded. We have been through so much together already.

We leave the hotel and head towards Unjaan and the Mall. He drives. We take a few wrong turns but eventually arrive at the Mall. He jumps out, and I head to Nimpura and Shakthar.

I get back to my house around midmorning. I let the cats out, and there's a message from Jai asking if have reached home. I tell him yes, adding that I miss him already and that I love him. He replies, saying he loves me too. He says, "Shall I stay another two days?" I cannot cope with the stress, so I tell him no.

I get to LOM later than my usual time, around 11.30. No one bats an eyelid. There was only one checkout, and no guests are checking in. So, I just do the normal schedule updates for the next couple of days. Nothing of note is happening at LOM today.

Around 4 p.m. I start my journey back to the mall to pick up Jai. He's waiting outside, and we head back to Unjaan.

On the way there, our conversation gets a bit deep. I don't know how this happens, but we talk about the future and even children. I say I'm not sure if I want children, adding that it might be too late for me anyway. I ask him if he wants children. He says, "Not now, but in future, yes. Who else will continue my bloodline and inherit my empire?"

I feel like this relationship has an expiry date. It cuts me deep when he says this. We have talked about our future together and have discussed building something ourselves, but all I can think about is me helping to build our future together, and then him going and marrying someone else to have children with. Where does that leave me? I'm twice his age practically. Where would that leave me in my old age? I don't say anything to him then, but the tender fault lines of my heart ache at the thought. I feel sick.

We manage to make it to the bus station through the traffic. I give him the twenty thousand rupees he had asked for. We hug while in the car, and then he gets out and leaves. The emotional strain of the last few days has taken its toll on me. I pull over to the side and have a cigarette. My mind is spinning from that last conversation.

After a short while I compose myself and start the drive back towards Nimpura. It's not that far, maybe half an hour.

Just as I get on the bridge to cross the Mondovi River, Jai calls my phone, saying he's on the bus. He says, "Thank you for everything. Let me know when you get back." I say I will, but I can't hold my emotions and I start to cry. I don't tell him why I'm crying. He says "bye" and hangs up.

Chapter 10

HIDE-AND-SEEK, PART II

That evening I go to LOM as if nothing has happened. The restaurant is busy. Harry and Jasmine are having dinner and chatting. I'm at a different table, sitting with Jag from High Life. He sometimes comes to join me for after his shift has finished. He's a nice enough guy, and it's good to have some company for dinner.

We chat about general things. He tells me about his work relationships, saying that he has a bad relationship with the German woman who does the bookings and with the owners of High Life. He used to work in Manali (North India) at a resort he used to run.

I listen and chirp in the odd comment. I'm actually glad he is there. I'm also glad that Harry is there. I feel that it somewhat takes the focus of any gossip that may be going around about me and Jai.

I want the people at LOM to think that I have other "friends" and keep them guessing. Not that anything is going to happen with Jag. My heart belongs to Jai.

It's getting late. Jag leaves. I go to chat with Jasmine. Harry is now at the bar, being the big man. He is making Jasmine a strawberry daiquiri and asks if I want one. I say OK. The drink arrives, and it's actually very nice. I drink it as slowly as I can. I'm actually exhausted. After a while I make my excuses and leave to go home.

I get home and message Jai. He's still on the bus. I tell him I was sitting with Jag. He says, "Damn, why do other people always want what I have? Even Neil." I tell him it's because they can't have me that they want me, adding that they probably think I am rich. He says he doesn't like me for that reason, for sure. He says he knows I have a heart.

He says how he wants me to be like a "sweet mother".

I'm like, "Er, what?!" He wants someone to care for him and give him affection, something he has not got from anyone before. I tell him I care, adding that sometimes I care too much, and it pains me.

He reminisces about the fateful night we first got together, saying how at first he was not interested and that he only wanted to help to set up LOM. But then the night in UV Bar happened. I had hugged him, saying I didn't want to kiss him, but then we kissed. Then came the end to his bachelor life once we had broken in that car. I ask him if he regrets it. He says, "*No.*"

We talk about plans for his next visit. We agree that he will come back for Valentine's Day.

We have some big conversations that night. He tells me not to compare him to my previous partners, saying that he is different. He says that he's not a kid anymore and that now he has to focus on his career. I ask him what he wants from me. He says he just wants someone to care about him. He says he has lost all his valuables and that he doesn't want to lose me either. He asks me to trust him. He says he's going to walk with me through my life. I tell him that all I've ever wanted is someone to share my life with.

He says that once he starts work, all money matters will be fixed, and he doesn't want us to fight about money issues. He says he will never ask for money again. I say, "If I don't help you, who will?" His family are not helping him. He says that's why he won't take advantage of me.

We talk about building a future. He says it will take time. He calls me once the bus has stopped for a break. We each say, "I love you." I'm very tired, and I sleep deeply that night.

Over the course of the next few days, we continue to message and speak. He's visited his grandfather and his mum's brother. He has requested that his identity papers be drawn up. He mentions that I was upset when he had called after he left, saying that he felt bad but could not talk on the packed bus.

We talk about me going to Gandabaan once I have finished at LOM, and then we'll take a trip to Pondicherry, where I've wanted to go for a while to explore yet another part of India.

I talk about how when I go home, I'm going to have a massive house party. He says he will be there for that.

So, after the last few days, we're both a bit more relaxed. He's starting to sort his life out.

It's busy at LOM, and the work is taking up a lot of my time. Guests turn up who had previously cancelled. Jake and his stepdad and mum, Cliff and Julia, had previously made a big booking at LOM but had cancelled. They ended up coming anyway as the other place they had booked was a bit of a hellhole. So, they were stuck. And Julia wasn't feeling great.

I put Cliff and Julie in 301, one of the deluxe rooms, and Jake in 204. They seemed happy enough.

They are from London, and we all immediately got on. And because they are English, I can't help but treat them with a bit of favouritism.

In addition, I have been dealing with other guests checking in and out. For some reason Shakthar has a bit of a vibrant atmosphere. The restaurant always has at least a couple of tables occupied during the day. At one point Jalan had said that people were beginning to really talk about Light of Moon. It is becoming the no. 1 place in Shakthar, and this is above Café Nu, which has a good reputation.

Guests are also extending their bookings at LOM. They originally book for one or two days but end staying another couple of days.

Locals are beginning to pay attention to what is happening at LOM. Again, Jalan said that one of the local dons had said he wanted to take over next year's season. I basically replied that no one else can do what I am doing or what the restaurant guys are doing. They are doing a really good job, not just in terms of the quality of the food but also in building relationships with guests and making them feel special. They have a number of large bookings coming in in the evenings for birthdays and various events.

The following day I am in LOM as usual. I am standing at the bar when an English couple approach me. The man says that he is Jake's brother-in-law and that he has lost his bank card. "Has anyone seen it?" he enquires. I ask around, but no one has seen it.

When leaving, he asks if I know anyone who sells any weed. I say, "Let's talk outside." We walk up the main entrance to the restaurant. I say, "Yes. I cannot buy it myself, but I can take you to someone." He says that the smokes are for Jake. We arrange to meet at LOM that evening to go to Anjaru. I put a call into Neil, who is more than willing to oblige.

That evening, I'm waiting for Jake, Abigale, and Kev (Jake's sister and his not quite brother-in-law) to arrive. Kev and Abigale are staying at a place in Obrah. Jake is still in his room at LOM.

I had briefly chatted with Jake, and it turns out that Abigale is a master at Connect 4, so we had arranged to have a little match before leaving. However, they all arrive late, and the match is called off.

Kev and Abigale arrive, but Jake is late. He is charging his phone in his room. I sit and chat with them both. Abigale lived in the United States for a long time and is very much into her yoga. Both she and Kev had done two yoga sessions that day. Kev was starving, so he ordered naan bread to tide him over.

But he doesn't look well after eating it. I see the immediate look of dread on his face before he pegs it to the washroom. Abigale and I look at each other in total shock.

At this point Jake arrives. He's brought Cliff with him. We all stand in the restaurant ready to go, waiting for Kev to come back from the washroom. When he does reappear, he does not look great. We all stand looking at him, which makes him even more paranoid. He decides he isn't up for dinner and that he just needs to get back to his room. It doesn't help that there are four faces of concern staring back at him.

Kev and Abigale go back to Obrah. Cliff goes back up to his room to check on Julie, who is still ill.

Jake and I head to Anjaru in my car. We had arranged to meet Neil at Angel on Anjaru beach. We don't see him, so we sit and have a beer. I allow myself only the one beer as I am driving.

We sit and chat for a while. Jake tells me about his job as an independent sound engineer and tells me about how he met Theresa May, saying she is the coldest, most serious person he has ever met. But I suppose you don't get to be prime minister by having a cheery disposition (didn't hurt Obama, though). He says that she doesn't like to be miked up and always have a standing mike, but on this occasion, it wasn't possible, so he had to mike her up under her clothing. He says she always has really pretty women working for her. We wonder about her sexual orientation.

In his spare time, Jake is an aspiring music producer.

Jake is a really cool guy, but he looks totally out of place. He's wearing jeans, a smart shirt, and a tweed-type jacket. He's tall with a slim frame and cute but in a mildly geeky kind of way. I'm not attracted to him, but we get on as we seem to have a similar perspective on life. But he is kind of a scatterbrain. The previous day he lost his bank card, which evidently was found in a pile of rubbish by one of the taxi drivers. Over the course of the next couple of days, he loses his laptop, which he left in the taxi when they all relocated out of LOM. He also leaves his electric toothbrush at LOM. This all means that he has to keep returning to LOM and collecting his lost items.

I give him a general synopsis of what has been going on with LOM. I also tell him about the Jai situation. It's a weight off my shoulders just to talk to someone about what has been going on, just as it was when Ryan and Samantha were here.

I'm realising more and more how British I am.

I give Neil a call, and he's at a place called Angel Bar on the other side of the beach. Jake and I finish our drinks and walk along the beach. I sort of know where this place is, along the right-hand side of the beach.

We manage to locate Neil in the Angel Bar. He is seated on his own on a small round table. I introduce the guys to each other, and we chit-chat for a while. Neil explains that he was sitting at Angel when the cops came and did a sweep of the beach. He saw a couple of other dealers being taken away. He saw what was going on and pre-empted any arrest by making a sharp exit at that point.

We order some drinks, and Neil gets a fresh rum and Coke. I am now on soft drinks.

Jake initiates the deal. Neil hands over a small package containing weed. Jake isn't well pleased with his purchase and says that it's half of what he was expecting for what he has paid. Neil refutes this and says that this is the deal he always makes. This goes on for a little while. It's all amicable and calm. Neil is a pretty chill guy, so things do not get heated. Neil then offers a deal on some cream (hash/resin, as opposed to weed). Jake doesn't have enough money, so I offer going halves on the cream, which he is happy about.

It is a credit to Jake that he held his own considering he is a skinny white English dude making a deal with Neil, a big African guy.

By now it's getting late, so I say it's my time to leave. It's around 11.30 p.m. I have left the cats out too, and I don't like leaving them out at night, although I know they can look after themselves. But they are still babies.

I drop Jake off back at LOM. He's hungry, but the restaurant is now closed. I tell him that I'm sure the guys will make him something to eat. We loosely hug and say we'll catch up tomorrow.

I get home. The cats had greeted me on the road as usual and walked with me to the house. They are the cutest and have kept me sane all this time. They haven't been spayed and neutered yet, which I must do soon before I have another set of kittens on my hands.

Once inside, I speak to Jai, updating him on the day's activities, including my little deal/purchase with Jake and Neil. He tells me how much he is missing me and says he wants to come back to Goa next week. I tell him no.

The next few days it's quiet at LOM with only four rooms booked. I decide to have some me time before the weekend, when LOM is fully booked.

Harry has also arrived at LOM. He does his usual milling around, looking like the big bossman.

I also make an appointment for the cats to be spayed and neutered at Worldwide Veterinary Service in Jaspore on Wednesday, 25 January.

Jai has been asking about a loan again to help him get started. He wants money for getting a bike, buying clothes, and paying his general expenses. He is virtually begging as his family will not help him. They are threatening to throw him out of the house if he starts to come in late.

He is saying that he even lost money, around sixty-five thousand rupees, to Harry.

To date I have lent him 1.6 lakhs, approximately £2,000. In the grand scheme of things, it's not a lot of money, but when will this end? He promises it will be the last time (where have I hear this before?) and that he will start to pay me back as soon as he gets a job.

He has started looking for work, but he doesn't have any of his documents ready.

I ask him why his parents won't help him. He says that for the five years he was in Hindavi, he didn't send any money home, adding that he had dropped out of engineering college when he was younger and that he had taken money from them and misused it by just going out and roaming. And now he has turned up back at home with just ten items of clothing.

He wants to show them that he can do something with his life without their help. But it's me who is funding him.

We talk further about the technicalities, about me opening a bank account for him in my name. I don't like this idea, but I try. It doesn't work because I am a UK national and I only have two months left on my visa. I don't feel comfortable about doing that anyway.

It's Tuesday, 24 January, and the previous evening I had arranged to meet up with Jake and his sister again. We are going to see Ishwari perform at Chakra in Anjaru.

I had asked little Jagu and Jalan to drive us in my car to Anjaru. After much misdirection, we manage to locate Chakra, just where I said it was going to be, but Jalan had insisted it was where I met Ishwari the first time we met, in the darkest depths of Anjaru down a maze of small streets, but it was just off the main Market Street by Anjaru Police Station.

So, we manage to find Chakra, but because of the little diversions, we miss Ishwari's performance. I introduce Ishwari to Jake and Abigale. We spend the evening talking and have dinner. The place is full of yoga hippy types, and there is an impromptu drum session taking place. The place is full of mismatched furniture and lots of low tables where you need to sit on the floor. It's quite relaxing with the drummers and other assorted instruments playing. A random puppy makes friends with us and is enjoying being cuddled. It's a lovely relaxing evening. We talk politics and get a little philosophical. Ishwari is quite the philosopher. We discuss how you meet people to serve a purpose in your life for that given period.

Abigale loves Anjaru for all its yoga and hippy-type clothing stalls.

It's getting late, so we decide to get a taxi back to Shakthar and Obrah. We walk Ishwari to a place near her house, and we agree on a price with the taxi driver for a ride to our respective destinations.

I message Jai to let him know I'm home, and then I go to sleep.

The next morning, I awake to messages from Jai. We message for about half an hour while I have breakfast.

He says the emoji heart I had sent him last night is still beating. We tell each we are missing each other. He says he wants to wake up with me. I tell him about setting up Jag from High Life and Ishwari as Jag had expressed an interest in her (but it never happened).

I tell him I might be going to Jungle Dance with Jag for the set-up. He tells me to watch out for the dogs. "Which dogs?" I ask.

"The big dogs," he says, "like the ones in UV Bar."

After a while, I get ready. I put the cats in the red basket to take them to the vets. I had already told Jalan I would go straight from my house, so he shouldn't expect me at LOM until later. Harry is there if there are any problems. I'm sure he can handle them, big bossman that he is.

The cats, especially Lollipop, are protesting about being in the basket. I try to calm her but to no avail. I drive the car down the drive to my house, get the cats in on the front passenger seat, and get on my way to Jaspore.

I head towards Obrah, thinking I'll have a peek at Amun Ra Café. It's like a sleeping giant. I still cannot believe what has happened. And I'm still here. It was just as much my dream as it was Jai's. Seeing the place empty with not even one lonely waiter breaks my heart. I don't tell Jai I went past.

So, after going through Obrah, Tarana, and Thairi, I take the opposite road towards Chatu and Gohar. Turning left at the cross-roads, I reach the vet's easily.

I check in at reception. I ask how long the process will take and say, "Shall I pick the cats up tomorrow?" The woman says that I have to wait while the procedures are taking place, which I am surprised about, but I don't complain too much. It's a valid reason to be away from LOM and Harry.

The receptionist asks me to go to the back-waiting area. During this time, I notice another woman next to me with her cat. We smile as I go the waiting area.

I am feeling nervous, and I don't know what's going to the happen to Brutus and Lollipop.

The other woman with the cat comes and sits next to me. We smile and say hi.

One of the nurse-type people calls out Brutus's and Lollipop's names. I wave to the nurse. He comes over and explains both procedures to me. He says the neutering is quite straightforward as it's an external procedure, but the spaying is more invasive and will require actual internal surgery, so it will take longer.

I take all of this in and am scared for my fur babies. I just hope they don't pick up on my nerves. They are still so small.

The nurse takes the red basket from the seat next to me, and I almost weep seeing them go.

I fiddle on my phone to try to distract myself, but there isn't any Internet or phone network. I can't even text Jai.

A few minutes pass, and the same nurse brings out a sack. I am horrified. I ask, "Is that my cat?" It's Lollipop.

The other cat woman says they need to weigh the cats, so they know how much anaesthetic to use on each cat. It's part of the process. The next thing is that Lollipop is taken out of the sack and placed on a table away from the waiting area. I can see her lifeless body but her eyes wide open. I'm so upset to see her like this. I go over to her and make sure she is still breathing. She is. I gently reassure her that everything is going to be OK, and I stroke her, hoping she can see, hear, and feel me.

I go and sit down. Tears are welling up in my eyes, and I can't help but let them flow down my cheeks. The other cat woman reaches over to comfort me, saying that my cats are in safe hands and that she went through the same thing when she brought her first cat in to be spayed. She offers me a tissue, which I take. I thank her for it.

We start to talk about general things about ourselves. I tell her about Light of Moon and how it's been my dream for the last three years.

Her name is Daphne, and she lives in Cotti, near the train station. She is a marine biologist and has worked and trained in the United States and Japan. I am totally amazed to meet an actual marine biologist, let alone an Indian woman marine biologist. Our views are the same in terms of how women are treated, and she says her father and family have never pushed her towards the more traditional route of getting married and having kids.

She is an amazing woman, and I have total respect for her. She tells me she has about twelve cats, and the one that's in to get done is mother cat to most of the others.

It's so lovely to have a conversation with an intelligent woman in the most bizarre of circumstances.

About forty minutes pass. Brutus is brought out. He is still unconscious, and the nurse gently lays him down in the red basket. He looks so small and peaceful. I stroke him and whisper that he is going to be OK.

Daphne and I continue to chat. She has made the whole ordeal a lot less stressful.

Another twenty minutes pass, and Lollipop is brought out. Her side is shaved from where they did the surgery. Poor baby is out cold. My heart goes out to them both, my little babies. They really have kept me sane and grounded throughout all of this. I feel completely responsible for them. I've had them since they could fit into just one of my hands. And I am really all they have ever known.

I really don't know what I am going to do when I leave Goa to head home.

The cats are given an injection to bring them round from the anaesthetic. They both slowly come around. They are still very groggy but have opened their eyes. They're curled up with each other. They look so adorable.

I turn to say goodbye to Daphne. We decide to swap numbers. I tell her to come by the restaurant, and she invites me to her farm. We hug loosely as near-complete strangers who have just shared a moment do.

On the way to the vet's, I was conscious that I needed petrol, so I ask Daphne and the nurse if there is a petrol pump nearby. The nurse says there is a big petrol station on the way to Gohar.

I put the cats in the passenger seat and go around the car to the driver's seat. I start driving and head towards Gohar. At the crossroads where I usually turn left, I go straight ahead. I'm driving, driving, and driving, and I manage to end up on a minor road through a village-type area.

I see some men in a van and pull alongside them and shout out the window. They look at me blankly. I repeat the question again, slowly, exaggerating "Petrol!" There is a car behind me beeping its horn. I slowly inch forward, but the driver is still beeping. I inch forward again.

Shit! The car has fallen into a ditch!

The front passenger-side wheel has gone into a waste channel of sorts, and the car is halfway in, with the back end at a forty-five-degree angle in the air. I get out and am totally freaked out by what I'm seeing. The bumper has come away from the car and is hanging off.

I'm dumbfounded. I just hold my head in my hands. The men from the truck have come over, and a few locals have come out to see what the commotion is.

I look into the car to check on the cats. They are still calmly sitting in the red basket. Well, they're probably still sedated.

I'm freaking, thinking, *Shit, who do I tell?* I should phone Robert; it's his car after all. I call him, but there is no answer. I send a message on WhatsApp saying I've had an accident. I don't call Jai. For some reason I am reluctant to tell him. I don't know why!

Some of the gathered men take a better look, and one of them brings a very large bamboo pole and tries to lever the car up. Another man gets into the driver's seat and tries to reverse the car. It doesn't work, so he tries again, revving more, and the car lurches backwards to a more stable position.

Thank fuck, is all I can think. I push the bumper back, and it manages to clip back in to a near-perfect position.

I check on the cats. They are still OK.

Once the car is safely on terra firma, all the men disperse, and it's just me and the old woman in the shop opposite.

She says something: "Tension … tension." I ask about the petrol pump again, and she points to her shop. She has a water bottle filled with one litre of petrol, which is pretty standard fuel availability.

I buy one litre off her. Hopefully it will be enough to get me back to Shakthar or somewhere closer. I'm a bit nervous as the petrol is generally of bad quality and only meant for scooters. But at this point I have no choice. I need to get moving.

I still don't know where I am, but I retrace my steps and then finally recognise the road leading up to the vet's. After a couple of U-turns, I end up on the road where Flash is, where I went on Christmas night with the Aunties. I keep driving and eventually reach the main crossroads in Thairi.

Thank fuck!

I turn left and head back to Shakthar, gingerly watching the petrol gauge.

I reach my house and take the cats in, opening the red basket. The poor loves are wobbly on their feet. I put some food out for them, and they start to wolf it down. They are starving as they have had nil by mouth since yesterday evening.

I check my phone and see that there are messages from Jai asking about an account at the HDFC branch. I don't really need this. I reply saying that I will check later, adding that I have just come back to drop off the cats. I tell him I'm going to LOM and will speak later on.

I get to LOM and order lunch and a drink. I'm hungry. I'm also wired from this morning's events.

As soon as I sit down, Satish asks about the Wi-Fi. The Airtel router isn't working. I call Vijay. He checks and says that the data limit has been reached and there's an outstanding amount from last month. So, it looks like a trip to Nimpura.

After lunch, Jalan and I go to the Airtel office in Nimpura. On the way we chat of general things. He asks me why I don't stick up for Jai when people talk about him. I'm taken aback by his question, and I tell him I don't want people to know what I am feeling.

He says he thinks that Jai is with Ravi in Hindavi. I ask him why he believes this. He says because they are best friends and they help each other out. After that the conversation turns back to general chit-chat, mostly about Harry and his antics. I'm only half listening.

We reach Nimpura. I park up outside the Airtel shop on a precarious corner. We jump out, and I pay the outstanding balance and next month's Wi-Fi balance. Vijay says that the router name will need to be changed and asks me to call him when we do that. I tell him OK.

I still need petrol, so we go to the main petrol pump in Nimpura, which is only a minute's drive away. We refuel and head straight back to Shakthar.

We arrive back at LOM, and I have a tea. I just want to get home and relax.

By the time I do get home, it's early evening. I just want to chill before another evening at LOM, especially with Harry and Jasmine there. I could really do without the false platitudes.

I call Jai and tell him about the mad, crazy day, but I leave out the bit about the little accident I had with the car. Then we message for a while. I try to sleep, but sleep eludes me. The cats are on the bed with me. They are still a bit subdued, but both managed to jump up on the bed. I can feel Lollipop wince slightly. They both climb up onto me and settle in for a nap. I let them and don't move.

I get a couple of hours of me time, then it's time to shower and get back to LOM.

My first job is to fix the AirNet Wi-Fi router. I ask Jalan to bring it down to me in Room 201, which he does. I call Vijay, and he talks me through the process of updating the router name via my mobile phone. After much repeating of instructions, the router is fixed and the Wi-Fi is up and running.

While I'm still in the room, Jasmine comes in with Hakim to change his nappy. I tell her about the cats and the little accident (I still don't know why I didn't tell Jai). She says I look tired and stressed.

I decide to get takeaway from the restaurant as I don't feel like being sociable. I ask Satish to order palak paneer and roti as a parcel to take home.

I get home, eat dinner, smoke a ciggie, and call Jai. We talk of general things and the plan for his next visit to Goa on Saturday. We end up talking for over an hour, and then we continue to message, sending random emoji late into the night.

The next day is Indian Republic Day. LOM is fully booked for the weekend ahead of the national holiday. There are six rooms to check-in today, so I update everyone to let them know. Harry asks if there are any free rooms. I tell him, "No, we're fully booked."

I make sure all the rooms are ready with Jalan and Amit, and I do a quick spot check of the vacant rooms. Everything seems to be in order.

I go over to Serenity Retreat to check in with Vijay Bhai to see about clearing the outstanding balance. He says he'll give me four cheques for smaller amounts so that large amounts of money are not coming out of his account or not going into my account. I decide to hang out there for a little while and message Jai.

After a while I head back to LOM, check that everything is OK, then decide to go back home to relax and get ready for the evening stint.

It's now early evening, and I haven't showered yet. There is a call from Satish, saying guests are complaining about a room. I ask him what the problem is. He says that they are angry about the room.

To my dismay, I drive back to LOM to manage the guests. They are a young Indian couple in their early thirties, I would say. They have a small child with them. I ask what the problem is, and they say they do not like the room, adding that it smells, there is no furniture, and they wanted a sea view room.

I reply that the booking was for a standard room, non–sea view. The woman checks the booking on her phone but cannot find the details. I tell her the hotel is full and that I will not be able to move them to a better room. The woman is adamant that they had booked a sea view room. I tell them that I will look for another room for them if they do not want to stay in the room that I have allocated them.

I walk down to Serenity Retreat to see if they have any rooms. Vijay is there, and he replies that they are fully booked. I then go to Arabian Waters to check there. They have rooms available, but they have a minimum of three nights' stay, and the rooms are three thousand rupees per night anyway.

I am getting stressed out about having to deal with these guests and their request. I let them know that there are no other rooms available in Shakthar because it is a public holiday.

Again, the woman starts in about the booking. I tell her that as they are only staying the one night, I had given them this specific room. I don't tell her it was the room of last resort. In addition, they arrived late in the day, and all other guests had already checked in.

We all still standing by the couple's car, a big SUV-type vehicle, discussing the booking. They are polite enough but are insisting on getting another room. At this point the child is getting restless and starting to cry. I apologise that I cannot give them another room.

It's now going on 8 p.m. The child is winging still. As a compromise, I tell them that it's late, so I will give them a complimentary dinner to compensate for the room. They seem to be happy with this. So, they get out of the vehicle and go into the restaurant.

I am not only stressed but also annoyed now. I can see Harry at the bar milling around. It annoys me that I have to deal with all the complaining guests, and he just watches and does nothing—not even a word to help. But if I'm honest with myself, if he did get involved, I would be pissed about him trying to take over. Also, he doesn't actually have to balls to deal with complaints.

The guests settle to have their dinner. I decide to hang around for a while to ensure everyone is settled.

I check in with Jalan, and he has everything under control from his side. He can be annoying, but he does build excellent relationships with the guests. He's there 24/7 to deal with any issues.

Once things are calm, I decide to leave, as I hadn't even showered yet. I approach a guest who is complaining about moving his big SUV. He asks where he can park the vehicle. I tell him there is parking at the back of the hotel. I tell him I will check if there is space.

Jalan accompanies me to the parking spaces, and he tells me that the landlord is having bricks delivered tomorrow for the building that he is planning to build behind LOM. I ask Jalan where the bricks will be unloaded. He said he doesn't know.

To avoid any potential damage to the guest's vehicle and to ensure no one is blocked in, I go to find the landlord to ask where the bricks are going to be placed.

The landlord is out by the taxi rank, sitting with Haroon, Jagu, and an assortment of other faces affiliated with LOM.

I ask the landlord where the bricks are going to be unloaded, and to my confusion he says to ask Harry. I say, "How will Harry know?" But he is insistent I ask Harry. He is in one of his weird moods and has crazy eyes. He seems to be slightly drunk and starts going on about Harry and how he is the boss, but I can't quite understand as he is talking in the local dialect.

I try asking again, and he gets agitated, saying I need to ask Harry. To get some sort of answer, I approach Harry and ask him to come to speak to the landlord about the parking situation. He says he doesn't know anything about it, but I ask him to speak to the landlord anyway. Harry follows me to the taxi rank.

As soon as Harry approaches, the landlord starts to shoot his mouth off at him. He's speaking in the local dialect, but I catch the gist of what he's saying. He's still pissed about the previous season's rent not being paid. He starts to shove Harry, and I shout out the landlord's name. I say, "No!" He continues to shove Harry, who does nothing but has a weird kind of smirk on his face.

A crowd has gathered. I say, "Someone do something," but no one moves. They are just sitting around watching the spectacle. The only person who tries to stop the landlord is his daughter Anjali. She is the only one who has any balls to stand up to her father.

I can't believe what I am seeing, a grown man acting like a bully to Harry. Even though Harry is my least favourite person, he does not deserve this unprovoked assault.

Eventually the landlord backs off, and Harry starts to walk back to the restaurant. As he does so, the landlord's elderly father goes to hit Harry with his walking stick. Luckily Anjali is close enough to stop him. I have to laugh at this, that the old man, probably in his eighties, thinks he can take on Harry.

Harry goes and sits down with Jasmine and their guest Katherine, who is staying at LOM.

I still can't believe what I have just witnessed. I go and stand out back by the kitchen to have a smoke. Jalan is with me, and we both have a giggle at what just went down.

The next thing we know, all the electricity goes off. This is nothing new in India, but I look around and see that all the neighbouring lights are still on. I realise the landlord has turned off all the electric to the hotel and restaurant.

Again, I cannot believe this is happening. The hotel is fully booked, and the restaurant is full. The kitchen is in peak service time, and the imbecile of a landlord turns the electric off.

I'm not even angry, just physically exhausted by the evening's events and by the last five months, but there and then I decide I have had enough of this. I cannot run a business like this.

I walk over to Harry's table and tell him that I've had enough and that he can have the business; I'm booking my flight home. He looks shocked. He doesn't know what to say. I walk away. I see that the guest has moved his car. I get in mine and drive home.

I am done!

Chapter 11

THE STRAW THAT BROKE THE CAMEL'S BACK

Following the events of the evening of Republic Day, I go home and phone Jai and tell him that I am leaving LOM. I talk him through the day's escapades and say that I've had enough. He tells me not to make any rash decisions and that he doesn't want me to lose out financially as he has done. But ultimately, it's my decision.

I really do feel physically and emotionally exhausted from the onslaught of being continually undermined by Harry and from the paranoia of working with people whom I cannot trust.

The last couple of days seem to have been filled with anxiety and bad omens: the trauma of seeing the cats going through the surgery, the incident with the car and the ditch, dealing with awkward customers, the brawl with the landlord and Harry in front of everyone, including a restaurant full of guests and customers, and then the final straw, the electricity being turned off by the landlord. How could anyone deal with that kind of onslaught all on the same day?

Harry messages me and says, "Please come back. And do

not worry." I phone him, and we agree to meet tomorrow to talk, but I tell him that I have made up my mind.

Jai and I message into the night, and we confirm that he will come to Goa in the next couple of days. We decide to go somewhere else in Goa to get away from Shakthar. He suggests somewhere in the south, either Vapur or Zeeri.

I switch my phone off for the night.

The next morning, I have a lie-in. I'm not in the mood to rush into LOM and arrive around midmorning. I have calmed down since last night and have decided that I can stick it out for another two weeks. That will give Harry time to find someone to take over for me.

I call Harry and tell him I'm at LOM. He's at his house and says he'll be there later. I tell him that I will work two weeks, but then I will leave.

Satish asks about the complaining couple from last night, specifically about their restaurant bill. I tell him to put the charge on my ongoing bill.

I see the landlord sitting at the taxi rank. I approach him. He is looking sheepish. I tell him that I am going to leave in two weeks, saying that I cannot work in this sort of environment. I tell him that what he did last night was wrong. He nods his head and says OK, but he doesn't say anything else. He looks shocked. Maybe he realises he is in the wrong. I will never know.

I hang around for a while and check a couple of guests out. One is a hot guy who had checked in late last night but was only staying for the one night. He's tall and very fit and handsome. For some reason we end up sitting down at one of the tables in the restaurant.

We chat briefly. I ask him where he's from. He's a model and lives in New York but is originally from Lebanon. I am suitably impressed. He asks, "Are you from London?"

I ask, "How did you know? Did the restaurant guys tell you?" He says no. I say he must be psychic. We have a little chuckle.

He pays his bill, and then gets a taxi from the taxi rank and leaves.

I hang around for a while. I message Jake and confirm that they are still going to the Goat Festival, a dance festival which is happening at Ibiza resort in Tarana. It starts today and goes for about three nights. There are a couple of DJs I recognise from the UK, but I'm not particularly familiar with their music. But it's something to look forward to outside of LOM where I can spend some time with people I can speak freely with.

I also tell Jake I have handed in my notice. I tell him I will fill him on the details later. He is stuck for a room for the next few nights. Unfortunately, LOM is fully booked, so I cannot accommodate him.

There are local elections happening in Goa, and as a run-up to voting, all purchase of alcohol has been restricted. No bars or restaurants can serve alcohol after 10 p.m. I am not sure what the purpose of the restriction is, but it's not helping business.

Even though LOM is fully booked, it's quiet once the guests have checked out. Jalan and Amit are cleaning the now empty rooms. So, I decide to go back home and chill for the afternoon.

This evening Faraz, the photographer who took the new pictures of LOM, and whom I know from Kovvi, is due to arrive. He's coming to Shakthar to meet Harry as he took photos of Veenram LOM. He had contacted me earlier to ask if there were any rooms at LOM. I couldn't accommodate him either, but he said he would come to LOM for dinner.

There's no sign of Harry, so I decide to go for a wander along the Shakthar shops before heading home to call Jai.

Once I'm home, he and I chat about general stuff and discuss when he will next come to Goa. We plan over the next few days. I wash some clothes and chill for the afternoon. The cats are playing outside. Everything seems calm.

I return to LOM and wait for Faraz to arrive. I sit on my own for most of the night. Harry sits with me for a short while, and we discuss the events of yesterday evening. We agree that I will stay for the next two weeks and then he will find someone to replace me.

Jasmine and Katherine are sitting at a nearby table. I say hi to them but don't interact with them. The restaurant is quiet this evening. Everyone else is just milling around. Jalan is carrying Hakim around. They really are the best of friends now.

Later Harry is sitting with the landlord; they are having a heated discussion. I don't know what it's about, but the landlord looks anxious. I don't bother to enquire, I have enough going on in my own head.

I message Jai while sitting on my own. I book his bus ticket for his arrival the morning after next. We chat about the events that have happened to the both of us since we each arrived in Goa. He jokes that I should have told Harry that I have taken on Amun Ra Café.

We chat about the novel and all the twists and turns. He says he is the superstar of the novel. I tell him he is the God of the Sun. He says I am the goddess! I say, "For it is written that Sabbie and Jai will be King and Queen." He tells me he doesn't want to dream without sleeping, and he needs to work on reality.

God, I love him so much, and I will do anything in my power to help him. I have never felt such a deep connection to another human being in all my life, not even previous relationships. It's like an invisible string that binds us together no matter how far apart we are from each other.

Faraz has arrived, accompanied by a beautiful, voluptuous red-headed woman. Faraz introduces us. Her name is Kate. She's from England.

They need to eat. Satish comes over to take their order. Faraz and Satish are surprised to see each other, and they greet each other with great glee. They know each other from Kovvi, where Satish used to work for Lucky and Bally. Faraz is good friends with Lucky and Bally. That's where I had met Faraz, on my first trip to Kovvi a couple of years ago.

It feels like a bit of a reunion.

Kate and Faraz order food. I have eaten already, so we chat while they eat. Kate used to work at a resort in Veenram, handling all the online bookings and enquiries. She didn't have any contact with the guests directly and only liaised with the on-site staff. Sounds like she had the right idea. She is a confident young woman, and I am secretly envious of her.

Faraz is fidgety and keeps getting up and leaving the table. I'm not sure if he's nervous or just hyper. I like Faraz. He has followed his dream of becoming a photographer, rather than acquiescing to the usual pressurised family demands. We had discussed this on our first meeting in Kovvi two years previously. He's a talented photographer, and I'm pleased for him that he is his own man. Dev Chef also comes out to say hi.

Kate and Faraz still haven't sorted any accommodation, so I say I will help them. There aren't any rooms available at LOM, Serenity Retreat, or Arabian Waters. Jalan knows people in the area, so I ask him if he knows anywhere. He says we could try the new resort next to LOM. So Jalan and I go on the scooter to enquire.

We get there and speak to the manager at reception. He says there is a deluxe villa available. We ask to have a look. One of the staff takes us down a path with solar lighting along the edges. The grounds are large with villas made of pine dotted around. There's lots of greenery and plants creating a tropical vibe. It's really very pretty in the night.

We enter the villa. I am surprised how nice it is. There's a four-poster bed with cream curtains hanging down. The bathroom is stunning. There's a walk-in shower behind a glass-panelled wall. The guy showing us the room moves a curtain in the shower room to reveal a small indoor veranda with plants and lighting. It's stunning. I take photos and send them to Faraz.

I ask about the rate. It's six thousand rupees per night. That's a lot, but I would definitely pay that amount for this room.

We go back to LOM and tell Faraz and Kate. We return with Faraz following in his car.

While we wait for Faraz and Kate to check out the villa, Jalan starts to talk to me, saying he and the landlord had a fight last night after I left LOM. He says that he hit the landlord, and they are now not talking. He says he wants to leave LOM and Shakthar.

I listen to him, but all I can think of is that Harry has caused this. He has manipulated Jalan and filled his head. Harry is poison and cannot see anyone being happy. He does this to cause division amongst people. He is paranoid that Jalan is telling the landlord what Harry is doing.

Anyway, I don't really care now as I have decided that I am leaving in two weeks.

Kate and Faraz love the place. We say our goodbyes, and Jalan drops me off at home, as my car is being serviced.

I get home, send the pics of the villa to Jai, and call to confirm plans for his arrival.

The next morning, I arrive at LOM at the usual time. Guests are dotted about, having breakfast. I do the usual updates and share them with the team.

There are a couple of guests due to check in today, so I hang around. One of the guests is Jakub and his pregnant wife from Poland. I was in communication with Jakub a couple of months ago and have built up a relationship with him over the period leading up to today. They arrive, and I greet them like old friends.

Their room is not ready yet, so they store their luggage in the reception area and then head to the beach to relax.

It is late afternoon when Harry and Jasmine arrive. I sit with Harry, and he starts going on with himself about how these people are backwards and how he built LOM up from nothing, having designed and built the kitchen. He goes on, saying these are uneducated small people. He tells me of how he left his home at the age of twelve and built up the name Light of Moon—his usual life history and escapades.

He is being sugary sweet and says both he and Jasmine talked last night about how great a job that I have done. He says that he considers me his sister.

He then turns the conversation to how he wants the money to be handled by Jasmine from now on, saying that the money will go into his account. I say that's fine and that I could do with the support (I lie). He wants a bill book to be made and for guests to sign the bills to ensure there is clarity and transparency with all the bills. He says that at the moment he doesn't know what money is coming in and that the spreadsheet doesn't really tell him anything. He mentions that I could be misleading him in that I may not put all the bookings on the list. I tell him that I have been completely open with him (this is mostly true—99 per cent).

Jasmine comes and sits with us.

Harry says that he doesn't want any more drama and doesn't want to repeat himself again. I ask him if he will give me access to the bank account so I can see what money is coming in and going out. He says that I just need to ask. I tell him I have asked for this since day one. He says he will the sort online access also.

I say, "OK, all of this is fine, and as there only a couple of months left in the season, I will stay until the season finishes. But I will definitely not be back next season, and next season I will be looking for a place for myself." He says that's fine and asks if he and Jasmine can come and have dinner at my place.

Jasmine gets up to deal with Hakim, who is crying.

At this point, I ask Harry if he will return the money that I have invested in the business, e.g. for the bedding, the lighting, and the paint. He says no, adding that it's my fault that I paid over the odds for everything. He is getting defensive.

I say, "OK, then will the same be applied to the furniture and equipment that you have bought?" He starts to get aggressive and starts to go on again about how much he has put in. I remain calm.

I can see that he is agitated now. Jasmine rejoins us.

Harry says that I am now in India and need to stop using my English brain. He says that he never listens to anyone, that he is his own man, and that he doesn't even listen to his wife.

Jasmine asks, "What's happened?" I tell her that I asked about my investment in the furniture and fittings and if I would get money back, telling her he said no, so I'd asked him if the same principle would be applied if Harry were to leave.

He starts to go on about how Jai and I conspired to get rid of Clive the chef and that he knows that I message Jai and that he visits me. I say that my personal life is separate from LOM.

At this point I lose it and fight back. I say that Clive left because Harry treated him like shit after he found out that he didn't have a penny to his name. He calls me a liar. I say, "*No!* You need to take responsibility for your actions and not blame other people."

He starts to ramble, saying that he if wanted to, he could get people to come and visit when Jai is here, and they will beat him.

At this point Jasmine pipes up and says to Harry that there's no need to get personal.

I get up from the table and say to Jasmine that this is the type of behaviour I have had to put up with for the last six months. I hold back because of her. I tell them I've had enough and that I am done!

Harry says something as I leave, and I shout back that I'm not the one who has built a business with other people's money.

I am fuming! Everyone is watching, the restaurant staff, the guests seated at the big table, and the usual people loitering outside the landlord's house.

I walk home.

I phone Jai and tell him what happened. He tells me to

rethink everything, but I tell him I cannot, not when I've been personally attacked.

I continue, telling him I've had enough of these fucking idiots and that I will not put up with personal attacks. He says not to make a decision in anger. I say I am sick of the lot of them. I was being reasonable, and it got thrown back in my face. Fuck the lot of them!

He says, "Don't worry, babes. I will be there in the morning. I just want you to be happy with your decision. But I feel bad that even you have lost money."

I tell him it just makes me even more determined to make a success of my own business one day. He says, "As you wish." I tell him nobody knows how strong I am. He says that even he doesn't know.

I tell him that everything I have accomplished in my life, I have done by myself. Why change now?!

I don't return to LOM that day. I am too angry. But in a way, I feel a weight has been lifted from my shoulders.

The car has been delivered to my house by Robert's son. At least I have my wheels back.

This evening is the second night of the music festival at Ibiza beach. I drive down there and meet Jake outside the main entrance. He is late as usual.

We go into the venue. It's full of party people, and the DJ is playing house music. The stage is small with a canopy covering. There is an island bar and lots of daybeds dotted around.

Jake buys me a beer, and we go and sit down on one of the beds. He knows some of what has been happening, and I tell him about the events of the day, adding that I have resigned from LOM.

I also tell him about the situation with Jai, and he says that he should have come to the festival. I tell him it would have been too risky for him.

I go into a little detail about our relationship, mentioning how I've bailed Jai out on the money front and saying that I still have reservations about the authenticity of the relationship, specifically Jai's reasons for being with me. But I do tell him that I love him.

Even in the haze of being in love, there is always a niggling feeling in the pit of my stomach. A gut instinct, I suppose. But we'll see what happens.

Abigale and Kev are due to meet us too, but they have gone to get something to eat. We meet them by the main entrance a short while later after multiple phone calls. These guys are so disorganised that getting them together is like herding cats. Ha ha!

Kev is a funny guy, and he proceeds to tell me that he produced dance music back in the day, but for whatever reason he lost his motivation. Later, while I am chatting with Abigale, she tells me she is a singer in a band. I'm impressed. They are such a musical couple.

We stand around at the back of the dance floor throwing shapes. The DJ is hit-and-miss. Kev and I critique the playlist with its ups and downs and lack of consistency. Jake is off somewhere on the hunt for a really good-looking Indian woman, but she is surrounded by a bunch of Indian guys. There's not a chance in hell of Jake getting anywhere near her.

Later I ask him if he is interested in Ishwari. He says she is lovely, but he is not interested in her romantically. He says he feels bad now, and I feel bad about my lack of matchmaking skills.

After a while, I start to feel anxious and feel like I need to go home, but I stick it out until 10 p.m. Jake mentions there is an after party, but I decline the invite. At 10 p.m. Jake escorts me back to my car, and I drive home.

I call Jai to confirm details for the morning. He has packed his bag. We decide I will pick him up from Unjaan bus station. I tell him I'm scared and that I just want to go away for a few days with him. He says we can decide in the morning where we will go. We say "goodnight" and "I love you."

I sleep. I am physically and emotionally exhausted from the day.

I wake up early to drive to Unjaan to pick up my big guy. I packed a small bag so we can stay overnight somewhere.

I make sure the cats are OK, and I leave. I arrive at the pickup point early.

The bus arrives fifteen minutes later, and my big guy comes around the corner. We loosely hug as we're in public. We decide to go to Mangrah. It's in the opposite direction of Shakthar, heading towards South Goa. I don't know the way, so Jai gives me directions.

I know Mangrah well as that's where I was based when I did the month's volunteer work three and half years ago.

On the way to Mangrah, we talk about everything that's happened over the last few days. It feels so nice to be with Jai. I feel safe and relaxed with him. I love him so much.

We stop off in Mangrah for lunch, and Jai books a place for us to stay in Zeeri, which is just past Mangrah near Vapur.

We talk more about everything that's happened. He thinks I have made a mistake, but I have made up my mind. I cannot deal with the onslaught of attacks or the fact that I cannot trust anyone.

To lighten the mood, I tell him about when I stayed in Mangrah previously and point out where the slums are where I used to teach as we drive through on the way to Zeeri.

We approach Vapur and Zeeri but stop to ask for directions. Generally, people just point in the direction we are asking about, with a little head wobble thrown in for good measure as a parting gesture.

Eventually we arrive at English Rose Villas. It's off a deserted main road. It looks like a small townhouse, and we park up. We are greeted by a friendly young man with a wonky face. One of his eyes is significantly lower than the other, but he gives off a friendly, happy vibe. There is another man inside the entrance, which opens onto a living room. He is not so friendly. I think to myself, *The guy with the wonky face seems happier than this "normal"-looking guy.*

We are shown to our room, but it's not ready. The guy needs to change the sheets. We say it's fine. We have a look around the room. It's small with a double bed. It looks like a kid's room.

I ask where the bathroom is. The man points to a wardrobe and opens the door, and through another door the bathroom appears. Jai and I are amused by the set-up.

There is a balcony through the French doors at the end of the room. The room has air-con and a TV.

The guy puts new sheets on, and Jai and I settle in for the afternoon once he leaves. I lie down on the bed as we have been driving for about three hours. Jai drove from Mangrah. Jai switches the TV on and lies down next to me. We have a cuddle and decide what to do with the day.

I feel like I'm in some crazy drama, on the run from an evil business partner. My head is full, and I just want to do nothing.

We relax for a while.

My phone rings. I look at it. It's Satish. I ignore it and let it ring out. It rings again. I ignore it.

Jai says I should answer it in case it's an important call. I say, "I don't want to speak to anyone. And how important can any conversation be?"

After a while my phone rings again. It's Jasmine. I reluctantly answer.

She asks how I am. I tell her I'm OK. She says she is sorry about how things have gone and that I have done a great job with everything. She says woman to woman that I shouldn't have to put up with that kind of behaviour.

I reiterate to her that I have had to put up with it since day one and that I actually held back my anger because of her. I add that I will not put up with being personally attacked. Again, I hold back and do not say anything about Harry. After all he is her husband. She will no doubt find out soon enough what he is like.

She asks when I will come back to LOM to do a proper handover. I tell her I'm not in Shakthar as I need to clear my head, but I say I will be there tomorrow to sort out the schedule and go over everything with her.

I update Jai on the full conversation.

It's now getting late, and we decide to go to Zeeri beach to check it out.

When we get to the beach, it's pretty much empty. There are only about ten shacks along the beach, which is probably a couple of miles long. It's beautiful though with hardly any people around. We go for a little walk along the beach, but we head back when Jai gets paranoid that someone will see him.

We end up sitting at the first shack/restaurant at the entrance to the beach. It's the usual fare: dirty tables and low bamboo seating. We order dinner and sit and relax. I order vodka and soda. I need a drink to de-stress.

I ask Jai about his job situation. He has been in contact with some agencies and needs to update his CV to send to them. But it's going to take time. He is also waiting for his new ID documents to be created. These will also take time. At least it's progress in the right direction.

We talk about what happens now with me leaving LOM. We decide I will go to Gandabaan, and I will fly back to the UK from there. He says he will look for a place where I can stay while in Gandabaan.

But I still have a few things to do in Shakthar before I head to Gandabaan. Firstly, I need to wait for the cheques from Serenity Retreat to clear, and secondly, I need to get some money from the landlord from the card machine payments. There is approximately four lakhs (£5,000) in the account, and I want to take some money out of this situation. But I want to make sure that the restaurant team have their costs covered too. I say I will speak to the landlord when I head back to

Shakthar. And I need to go back tomorrow anyway to hand things over to Jasmine.

It's lovely just to sit on the beach and watch the sunset. We sit and chat for a while and then head back to the room.

We sit in bed and watch TV. It's nice just to relax and watch a film while cuddling without any pressure. I eventually fall asleep while Jai continues watching TV. It's just lovely to have my big guy next to me.

The next morning, we awake, and Jai asks the room guy to make us breakfast. He orders omelette, toast, and coffee. While we wait, we shower and get ready. I need to get back for the cats and then go to LOM to meet Jasmine.

On the way to Shakthar, we stop off at Café Coffee Day in Unjaan opposite the mall. We talk about what Jai is going to do while I go back to Shakthar. We decide he'll watch a movie at the mall and wait for me to return.

Ten minutes after I leave him and start the drive back to Shakthar, he calls me. I'm in traffic. I answer the phone. He's in a panic and says he saw the LOM landlord at the entrance to the mall.

I turn around and pick him up at a little roadside restaurant he has hidden in.

He says he saw the landlord as he was crossing the road. But luckily the landlord didn't see him. We wonder why he would be standing outside the mall. We guess that he must have something to do with the election. Maybe he's a driver for one of the candidates. Anyway, Jai wasn't spotted.

Having decided not to take the main road back to Shakthar, we end up going through some village and then get back onto the main road near Nimpura. Jai will hide out in my house while I meet with Jasmine.

It's now the middle of the day, and it's risky bringing Jai back to my house, but we have no other choice. I drive the car directly to my front door, and Jai quickly enters the house.

I make sure the cats are OK and let them out to play. I

depart for LOM, leaving Jai hiding. I tell him to lie low in case the pregnant landlady comes by. Luckily there was no one around when we arrived.

I get to LOM and am greeted by Satish and some of the other restaurant guys. He asks where I have been and why I am leaving. I tell him I went away and that I will not be returning. I say, "How can I work at a place where I am being attacked all the time and where I cannot trust anyone?" I add that whatever I say makes its way back to Harry.

Jalan is hovering around in the background. I just say hello to him, and he replies. He is looking very sheepish.

Satish retorts that no one has said anything to Harry and mentions that they all know what he is like. He says that it's probably the room boys who tell Harry everything.

And then it all clicks into place. Jalan! He's the one who tells me everything about Harry and all the stuff about the restaurant guys. So, it makes complete sense that he would probably tell Harry everything about me, including what I do and who I see. He had admitted to me already that he and the landlord go roaming at night as a timepass and they had seen Jai's car parked by my house when he was still in Amun Ra.

I feel completely betrayed by Jalan. I cannot even look at him. Otherwise I would lose my rag at him. But I'm not going to give them the satisfaction of making a scene. There has been enough scene making to last me a lifetime.

Satish asks about the restaurant bills for the month, and I tell him I will sort them out with the landlord. He says OK.

One thing is clear: I will not cheat the restaurant guys out of what is owed to them. At the end of the day, they are here to do a job. They are hard workers, and I have worked well with them, even though I don't trust them. They have salaries to pay, and I won't take any frustrations out on them.

Eventually Jasmine arrives. She asks how I am and says she's sorry things have turned out the way they have. Harry has gone to Hansari. I'm glad I don't have to see his face.

We sit down, and we go through everything from the Bookings.com extranet site and the phone app. I tell her how I take the bookings and update the schedules. I show her the messages from guests on the phone app and the emails. She downloads the app so she has access to it. She changes the email password, so she remembers it. I'm happy to no longer have access to these.

I go through the breakfast bill with Satish and Jasmine and work out how much is owed each month from the room money to pay for inclusive breakfasts. We also go through my food bill, the credit card payments, including how they are divided between the restaurant and rooms, and the spreadsheet that I created to record each transaction. I tell her about booking taxi pickups with the landlord. I say to myself, "Good luck with that," considering she is Harry's wife.

A couple of hours into the handover, Jasmine looks shell-shocked. And my head is mashed from having gone through everything with her.

By the time I get back home, it's late afternoon. Jai is relaxing—well, as much as he can while hiding out in my house. The cats have followed me back into the house too.

We decide what we want to do for the next couple of days now that I do not need to go back to LOM in the morning. He says that we can go back to English Rose Villas, and he rings the owner, who says it's fine.

We chill out for a while. I decide to take the cats with us as I don't want to leave them on their own in the house for two days straight.

We wait until it's dark. I put the kittens in the red basket. Lollipop protests as per usual. I bring the car down to the front of the house, where I load the luggage and the cats, and then we head back to English Rose Villas.

By the time we get there, it is late in the evening. We didn't stop for lunch, so Jai goes out to Domino's Pizza, which we had passed on the way, and brings back pizza for dinner. We eat while watching TV. It just feels perfect.

The cats settle in the small room, and they explore and jump about. I tell Jai I'm happy that I have my three babies with me.

The next couple of days we chill, watch TV, go back to Zeeri beach, and just relax. We discuss my plan to go to Gandabaan and also what I will do with the cats. There is no way I am going to leave them at the house in Shakthar. I debate whether to leave them with Daphne, the lovely woman whom I met at the vet's when the cats were spayed and neutered. But in my heart, I want Jai to take them. He is reluctant to agree to this as he will be living with his parents. But I say I have never asked anything of him, only this one request. He thinks about it and, over the course of the two days, agrees.

We talk about when I want to go to Gandabaan and how I'll get there, and now with the cats to consider. I tell him I still need to be in Shakthar for a few more days and that I will confirm dates later on. We also talk about his credit situation and what he needs money for. This is an ongoing reluctant discussion. He still doesn't have a bank account sorted, so as an interim measure I have given him the bank card drawing on my ICICI account. There are about three lakhs in there to help him sort out his identity papers and also to put any deposit down for a place for me to stay.

On the odd occasion, Jasmine calls with queries about the bookings. I help as much as I can. Jai pipes up, asking why I am helping now that I've left. I say that I don't want to leave on bad terms. And it's not Jasmine's fault. I tell her I will come by LOM when I get back.

On our last day, Jai and I venture to Vapur beach for lunch. It's as I remember it. The shacks are run down and dirty, and I don't want to eat there. I'm sick of the same old menu on offer. Jai mentions a place that a friend of his from Hindavi runs. It's called Santa Porto.

We manage to find it, just off the main street in Vapur. We

park in the car park, and Jai goes inside to enquire. A few minutes later he calls and says to come inside to reception. It's a big luxury hotel resort. I'm impressed there's a place like this in Vapur.

After a while an older Indian man comes out, and Jai introduces us. His name is George. He is the general manager. We talk about how the place is run, and I give him a brief overview of the things I did at LOM. It feels like Jai has introduced me as a business/investment contact, which is fine with me, I suppose. It's not like he can introduce me as his girlfriend.

The decor looks expensive and plush. There are various works of art on the walls, some abstract, some depicting historical Indian scenes, the typical maharajas on elephants and sari-clad water-women carrying earthenware pots on their heads. There are Buddha status dotted about. There's lots of dark wooden panelled walls. I check out the washroom, and it's on a par with any high-end hotel back home.

We walk around the grounds, which consists of high-end chalets and apartment-type buildings. There's an outside pool and separate bar and restaurant. Jai and I sit by the pool and smoke a cigarette.

We decide to have lunch here. The waitstaff are attentive and professional as we sit at a well-dressed table. I order a veg lasagne dish, and Jai orders chicken biryani, his standard. The food is nice enough.

After lunch We head back to English Rose Villas, where we chill for a little while. We had booked Jai's return ticket earlier. He is heading back this evening to continue with his job search and to look for somewhere for me to stay.

It's been a lovely couple of days relaxing in each other's company, but it's time to get back to reality. For me it's felt like I've been with my own little family with Jai and the cats. However, I need to head back to Shakthar to start to sort my shit out. I need to pack up and plan how to get to Gandabaan. I need to let my house landlord know I will be leaving, and I must also tell Robert about giving the car back. I'm not sure how they are going to react as I will be ending my stay in Shakthar earlier than anticipated.

And most importantly I need to decide how I'm going to transport the cats and get my money.

Chapter 12

LEFT BEHIND ON THE WAY TO GANDABAAN

Secrets and Lies, Part I

I arrive back in Shakthar in the late evening. I feel at a bit of a loss, but I have things to do. I want to get the money situation sorted first.

The next day I go to LOM to help Jasmine with the bookings. I am sitting at the restaurant table waiting for her. Satish and Dev Chef are chatting, and Dev Chef asks why I am angry at them. I say I am not angry but that I can no longer work there with Harry. Satish says he knows what Harry is like and tells me that they have told Jasmine that I was completely up front with everything I did.

I also go to see the landlord about getting my money. I tell him I want two lakhs from the credit card machine account, and the rest will go to pay Satish to cover the restaurant payments and bills. He seems happy with this and says he will give me cheques later in the week.

The local Goan elections are still in process, and the banks are closed for a few days.

Jasmine arrives with Harry. He doesn't say a word to me and loiters in the restaurant. Jasmine comes and sits with me. She opens her laptop. She has only just bought it, and it looks like she has been sold a cheap one with software which is at least five years old. The operating system is Microsoft Word XP, the 2007 version. My laptop has Windows 10 and Office 2013, so some of the documents I have emailed to her are not opening.

She has created her own version of the bookings schedule, and when I check it, it's missing a load of bookings. We discuss this, and she gets upset and starts crying. She is completely overwhelmed, it seems. I help her as much as I can as I do feel bad for her, but it's not my problem now.

I leave as quickly as I can. I don't want to hang around any longer than necessary.

I end up staying in Shakthar for another couple of weeks to sort things out. I want to see Ishwari before I leave. She has been a good friend to me, and she's helped by talking things through impartially, as she is not affiliated with LOM whatsoever. She is in Hindavi seeing her family until 10 February.

In the meantime, Jai has been looking for a place for me to stay in Gandabaan. We planned that he would come and collect me in a car and drive us back to Gandabaan. But he couldn't come to Shakthar to do that, so I booked a place in Unjaan to stay for one night, and he said he would meet me and the cats there.

Over the course of the next ten days, I meet various friends for dinner just to keep myself occupied. I met Neil and Jake one evening to score for Jake again. One evening I went out with Jag from High Life.

I let my house landlord know that I am leaving. They are not happy and ask to speak to Jalan. I call him, and they speak briefly. I am not sure what the purpose of the call is, but hey ho, it's what these people do.

I go to the pet store next to the mall to get a new crate for the cats, as they are outgrowing the red basket, and also to get some provisions for them.

The cheques from Vijay at Shakthar retreat clear. I had picked up the cheques from the landlord, and those too have been deposited.

When I went to pick up the cheques, the whole family had gathered and asked where I was going and when I would be back. I said, “I am going back to UK, and I will not be coming back.” It was difficult to hold my emotions. The family has been good to me. They took me in as if I were part of the family. I’d often be invited for lunch at their house, especially on vegetarian days.

In the bank I see Munni from Arabian Waters and I tell him that I’ve left LOM. He asks why. I tell him because of Harry. He says Harry always does this. I don’t go into details, but I say there is something wrong with his brain, then I promptly leave.

I let Robert know that I will be giving up the car rental. He is annoyed and says that he will lose money, adding that he had given me the car at a discounted rate in good faith. He says that he will be short ten thousand rupees and that I have to give that to him to cover his losses. I tell him I too have made a loss. However, I am too emotionally exhausted to argue, so I make the transfer of ten thousand rupees (about £100).

I feel like everyone is out to get something from me, and it’s all about money. But I just want to get out of here now.

Jai and I message throughout the days. We miss each other like crazy, and we say we love each other often. He keeps me updated on the search for a place for me to stay, and I tell him what I’m doing. Even though he is halfway across the country, the bond between us is strong.

He tells me about Gandabaan and the places we can go. They biggest mall in India is in Gandabaan. He says we can do timepass there.

I find a place to stay in Unjaan and confirm the cats can come also. The owner is fine with that.

I clean my house and find the secret place where the cats pooh in the night. I thought they poohed outside, but as there isn't a litter tray, they found somewhere in the house. No wonder it stank even when I cleaned the place. The secret pooh place is behind the gas cylinder in the kitchen, under the counter. Anyway, I clean it up. I don't want to leave it for the house landlady to do, not in her heavily pregnant state.

I sort out my laundry and pack the kitchen items and my bags. I also take some of my luggage to the hotel I am staying in at Unjaan so that I don't have to take everything in one go. Everything is confirmed with Jai: he has got a car and will meet me in the morning.

It's the night before my last day in Shakthar. Ishwari is performing at a place called Jungle Dance Temple, on the way to Anjaru. She put me on the guest list to see the show. I didn't get a chance to see her earlier, so I go and find somewhere to sit by myself.

Jai is messaging, saying he is leaving Gandabaan

There is a stream of performances in fusion belly dance style. Some are good and some are not, but it's an entertaining evening and a nice way to spend my last night in Shakthar. After the performances I meet up with Ishwari. She doesn't seem her usual, ethereal self. She has gotten something to eat. We sit and talk.

She has just come back from Hindavi and is exhausted. She tells me about her relationship with her father and how it's emotionally draining as he is very controlling and overbearing. I feel for her. She looks visibly distraught. She is upset as she messed up her performance, but I tell her nobody could tell and that her smile and her love for what she does shone through.

We talk for a little while longer and decide we don't want to stay for the after-party events. I drive her home, and we say our goodbyes. She has been a good friend. I hope I have been there for her too.

For my last day in Shakthar, I had arranged with Jagu the

taxi driver to come take me to Unjaan. This is a bit of a risk as he is one of the landlord's drivers, but I feel like I can trust him not to say anything to anyone. Someone once said he has a soft spot for me, so I am taking advantage of that. He has always been good to me. He will arrive at 12 noon to come collect me.

In the meantime, Robert is coming to pick up the car. He has messaged to say he hopes there isn't any damage to the car, I say I hope so too.

He arrives, and I meet him at the parking spot. He looks around the car and mentions some scratches that were not there before. He says that he will be getting rid of the car at some point but will need to cover the cost of the paintwork. Then he goes into detail about how much work will need to be done and mentions the cost: RS2,500. It's not as much I as expected, but I still negotiate it down to RS2,000.

We walk down to my house, and I go inside to get the money. We stand outside on the veranda and talk of general things. I tell him why I am leaving LOM and Shakthar. He says that there are nasty people out there and not to trust anyone outside of Goa—all other people are just con men. I listen and don't say anything, but I am thinking about what happened to Jai and Amun Ra.

I tell him that it's been really upsetting and that I had put my heart and soul into that place. I get emotional, and tears well up in my eyes. I tell him I have to go, then I say, "Thanks for everything." I quickly go into my house.

I let the tears fall for a moment, but then I compose myself. Everything is still raw, and I can feel the emotions pulsing under my skin and in my belly.

A few moments later there is a knock on my door. I open it. It's Robert. He says that if ever I need anything to let him know. He says that I am like him and that I am special to him from now on. My tears well again. I say, "Thank you." He gives me the RS2,000 back, pats me on my cheek, and leaves.

I don't know why I cried in front of him. It just happened. I don't tell Jai about this.

Again, I compose myself. I go to the kitchen to smoke a cigarette. I am all packed up and just need to put the cats in their new cage. There's half an hour left before Jagu arrives—my last few moments in Goa.

My period still hasn't come. I'm late!

Jagu arrives. We load the car with my suitcase and a couple of boxes. The cats are in their crate, and they go in last. Lollipop protests.

On the journey I'm still emotional and try to keep it together. Jagu and I make small talk about what has happened and about Harry, but mostly we sit in silence. At times Lollipop cries out, and we giggle at her. I tell her to be quiet, not that she listens.

It's now around 1 p.m. We arrive at the hotel in Unjaan. Jagu unloads the car. I take the cats into the reception area. I pay Jagu and tell him, "Thank you. Please don't tell anyone where I am."

He says, "Don't worry." We shake hands, and he leaves.

I call Jai, but there's no answer. I assume he is driving. I message him to tell him I'm at the hotel. I check in and pay the hotel owner. He takes my ID for the C form.

Jai messages, saying he's nearly there, and asks me to order food, saying he is starving. Poor boy has been driving all night. I ask the owner for food options, and he says there is a nice place that delivers. I order the food and take the cats up to the room to get them settled.

It's a nice room, small but comfortable. There are windows all along one side. I check them to see if they open. They do, but there is no wire netting, so I cannot open them; otherwise the cats will jump out. Unfortunately, it's a non-smoking room. Jai won't be happy about that, but it's only one night.

About fifteen minutes later, Jai arrives. I go down to meet him. He looks tired. I take him up to the room, and we hug. I had switched the TV on. We both lie down. He asks about smoking.

I tell him we must go outside. He chastises me for that. I tell him it's only one night, for God's sake.

The food arrives, and we eat in the room with the food laid out on the bed. We talk while we eat. I'm still feeling a bit emotional, but I don't show it. I just feel exhausted. We both are. We just lie down and go to sleep.

We awake in the early evening with the cats curled up between us. This is my idea of heaven, my big guy and my two baby cats. Only Lizzie is missing from the scene.

Jai goes out to get some alcohol for us, and he orders food from the same place for dinner. I wait for him to return. In the meantime, I watch TV and watch the cats playing. They are amusing themselves by jumping up and down from the bed and hiding under the bed, which Lollipop finds very amusing.

I'm feeling a little relaxed, but a sense of emptiness is creeping into my soul. I suppose leaving LOM and Shakthar behind leaves me at a bit of a loss without a purpose. But I am looking forward to spending quality time with my big guy in his home town before I head back home to England.

The food arrives, and so does Jai with vodka for me and Blenders for him. We eat and have a drink and chat away about our plans in Gandabaan. We talk about going to Pondicherry for a little trip and discuss other places we can visit. I fall asleep while watching TV.

We wake up early to head on our way to Gandabaan. We have breakfast in the room and then shower and get ready. I'm mentally preparing myself for the nine-hour drive. I pack up all the cat's stuff. Lollipop has decided to hide under the bed. I try to entice her out with chicken from Jai's dinner last night. Eventually I manage to get both cats into the crate. Lollipop does not like being confined, but Brutus is chilled as normal.

We go downstairs and load up the car. I say thank you to the owner, and we head on our way.

The journey itself was physically draining even though we're just sitting. We listen to music on the way. Lollipop is crying and trying to scratch her way out.

We take a detour as Jai want to get some booze for his uncle and friends, as it's cheaper in Goa. We are at a town on the Goa-Karnataka border. We end up driving around in circles for a while until we find a liquor store, which probably added an hour to our journey.

At the border patrol, the guards enquire about the bottles, which were on full view. It's illegal to take alcohol across borders apparently. Jai manages to either pay the guards or persuade them to let us cross with the bottles.

We stop off for lunch on the way, and again manage to get lost from the main highway. Jai is frustrated with himself for getting lost, but I take in the scenery. We go through old villages and small towns. Jai remarks at the buildings on how even villagers are building nice houses.

This is part of the real India tourists don't see. Jai points out various points of interest along the way and keeps saying shall we go and see. I say another time. We're both relaxed and have a laugh and joke along the way.

It's now dark and gone 9 p.m., and we've just reached the outskirts of Gandabaan. It's congested and dirty. The roads don't make any sense to me. There are road works everywhere. It seems like chaos, with cars, bikes, buses, and trucks all vying for the next inch of space to get a little farther.

We drive through suburban type areas, with small shops along each side of the road. There is multitude of different types of shops selling street-side snacks. Auto parts, types, clothing from Western and traditional Indian. Kitchenware and household goods.

As we approach the centre of Gandabaan the shops get bigger, and more modern. There are furniture stores, lighting stores. I notice a lot of gyms, all promising sculpted bodies. The neon lights light up the streets as if it were daytime. Restaurant selling international cuisine. There is the obligatory Domino's Pizza, which are everywhere.

There are people everywhere, from street sellers, to office workers, to "untouchables" in their dirty rags, drunks lying on the streets, young people in their trendy Western clothes.

The pungent smells seep in through the air-con vents. Fried goods, smoke, piss, and shit, and the general garbage which is just thrown on the side of the roads.

Of course, there are the cows which just roam about at their own free will, in the middle of the road, side of the roads eating garbage, and just generally acting as if they own the place.

And dirty mangy cats and dogs accompanying the cows. I feel sorry for the cats and dogs though.

We approach a flyover, and Jai puts his foot down on the gas. By now I am used to his crazy driving, weaving in and out of speeding traffic all the while bibbing the horn to let the motorist in front to get out of the way. There are massive billboards on either side. There are huge high-rise apartments lighting up the dark distant skyline.

We pass a few shopping malls. All the modern, trendsetting designer brands are here. This is truly the modern India that I had wanted to see and experience.

From the flyover It still takes us over an hour just to get from one side to the other and then to our destination.

Jai suggests we get some food before we get to the apartment, so we get some dinner from a takeout place on the main road, so we pull up outside a small roadside restaurant. Jai goes inside and places the order, and I step out of the car to stretch my legs. Lollipop is still screeching. I try to calm her down, but she is having none of it. I feel her frustration being stuck in the crate for over ten hours now.

Jai returns with the food package and we set off again. I still don't know how long we'll be. I ask Jai he says not long.

We do a U-turn, turn right onto a little dirt road from the main road into a residential area. Another left turn, and Jai says we're here. Relief is an understatement! The building manager and another young lad are there to open the gates, and Jai drives into the driveway.

I get out, I am exhausted. I don't even have the energy to talk. I just say Hi and get the cats out of the back of the car. Lollipop has quietened down now. Maybe she is confused as to where she is.

Jai directs the room boy with the bags, suitcase and boxes, and I take the cat carrier. I follow the Building Manager up the staircase to the second floor. He opens the door, and we enter. Jai is still downstairs.

We enter into a large open plan room. It's modern and clean. There is a TV on the wall, two single armchairs, and a table. There are two doors to the bedrooms. One to the left and the other to the right. The open plan kitchen is around the corner, and there is a washroom just off the living area.

It's nice. I like it.

Jai and the room boy arrive with the luggage and leave it in the living area. I put out food for the cats, and their litter tray at the far end of the living area. I decide to let them out in the bedroom to the right just, so they can get used to one room at a time. But as soon as I let them out of the crate, they are running around like lunatics. Being cooped in the crate for nearly ten hours, they must have gone stir-crazy.

We sit in the armchairs, I kiss him on the cheek and say thank you for getting us here safely. And now we can relax.

Jai orders some drinks for us via the room boy, and we sit and eat our dinner. Jai had turned the TV on and we sit and watch some film. I am too exhausted to even notice what it's about.

After a while I select the bedroom to the right as that has the en-suite bathroom as my bedroom. Not sure where Jai will be staying. I unpack my washroom things and get freshen up. It's now late and exhaustion is hitting me hard. I get ready and go to bed. The cats join me, and Jai comes to bed after some time. Sleep!

The next day I realise my period still hasn't come. I am now over two weeks late. I mention this to Jai. He suggests getting a test, I say OK. I don't feel like I am pregnant, just the usual water retention, minor twinges and boobs ache a little. I don't feel sick or anything. But I do feel like I have put on weight round my middle.

Now that we are free to do pretty much as we please, however Jai now needs to contend with the fact that we are in his home town. He has been living at home but with me being in Gandabaan, he will have to manage his relationship with his parents. I don't know how much time he will be able to spend with me.

The next day we lounge around the apartment. We're both still tired from the long drive. We sit and watch TV, drink coffee and tea, and smoke cigarettes. We decide on what the plan will be for the day. We decide to go to the cinema that evening.

We also talk about the places we can go and visit. We had previously talked about going to Pondicherry, but it's a good eight-hour drive. I don't want to leave the cats and I don't want to put them through another long drive.

Jai suggests Tarakeen and Sakana which are close enough to reach within a two- to three-hour drive. He has the car with him, so we can go at our leisure.

So, the next few days are spent chilling at the apartment. Jai has spent some time at his parents just to show that he is still around. We both seems to be completely run down. The last six months have taken it out of us both. Jai is still hurt from everything that has happened. I'm hoping spending time together before I go home will help us both to relax.

It's 14 February, Valentine's Day.

In the morning I wake up before him. He's sleeps like the dead. I let him sleep. My phone needs charging, and there's only one charger between us which is plugged in the living area. Jai's phone is plugged in.

I unplug his phone, and see that there are WhatsApp notifications from Anisha, his ex-girlfriend. I didn't intend on reading them, but she has replied that she is actually going to be working on Valentines.

I'm not sure how to feel about this, but obviously she is replying to his question as to what she will be doing. So, he has asked her what she will be doing on Valentine's Day! I put it out of my mind, or at least make a mental note of the message.

I had previously bought a card to give Jai. I had already written in it and put it in front of the TV for him to notice when he got up. I had written about how much he meant to me, for being my best friend and being the only person that I could rely on while all the time in Goa, and that even though I had gave him a hard time about the money situation and he had always stuck with me, that I will love him forever just for that.

After a while he gets up, see the card and opens it. He says thank you, reads it, and puts in on the shelf in the bed room. But I feel a tinge of disappointment, that I don't even get a hug or anything! I know he is penniless, but how much would a small gesture have cost? I leave it and don't say anything.

That evening we go to Captains Road which is one of the main shopping streets in Gandabaan. We mooch down the street checking out the shops. There are designer shops, middle of the range high street shops, and a lot of shops selling local tat. It's busy with all sorts of people milling along the street. In addition, it's Valentine's Day, so there are a lot of couples walking about holding hands.

We go into Calvin Klein. Jai looks at a few items of clothing, and I have a look at the sale items. Jai is talking with the sales assistant, and I find a nice grey jersey dress.

I decide to try it on. I go to the changing rooms and put the dress on. I am completely disheartened. I can't believe how much weight I have put on in the last couple of weeks. I can see all my lumps and bumps. I feel horrible. Every insecurity comes to the surface. I feel like I am a hundred years old. I look at myself and think how can Jai even find me attractive, how can he even love me? How can we have a future when he is only in his mid-twenties and I am fast approaching my next birthday. I feel like I want the ground to open up and swallow me. I feel disgusting.

I get changed back into my clothes and go back out into the store. Jai is still talking to the sales guy. He is looking at belts. He sees me and asks about the dress. I say it doesn't look nice.

Jai decides to buy a shirt and a belt. He asks for my debit card. I hand it to him and wander to the doors and wait for him. I don't want to speak to him or even look at him.

I tell him I want to go for a drink. We walk down a side street, and one of the hawkers approaches us with some roses. Jai nudges him out of the way and says some like why simply waste money and smirks at me. I don't say anything. Again, I feel completely disheartened. It's Valentine's Day and he can't even get me a rose.

He takes me to a pub and we sit at a high table. I order a beer and light a cigarette. We sit in silence. He is looking at me. I avoid his gaze and look around the place. It looks like a typical pub/bar as if I was back home, but all the faces are brown.

Jai orders some munches to go with his Blenders and coke. I don't feel like eating

There is an atmosphere between us. I don't know how the conversation was started, but it doesn't go well. I still feel horrible and now I also feel rejected. I know he senses something is wrong, but he doesn't know what to say. Eventually he says why I am I silent. I feel like crying and hold back my tears. I say that how can we have a future, when he is going to get married and have a happy life. He says that he loves me and that he doesn't want to lose me.

All I can think of is that he doesn't want to lose me because

I am the only one that is supporting him. It makes me doubt his motives for being with me.

After a while we finish our drinks and head back home. I don't say much in the car just watch the scenery go by.

We arrive back home, and he pour us some drinks. We don't say much to each other. We sit and watch TV. We're both on our phones as the apartment has Wi-Fi.

I go to bed as I have had enough of today.

The next couple of days is spent with me chilling at the apartment, and Jai is off doing his chores in the daytime, and then comes back in the evening to the apartment. We go to the cinema and visit a couple of malls.

My period has still not come, and I remind Jai to get me a test.

One of the days we go to Bannerghatta Zoo in Gandabaan. It's the National Zoo for all of India. We arrive midday, and it's starting to get hot. We enter, and the place looks a bit rundown if I'm honest. We start walking round following the designated path.

I'm not really a fan of zoos as I think animals should not be kept in cages.

Jai says he came here years ago on a school trip. He is not impressed and jokes about complaining to the authorities. Says it's a disgrace that this is meant to be the National Zoo of India. All the cages look rusted and the whole place has not been maintained in years by the looks of it. The animals look miserable, and I feel sorry for them.

We walk round, see some crocodiles, hyenas, lots of varying species of monkeys and birds.

Jai intermittently looks at his phone and seems to be sending messages. At one point he takes a phone call. I try not to eaves drop but he says the usual intro and asks if they have had lunch. He goes on to say, that he can't say where he is. I don't understand why he says this to whomever is on the phone. What is he hiding from this person? I don't ask but walk on further down the path and leave him behind on the path.

I start to feel annoyed and I distance myself from him, physically and emotionally. I can feel myself becoming closed.

He catches up with me, and we approach a small lake offering rides on a pedalo-type contraption. He asks if I want to go on it. I say no. He says he wants to go on it. I say you can go, and I will wait in the car. He says why would I do that? I say because I don't want to go on the ride.

We decide to leave but stop off to have a coffee at a small stall. We sit but we can't smoke. I don't say much. The little messages and calls are beginning to bug me.

We start to head back to the apartment. Jai apologises about the state of the zoo. I think he wanted to impress me but is disappointed. I say, "It's fine."

We chill in the apartment until evening time, and then decide to go out in the evening for dinner. He takes me to a really nice place not far from the apartment, called Social.

We stand at the bar, and order drinks and food. He goes off for a little while to find his friend who owns the place. He comes back, and we are seated at a table overlooking the downstairs level.

The place is very modern and there is a lot of greenery on the walls and in the atrium. The place is filled with young Indians and a few foreigners having a good time. It's good to see young Indian women enjoying themselves having a drink. This is modern India, even with all the constraints which still exist.

I feel a little more relaxed after a drink and we chat about general things. Jai tells me about how much it would cost to get a place like this started, which is way beyond any budget which I might have. Not that he was saying he wanted me to fund anything like this.

We eat dinner, and I'm a lot more relaxed after having a

drink. I watch the people downstairs dancing having a great time, which I find amusing.

Back at the apartment, we resume our seats, watch TV. We chat about our sightseeing trips. The cats are having their night-time manic phase and run from one room to the other. I am loving seeing them so happy running around like little loons. They make me so happy.

It's the weekend and we plan to visit Tarakeen. Jai had asked the room boy to check in on the cats' food while we are away for the night. My mood has cleared somewhat, and I'm looking forward to having a road trip. Jai tells me about the sites to see.

We head off mid-morning as it's going to take a few hours to get to Tarakeen. We drive through Gandabaan city. Again, Jai points out various buildings. Somewhere the big IT companies are housed. We reach the outskirts of the city and stop off for some takeaway lunch.

I'm feeling relaxed, but my mood is still a little low. We chat about general things. I still need to book my ticket for going home, he reminds me to book it when we get back. I say, "OK, we will sort it."

A few hours later we reach Tarakeen and stop off at a Coffee Café Day (CCD). The area is very hilly and there are mountains in the distance. It feels like we have reached some Indian version of Swiss valleys. But not as clean and not so snowy.

We order coffees and I look on my phone for somewhere to stay. We book a place about half an hour away. We finish our drinks and head off. It's now getting dark, and we drive along a windy road along a cliff edge.

Jai jokes that if a body was left here, it will never be found. I laugh and say there's only one person that would need to be ditched here. We don't mention names, but we both know who we mean.

We find the hotel and check in. I go to our room. It's a large room but sparsely decorated with wood-panelled walls. There's a TV mounted on the far wall. At the back it looks like a garden with a kids' play area.

I lie down on the bed. It's comfortable enough. Jai goes back out to get us some drinks, and I order food with the hotel manager.

Jai returns, and the food arrives. We eat and have a couple of drinks. It's nice. We both relaxed. We actually have a cuddle and a laugh. Cuddles have been lacking up to this point. I think the stress of everything has been getting to us. I actually feel close to him again since coming to Gandabaan.

The next morning, we wake up early and start our day of sightseeing. First, he takes me to King's Throne. It's a large garden area with an outdoor balcony at the far end overlooking the hills of Tarakeen. It's a great view but not much else to see. We don't stay long.

Next, we head to Abbey Falls, a waterfall in the hills, a half hour drives away. We walk through wooded area along the path. It's steep, and I have to catch my breath a couple of times. God, I realise how unfit I have become. We reach the waterfall. It's just a trickle of water with a shallow pool at the bottom.

There is a group of young lads taking photos. Jai asks if I want a photo taken. I say no. Again, we don't stay long, and head back to the car.

Next stop is Talacauvery Sacred Temple. Apparently, there is an amazing view of the Dam from the top. The temple is on a hillside and the view from the main square area is stunning. A panorama of plush tropical jungle rising up the mountain and flowing down to the valley below.

We must take off our footwear to enter the temple area. And I have to cover my legs as I'm wearing leggings which reach only my knees. I have to hire a sarong type thing. It's now midday and the day has heated up. So, we start to walk up the 150 steps. My feet are starting to burn on the hot stone steps as we reach halfway.

Jai stops and speaks to some random guy. He asks, "Is the dam at the top?" The guy says there is no dam; it's just what they say.

I say, "I'm not climbing up the steps if there is nothing to see. In addition, we were not allowed to bring any water in with us."

So not only is it sweltering, my feet our burning, and gasping for water, there isn't anything specific to see. I tell Jai I'm not climbing the rest of the way. He agrees, and we start to head back down.

He is complaining as to why these people say things when they are not true. He says it's simply a waste of time and fuel. And also hiring the sarong, he's saying that all the want is people's money. He's not happy but he gets over it.

We leave and, on the way, back we stop of at a roadside stall to have coffee, as I'm feeling a little faint. The young girl serves us hot sweet coffee, and we get some biscuits. I felt like my sugar levels were low and just needed a boost.

He says we'll go to Little Tibet next, so we get back in the car and head along the windy hillside roads. Jai drives his usual crazy way, and I have to clench my buttocks on more than one occasion when there is a big truck heading straight towards us but manoeuvres out of the way at the last second.

About an hour later, we reach Little Tibet, and I can see the Golden temple in the grounds from outside. I am actually impressed. It's beautiful glistening in the midday sun. Along the road to the entrance there are prayer flags hanging from wires. There are a few shops selling wooden ornaments.

We park up on a street next to a square with souvenir shops around the edge. We enter the temple into a large outdoor square. There are Buddhist monks milling around in their orange robes, some old some young.

We walk through an archway and ahead is a blue and gold temple shining brightly, with a large picture of a monk on the front. If it's an actual special monk but I didn't ask who. There's are circular halo on top of the temple. It really is pretty.

There's a lot of tourists. Some families, and it looks like children on school trips.

We turn right and there is another building. It looks like a large villa decorated with colourful paintings of various Buddhas. We put our shoes in to the cloak room, and walk into the building, again with multicoloured paintings. There are three giant gold Buddha statues in front of us surrounded by colourful depictions of various events. It's Stunning!

We decide to sit down on the marble floor to take in the calming atmosphere. There are small children on a school trip ahead of us. I watch them and am amused by the kids taking selfies with their sunglasses on.

Jai asks if I want a photo. I say OK and pose sitting down. He shows me the photos. My face looks so fat and dark. I don't like them.

He says to take a photo of him. So, he poses in front of the statues trying to look all-natural talking on his phone.

We stay for a little while and decide to check out the shops. On the way through the grounds I say come take a photo with me. I thought he would at least stand next to me, but he just loiters in the background while I take a selfie.

Its stuff like this that really gets on my nerves. He is meant to be my boyfriend, but he acts like a nobody. As if he doesn't even know me. I don't say anything.

We head to the shops, and he wants to buy a Buddha for his Mum but doesn't want to spend a lot of money. He messages her, and she wants a specific Buddha. I leave him to look around in one shop and I go off along the row of shops. I want to buy a Buddha too, but I'm not really in the mood. I don't buy anything.

He calls me to find where I am. I ask did he buy anything he says no. The one that met his Mum's requirements was RS2,000, and he didn't want to buy it as it would mean he was spending his credit, and he didn't know if he would get the money back. I say, "Fair enough."

It's now late afternoon, and it will take us a few hours to get home, so we decide we've had enough for today and start the drive back.

By the time we reach Gandabaan, it's early evening and dark out. I remind him I need the test. He stops near the apartment and jumps out to get the test. When he returns, he hands it to me in a brown paper bag. He has also bought me some nail varnish remover, which I had previously requested.

We get back to the apartment. I make sure the cats are OK and have enough food. They have pooed on the floor as the litter tray was full. I clean up their mess, and we both resume positions on the chairs with the TV on.

In the morning I get up before him and do the test. I patiently wait for the lines to show. It's negative. It's a relief but I don't really feel anything. I leave the stick on the back of the toilet, so he can see it when he gets up.

After an hour or so he wakes and goes to the bathroom. He comes out and say it's negative. I say yes. He asks if I am OK. I say yes. He says something to the effect of if it had been positive, he would have been OK with that. I don't say anything but look at him, trying to figure out if he is just saying that or if he really meant it.

He says he needs to go back to his parents and gets ready and leaves soon after. I just chill in the apartment. I'm happy with him going. I want to be on my own. I feel numb.

In the evening he comes back, and we go out for dinner and to the cinema. He has also brought two small notebooks back with him. This is to record his purchases and to add to his outstanding credit from Goa, and what he needs to get him set up in Gandabaan.

We calculate currently he owes me £3,000.

The next couple of days are spent like this. While he's out to maintain things with his parents and do his chores, I go to the pet store to get some supplies.

One of the evenings we take the cats to the vets to get them checked and to get their deworming treatment up to date.

Some days are spent going shopping, visiting various malls, going to lunch, and generally roaming the sites of Gandabaan.

I'm still curious about the extent of Jai's relationship with his ex-girlfriends, and I know he has talked to other women while we have been together. I don't have an issue with him having women as friends, but if he is hiding things from me, then I do have an issue.

One day at I lunch, I casually ask him if he has told his friends about me. I ask him if he still talks to his ex-girlfriends. He looks at me with guilty eyes. He doesn't say that he has told them about me, but he does say he still talks to a couple and that they are close. He says that they are married now anyway. One name he mentions is Anisha's. I ask him what he has told them. He says he told them about Goa but not about everything that has happened.

I know he is hiding information from me. I can see it in his face. I don't press him with any further questions. The look on his face says it all. My emotional barriers slide up a little higher.

The days are spent milling about, making plans for what we want to do next. He has mentioned that he is invited to a wedding in Chennai on 4 March, which will mean an overnight stay. I say, "OK, no problem."

For our next trip we plan to go to Revolution Film Studio and Wonderful Water Park. Jai doesn't have the car for this trip as he has given it back to his uncle, whom he had borrowed it from, so he arranges a car and driver for us.

We get up very early as the drive will take at least two hours. Around six o'clock I start getting ready for the driver, who will be picking us up at 7.30 a.m. Jai is being his lazy self. He is terrible about getting up in the mornings.

I have breakfast, get showered, and make sure the cats have food and water. Jai eventually gets up. I make him a coffee to get him moving. He gets ready, and we go downstairs to wait for the driver, who arrives a few minutes later.

We head out through Gandabaan city, to the suburbs, and eventually the countryside. I'm beginning to get my bearings, and I recognise the routes we take.

As we reach the outer perimeter of the city, I feel sleepy and I nod off, leaning my head against the window.

I am actually fast asleep but am awakened by Jai talking on his phone. He is speaking in a low, soft voice. I don't move, but I listen as I slowly wake up. He's making a few "uh-huh" noises and asking, "What did he say?" I can hear a female voice on the other end of the phone. I keep my eyes closed. He closes the conversation with "OK, babe. Talk to you later." I am seething inside. I slowly stir to make him realise I am awake.

I turn around to him and say, "Well, that was a cosy conversation." I can see he is visibly uncomfortable. He says it was just a friend and that she is having problems with her manager or something like that. I ask if he always calls his friends "babe". He says he speaks to all his friends like that. He asks if the phone call woke me up. I say yes!

I want to kill him, just push him out of the moving car. He thought I was asleep, so he felt it was safe to make a sneaky phone call to his "friend". I feel completely disrespected. I am meant to be his girlfriend, and he is talking with another woman, calling her "babe". I feel so alone in the taxi. Tears well up in my eyes, but I don't cry, not in front of him or the taxi driver.

I don't speak unless necessary for the rest of the journey.

We arrive at Revolution Film Studio. There's hardly anyone there. Jai gets the tickets, but the place doesn't open for another half hour. There is a big hall by the ticket counter. It's the size of two tennis courts, full of antique and art deco tables and leather couches with artwork depicting animals on the walls.

Jai goes in, turns left, and goes to sit on a couch. I enter and head the opposite direction, lying down on a couch so that we cannot see each other. I have never felt so alone in a foreign land in all my life. I just want to go home, but I'm stuck here, not only for the day with him but also until I get on my flight home.

Can he not realise what he is doing and how it's hurting me?

We spend the day making polite conversation, wondering around the tacky attractions of Revolution Film City. We wander around a film studio exhibition about some famous Indian actor from Karnataka. We take photos of each other in the Diary Chair of *Big Boss House* (the Indian equivalent of *Big Brother*) and find the most dire and saddest-looking dinosaurs in the prehistoric garden.

It's now midday, and the sun is bearing down hard. We hunt down the driver and the car and head towards Wonderful Water Park.

When we arrive, there is only an hour left until the place closes, but we decide to go in anyway. It's lunchtime, and we're both hungry. We find the canteen-type restaurant. It's mainly sandwiches and fried foods. Reluctantly we order. We sit on opposite sides of the table but not in front of each other. I check my phone even though there is no network, but it's a distraction from talking.

There are a lot of schoolchildren roaming around. Some of them are soaked in their swimming costumes from the water rides. Their excited little faces show they are happy to be away from school. I notice that all the girls are wearing long pants and T-shirts, while the boys are in shorts with no tops.

There is a person dressed as a dinosaur, and kids are taking selfies with it. It's all a happy scene compared to what I am feeling inside.

The place is like Alton Towers but rough around the edges.

After lunch we walk around the attractions. They are all near enough to closing and therefore are empty. We come across a small cinema showing a short film about some monkey. I'm presuming it's the mascot for the place. The next showing is in ten minutes, so we decide to go in. As we enter, we are handed 3D specs. We sit near the middle, and there are kids behind us, all very excited and cheering. We check out the seats, and they look to be mechanical. We wonder why that is.

The film starts, and it's animated. We put on our 3D specs. The monkey mascot is on some secret mission and goes off to complete said mission. The seats start to move in time with the action that takes place on the screen. There are puffs of air and snowflakes squirted in our faces from the backs of the chairs in front of us. We chuckle like little kids. The children behind us are shrieking with joy. Bless them, they probably haven't had this much fun before.

The film lasts ten minutes, and despite my reserved mood, Jai and I both actually enjoy ourselves with the pure infantile pleasure of being jolted about in our seats.

My mood is lifted somewhat.

The place is starting to close, so we walk back to the car and head back to Gandabaan.

The day after, I book my ticket to return home to London on 7 March.

Hurrah, my period has come! It's over two weeks late, but I have never been so pleased.

The next couple of days are spent shopping and going to the cinema.

Over the course of the month in Gandabaan, Jai and I must have gone to see a film about ten times.

Most of the films we saw were action-packed, gun-fuelled beat-'em-ups, Jai's choices. I soon got bored of them. Jai says he is learning from them how to be an assassin. I just look at him and laugh. He can be so silly sometimes. One night, at my request, we go to see *Lion* starring Dev Patel. It's an emotional film, and Jai is moved. Afterwards he says he is going to adopt a little boy from the streets. I won't give any spoilers away, but is the best film we've seen, in my opinion. How could it not be with the delicious Dev Patel starring and with the little actor playing the other main character being so cute?!

Jai asks the question of where I want to visit next before

I go home. He suggests Sakana. He starts to tell me about the places to visit in Sakana, including a palace. I agree to go there, and he arranges the same taxi driver as before for the next morning.

Again, it is a very early start in the morning as it will take three and a half hours to get to Sakana. En-route we stop off to get breakfast at a big outdoor restaurant. I fancy an omelette and toast, but Jai says we won't find that here, that it'll be more local food. So I have dosa, which is a very fine flat pancake made from rice flour served with curry-spiced mashed potatoes, coconut chutney, and a curry sauce. It's one of my favourites, so I don't complain.

We arrive in Sakana. It's beautiful. There are wide boulevards, and the streets are clean. There's a lot of greenery with big grass parks. In the middle of the roundabout is a massive statue of some raja who resided at the palace. The place has a regal feel about it.

We park up and queue to get tickets for the palace. It's getting hot again as it's midday. We queue to put our shoes into the cloakroom and then walk round to the entrance.

It's magnificent, just as an Indian palace should look. There are gigantic marble domes on each of the spires, and the great many windows are decorated in gold and white. This is the epitome of Indian regal culture. Jai says at night the palace is lit up.

Inside it's just as wondrous. We are not allowed to take photos. There are giant elephant tusks and paintings of the old royal family in the regalia. There are artefacts made of gold and ivory, and old weapons in dusty cabinets. We walk around a corner and exit into an open-air pavilion. It's huge, facing the open grounds and gardens of the palace. The tiered seating rises high above us.

I am suitably impressed with the palace. As we move onto the walkway leading to the exit, there is a small Hindu temple with multicoloured gods.

It's lunchtime, and we're both hungry. We find a nice hotel/ restaurant and decide to have the buffet lunch. We walk downstairs through an entrance which is like a giant barrel. We laugh at the entrance but are impressed. We enter into a pub-type room with the buffet laid out in the middle. We eat lunch. We're both in a good mood.

After lunch we head to Sakana Zoo, and it's much better maintained than Gandabaan Zoo. There are actual animals that don't look as if they are ready to top themselves. There are lions, bears, elephants, and monkeys, along with the all other animals one would find in a zoo.

We walk round chatting away. Jai is being cheeky, saying the monkeys are my family. We stand and look at the lions. Then we walk through some aviary with different varieties of birds, including pelicans.

Jai goes through the reptile enclosure. I give this a miss as snakes freak me out. I sit on a bench outside, waiting for him. By now my back is killing me from the walking and because my period came.

We're both having a nice time.

The next stop is the Royal Orchid Gardens. It's now around 5 p.m. There is a water and light show at 6.30 p.m. We discuss staying for it. We walk round the garden and up to the top of the hill to get a better view. The garden is very pretty, but by now, after a full day of walking in the hot sun, I'm beginning to feel weary. In addition, it will take us a good three to four hours to drive back. So, we sack off the water and light show and head back home.

Again, we locate the driver and car and start our journey back.

We had noticed before, but the driver keeps spitting out the window while driving, which is pissing me off and annoying Jai, but he says, "What can I do?"

We get home late in the evening.

A couple of days before 4 March arrives, Jai needs to get

some formal clothes, so we go shopping to get him a shirt and trousers, which he can also use for work. We leave late in the day, and after shopping we go for dinner at the Irish bar we had been to on a previous night.

It's a nice modern place. It looks like a typical Irish pub you would find in any UK town. We order food and drinks, and both of us are relaxed. I have put all the talking with his exes to the back of my mind. I realise that I'm not going to be in Gandabaan much longer, so I want focus on me and him and not worry too much—at least try not to.

We chat about me booking my ticket and what I will do when I get back home. He says that I am leaving him. I look at him. He looks slightly sad at the thought of me going. I tell him I have to go home sometime.

I think he has been feeling the distance between us too. Maybe the calls to his "friends" have been a way of feeling close to someone else. But he never talks to me about what he's feeling. I'm not a mind reader. But on the odd occasion says he loves me.

Our food and drinks arrive. We chat some more about general things. There is music playing, and we relax some more. He says that his tolerance for alcohol has increased and he doesn't get drunk any more. I, on the other hand, am becoming a lightweight. After two double vodka and sodas, I am feeling a little tipsy.

By the time we get home, we're both chilled. There is some weed left over from Goa, so I make us a little joint. This is the first time since getting to Gandabaan that we actually feel completely relaxed, so I let him get close to me. We both need the closeness as we have felt distant from each other.

In the morning, he leaves to go to do his family chores. I laze around the apartment. I want to go to the pet store to get some food for the cats.

We message each other to see what each other is doing.

He is at his parents' waiting for his mother to arrive, at which point they'll take his grandfather somewhere.

I decide to tidy up the bedroom as there are clothes everywhere. Jai is so messy. His holdall bag is there, so I start to fold his clothes and put them in the bag. He has a bottle of whisky in it. I move it to put the clothes in, and I notice there is a box of Manforce condoms in there. I assume they are from when we were at English Rose Villas, but they don't look like they have been opened. I leave them there without inspecting them.

It's now around midday, and I still haven't showered. Suddenly I start to get a stomach ache. It's like I need to go the toilet, or it's food poisoning pains. I break out in a sweat and lie down, doubled over. I can't think what might have caused this. I haven't had any meat. These pains were the reason was why I went veggie in the first place, when I had first experienced them two years ago.

I message Jai, telling him I'm in pain. He says he will be back soon. I google my symptoms. It seems it could be a waterborne infection. I message Jai and ask him to get me some cranberry juice. I tell him I might need antibiotics. He says he might need to take me to hospital. I say, "No, I don't want to go." He says he needs to make sure I am OK before he leaves for the wedding tomorrow.

I take some paracetamol and go to sleep for a couple of hours. I'm afraid it might be like the last time I had these symptoms, when I was in pain for two days. I don't want to be laid up and end up in hospital when I am due to fly home in a few days. The last time I was in hospital in India, I had to undergo surgery for an abscess below my left buttock.

Now that I've slept for a few hours, the pain has subsided. Jai isn't here yet. I decide to take a shower. While I am standing in the shower, the pain returns. I go down into a crouching position. I take deep breaths to alleviate the pain. I sit on the toilet as I feel like nature is calling. Immediately the pain subsides. I am literally relieved. I shower, get dressed, and go back to bed.

Early evening Jai arrives. I let him in but go back to bed. He asks if I want to go to the cinema. I say no, as I don't want to get stomach ache there. So, we stay in and order dinner and watch TV.

The next day Jai leaves with his friends to go to the wedding. They are riding in one of his friend's cars, a big four-by-four SUV-type thing.

I relax in the apartment, but I need to get an extra bag as all my clothes and the gifts I have bought for the family will not fit in what I have. Late afternoon, I get ready and walk to DMart, a big supermarket about a mile down the road from the apartment.

I find a big holdall bag with a handle and wheels. I also pick up some snacks and food for myself for the evening. It feels nice to have some space to myself and to do things for myself, rather than having to rely on Jai all the time, which I sometimes find frustrating.

In the evening I chill, have my snacks—hummus and nachos—pour myself a vodka and Sprite, and relax. The cats are running around as usual. I watch them playing, and it makes me feel happy but also very sad. I will be gone in a few days and will be leaving them with Jai to look after until we sort out their export to the UK.

Jai messages to make sure I am all right, which I am. He asks if I can postpone my flight. I check online and see that it will cost me a lot to reschedule. I don't want to leave him and the cats, but I have to go before my visa expires on 23 March.

There is also a little bit of weed left, so I roll a joint to relax and watch TV.

In the morning after breakfast, I start to pack my bags. God, I have so many clothes, and I have done a lot of shopping for the family back home. I go through each item, deciding whether to take it or not. One pile is for packing, another is for getting rid of.

My big suitcase is packed, as is the black holdall. I don't know how much they are going to weigh, but they are heavy. The baggage limit is thirty-five thousand kilograms for the flight, but I will just have to risk it—or pay the excess at check-in.

Jai hasn't arrived back yet from his wedding trip. I enjoy the time with just me and the cats. I am going to miss them so much. The little crazies have kept me sane all the time I've been in India. But I am looking forward to getting back home and getting my Lizzie back. I have told Brutus and Lollipop about their big sister back in the UK.

It's my penultimate night in Gandabaan. Jai has arranged for some of his friends to have a little party in the next-door apartment. I'm not sure if it's a send-off for me, but it's a nice thought, and I'm glad that he feels safe enough to introduce me to some of his friends. Obviously, it won't be as a girlfriend. I'm not sure what he has told them about me.

Gradually people arrive. There is a group of five lads, and then later two young women and another guy arrive. They are doing a barbeque on the roof terrace, so we all relocate there. It offers a great view of the adjoining apartment building. The weather is still warm.

Drinks have been bought, and we all hang out chatting. Music is playing on my Bluetooth speaker. They are cooking chicken, so Jai orders me some veggie food, and there are crisps.

They are all in their early to mid-twenties, I would say. Three of the lads, including Jai's cousin Lagan, all went to University of Southern England, so I chat with them about their experiences. They are all stoners, but all hold down professional jobs. This is modern India. I speak to the young women, Debbie and Sarah—they are sisters—and Sarah's boyfriend Jonny. They are all really sweet and ask me about general things. I speak to Jonny about music, and he tells me about Sky Bar, which is one of the happening places in Gandabaan.

Jalil is making the chicken on the barbecue. I chat with him. He is one of Jai's best friends. He's a cool, sweet guy.

Jai is milling around, chatting with Lagan, and having a laugh. He comes over to me on the odd occasion when I'm chatting with Jonny and the girls.

I feel welcomed by his friends. I know I am a lot older than all of them, but I know I can hold my own in conversation, and Debbie and Sarah are saying I am very lucky to have my freedom. I empathise with them. I know what it's like to be confined by the Indian culture. Even though it's modern India, the restrictions on girls especially, and boys too, are still part of everyday life. I feel for them, but I have fought hard all my life to break through those cultural barriers.

There are drinks being poured and joints being passed around. I take it easy on the joints. Everyone is having a great time.

It's approaching midnight, and the women need to get home, but the men are not moving. It takes about an hour for them to actually leave. Jai says he is going to go with Lagan and the rest of the boys for a while and asks if that is OK. I say, "Yes, it's fine," and leave them to it.

I'm happy that he is reconnecting with his Gandabaan crew after having spent the last five years in Hindavi and then his time in Goa. He needs to rebuild a life here now, after everything that has happened, and this is part of the process to re-establish himself. I want him to be happy in his new life.

I go back to my apartment and chill for a while on my own, which I'm more than happy about. Later, Jai tells me that a couple of then me have gotten sick. They had taken a whitey because they drank and then smoked too much. I have to laugh. I think to myself, *Youth is wasted on the young.* Ha ha! But we've all been there.

It's Monday, 6 March, my last full day in Gandabaan with

Jai and the cats. I'm feeling very emotional, but I don't show it. Again, it's a lazy morning. We sit around drinking coffee and smoking cigarettes, which has become our routine while being here, two empty bodies in a room, coexisting separately. I can still feel a distance between us. Maybe it's me closing myself down so that I do not feel the grief of being separated from Jai and the cats or the hurt from the messages and cosy telephone calls—or both!

Jai asks what I want to do. I say, "I don't know. Maybe finish off the last of my shopping for the family back home."

My flight is tomorrow at 8 p.m. We talk about how we're going to get to the airport. Jai says he'll get the car later so I don't have to get a taxi. He will drop me off.

By now it's lunchtime, and we order in (again). He says we'll go out for dinner for my last evening. I say OK. So, we just sit around, not saying much. I don't know what he's thinking.

I decide to tidy the bedroom to put the last of my things away, but also I just want to do something. I don't want to just sit. Jai's bag is still there from his wedding trip. I am curious about the condoms I found a few days ago. He is in the shower, so I have a look. The condoms are there, but it looks like the packet has been opened. I don't remember them being opened the first time I saw them. Again, I feel betrayed, but I don't want to jump to conclusions as I'm not sure. But the hurt reinforces itself in the pit of my stomach. I leave the bag where it is.

After showering, Jai says he'll be back later then leaves to go to his house. I smoke more cigarettes, trying not to let my mind run away with me. I just think to myself, *Only one more day to go and I will be out of here.* I keep myself calm, but my stomach is in knots. I am having many mixed emotions, not only the hurt and mistrust, but also the pain of leaving him and the cats. The cats! My heart feels like it's breaking, and my head feels like it's going to burst.

After a long while of what feels like an emotional hurricane, I get showered and get dressed.

Jai comes back in the early evening without the car. We order a cab, and we go out for dinner at a nice trendy place called Rasta, a bar and restaurant. We sit outside on the veranda at a high table. The conversation is strained. Again, he talks about his coming to the UK as soon as he can. I talk about getting home and moving into the spare room as my friend Paul is still renting my place. We talk about the cats and how he's going to look after them at his house. I ask him if he has he told his parents, and he says, No. But they will have to "accept my decision", He says.

I'm happy that he is going to have the cats, but I also have reservations. I know how flaky he can be, and he is easily distracted by other things. Also, when he starts to work, who will look after them then? I am worried that they are going to be neglected, but there is nothing I can do about it now. I think to myself I should have left them with Daphne, the lovely woman I met at the vet's when the cats went to get sterilised.

Jai seems to be in a bad mood. I can't tell what he is thinking. Is he upset? Is he pleased that I am leaving so that he can get on with his life with whomever?

He says he is going to miss me. I say I will miss him too.

We eat our food and finish our drinks. Jai orders another cab to take us back to the apartment.

We get home and resume our positions on the chairs. We are both subdued, both aimlessly looking at our phones. I message my cousins and brother at home, saying I will be back in the UK by tomorrow evening.

Jai and I drink some more, and I'm now tired. I decide to go to bed and leave him sitting in his armchair.

After a while he comes to bed. We cuddle. It's my last night, but we don't make love.

I feel so lonely, rejected, hurt, and ugly.

I wonder where the love has gone that we felt so deeply between us in Goa. What happened on the way to Gandabaan?

Did that love get lost somewhere on the highway? I don't understand what happened.

I turn my back on him. Sleep slowly comes to me with Lollipop snuggled by my legs.

It is now my last day in Gandabaan. My flight is in the evening. It's going to be a long day of waiting to leave for the airport. Jai and I agree that we should leave the apartment by 5 p.m. to get to the airport in time for check-in.

Jai leaves early to go pick up the car from his uncle. I laze around for a while. My emotions are high, and at times I have a little weep. I cuddle Brutus and Lollipop and tell them they will be with me soon and that I have not abandoned them. I tell them how much I love them. Cats are meant to be intuitive, but I cannot tell if they understand me. They are being their normal selves.

I wonder if Jai thinks I have abandoned him, but what can I do? I need to go home and start to earn money again. I don't know what is going to happen with us. When I get home, I don't even know if we'll even keep in touch. Perhaps things will just fizzle away into nothing.

We have been through so much together; this thought makes me cry.

To keep the emotions at bay, I decide to make these aloo tikka things from a packet mix that has been in the kitchen cupboard. I think I should make them before I have a shower; otherwise I will stink of cooking.

Jai messages, saying he will be back soon, around two-ish.

When he arrives, I am all ready. My bags are packed. I have put them in the living room. The cats get all excited and jump around on the bags.

Jai and I have lunch, and after a while I go and lie down. I feel emotionally raw, and I can feel the grief of leaving the three of them coming to the surface.

Jai comes and lies with me. We cuddle, but I hide my face. To make light, he starts to say that when I get home I should lose weight, and shave my moustache, and get plastic surgery. In that moment I hate him. I get up, go to the en-suite bathroom, shut the door. I cry.

He gets up and calls out, "Sabbie Boss, please don't cry."

I ask him, "Why are you being so horrible? Can you not see how upset I am?"

He pulls me out of the bathroom, and I sit on the edge of the bed. He tries to console me. He says he is sorry; he was just trying to make a joke. I tell him it wasn't funny. He strokes my hair and undoes my ponytail, saying I have blow-dried it nicely.

I go out into the living room and light a cigarette. He follows me out. He again says he was just joking. I am angry now, and I say to him, "Have you seen yourself in the mirror?" He tries to laugh it off, but I know the comment has pricked him.

By now it's approaching 5 p.m., and I say, "Let's just go." I am still upset. I try to catch the cats to give them one last hug, but they don't want to be caught.

Jai calls up the room boy, and he takes down the big suitcase. I take my laptop and handbag. The room boy comes back up for the other black holdall bag.

The car gets loaded up, and we head off to the airport. I am still upset and don't say much. Jai makes small talk.

He also says that I am leaving him. I look at him with tears in my eyes, then look away. I think he is hurting too but doesn't know how to show it.

We arrive at the airport, park up, and get a trolley for the bags. Jai and I have one last cigarette together in the carpark. He tells me he is going to wait for Jalil as he works for customs. I say OK.

With our cigarettes finished, Jai walks me to the departures entrance. He is not allowed to come in. We loosely hug, but I cannot look at him. He says, "Bye. See you soon."

I can't believe that this is how we are saying goodbye to each other, as if I am just going to the shops. We can't even look at each other. I don't even know if we'll ever see each other again. The casual goodbye kills me.

I walk towards the entrance, holding back the tears.

I get out my passport and my phone with my ticket details. The security guy checks them and lets me in to the airport.

Once inside, I pull myself together. I don't know why, but something about airports makes me optimistic. I suppose it's the thought of new adventures, but this time the adventure is over, and I am going home.

I reach the check-in desk. The clerk checks my ticket and passport, and I put my bags on the weighing scales. As suspected, I am way over my luggage allowance. I ask how much it is going to cost, and he calculates over thirty-five thousand rupees (£300). I am shocked, but there is nothing I can do about it.

I have to go to the Emirates ticket desk to pay for the excess luggage. One other official comes to take me. I pay up with my credit card and then head towards the departure gates.

On the way I reach the international flight immigration desk. I wait in the queue for the Foreign Nationals desk to open.

The official immigration guy arrives at the desk, and he waves me over. I walk over and hand my passport to him. He takes a while to look at my passport, simultaneously looking at a computer screen behind the counter. He asks me to look at a camera behind him, which I do.

He looks at me and says that I have exceeded the maximum 180-day stay on my visa. I say, "Sorry, but my visa doesn't expire until 24 March." He says that each stay within the visa period can only be 180 days. I have exceeded by four days, and I will have to re-register in India before I can leave.

I ask him, "So, can I not leave?"

He says, "No!"

Chapter 13

EXIT DENIED!

Secrets and Lies, Part II

I don't understand what's going on! What the fuck? I cannot get on my flight to get home?! Am I stuck in India? Is this a criminal offence?

Outwardly I am calm and collected. Internally I am confused as hell.

The immigration agent says that I will have to contact the FRRO (Foreigner Regional Registration Offices) to get an exit permit. He calls a colleague over, who walks me over to a desk. He says I need to fill in some details in a book he indicates.

I say I need to make a call, which he allows. I call Jai and tell him they won't let me go. He is just as shocked as I am. I tell him I have to go to some government office and get a permit to leave. He says, "OK. I will wait for you outside." He adds, "Lucky I didn't leave."

I complete the entry in the book with my name and passport number. I ask, "What happens now?" The man explains I need to go to the FRRO and gives me a small rectangle of paper with an address on it. He says I will need to complete the online exit permit request and then go to the FRRO to register as a tourist. After that I will have to apply for the exit permit.

I have never heard of this process before. And I would have thought they would have wanted to me leave India if I had exceeded my stay.

I ask about my luggage. The agent makes a phone call, and soon the guy who had taken me to pay for my excess luggage comes up to meet me. He says to follow him to the Emirates desk. I follow him. I ask him, "What happens with my payment?" He says they will give me full refund on the card I paid with; that's not a problem. At least I won't lose that £300. I am relieved.

The Emirates guy makes another phone call and tells me to wait for my luggage to be brought back to me. I sit in the waiting area by the desk where I paid.

I phone Jai again. He is outside waiting for me. He says that normally he goes straightaway, but something made him wait. He had gone to have something to eat. I tell him I have to wait for my luggage. He says OK, telling me to come out to the car park when I am through.

I am in shock, I can't believe I cannot go home. I will have to phone Mum and Dad at some point, but not at the moment. I keep wondering what Jai will think and say. Will he be annoyed at me? Will he think I am stupid for having let this happen? Will I be an inconvenience to him? One thing I know is that he won't shout at me; whatever he will say will be in a calm voice. But what will he say?

The luggage is taking ages to be brought back. I ask one of the Emirates guys about it. He says the luggage was already loaded onto the plane, and it's taking time to locate it. I sit back down and wait.

I can't believe this is happening to me. I think to myself, *Why is the Universe doing this to me?*

One positive is that the immigration and the Emirates guys were very nice and polite about the whole situation. At no point did I feel I was being attacked or interrogated. They were calm and professional. This was a genuine mistake, and maybe they realise this. After all, it is only four days over the 180 days.

What the hell am I going to say to my Mum and Dad?

It's taken nearly thirty minutes for my luggage to reach me. The refund has been completed, and one of the Emirates guys escorts me out of the airport building. I phone Jai, saying I'm out, and I push my trolley with my luggage towards the car park where we had parked.

I see him walking towards me, and he says, "What happened?" I try to explain the best I can that I have exceeded the 180-day maximum stay and that I need to obtain an exit permit from the FRRO. He says that I should have booked the ticket and gone last Friday. He calls me a child (again) and adds that I should know these things.

As if I'm not feeling bad enough, these words wound me deeply. I just want the earth to open up and swallow me. I am feeling lost and alone. I just want to go home now. But I am stuck here in Gandabaan with a man I love and who loves me or, so I thought. Now we are just strangers, and I am stuck with him in this strange land.

He shows me his phone, which has the FRRO website and exit permit details. I read some of the small text, but I can't focus. My head is spinning. I feel like I'm not there. My body is not even real.

Jai says that Jalil is nearly finished work and that we'll give him a ride home. He tells me I should sit in the back seat as it wouldn't look good for me to sit up front. I say fine and sit in the back seat with my luggage.

We drive round to meet Jalil, and he gets in the front seat.

On the drive back, they talk in their language. Jalil asks me what happened. I tell him. They continue to talk, with the odd word in English. Jalil says something about a girlfriend. Jai replies, but I don't understand what he says.

I just want to die. What has happened to me and my life?

Why the fuck did I ever come to India? Why the fuck? Chasing a stupid dream which has turned into a nightmare! The love has turned to pain and anguish. My heart is breaking!

The Gandabaan skyline is just a blur of colours. It's raining, and I can't even see out the window. I light a cigarette. Jai asks me something. I can't make out his words.

We drop Jalil off, and he says, "Don't worry. Things will get sorted."

I say, "Thanks. Goodbye."

Jai and I reach the apartment, and the building manager is there. He too asks what happened. Jai explains briefly. The luggage is taken back upstairs. I just sit in the chair. I am in shock. The cats are still there, and they know nothing of what has happened.

Jai comes in and sits down. I don't want to talk. He says I should have booked the ticket sooner, but he tries to console me, saying, "Don't worry. I am here. Everything will be fine."

The rest of the night is a blur. He orders dinner for me. I need a drink, so he gets some vodka.

The next morning, he leaves early to go to the gym, which he has been doing most mornings, with a membership that was bought with part the money I lent him.

I am happy to be left alone for most of the day. I need to gather my thoughts and see what needs to be done. I go onto the FRRO website and read it properly. I need to complete the online application and then make an appointment with the actual centre.

The online application asks for details of where I have been staying, including actual landlord receipts. Fuck! Does this mean I have to go back to Goa to get all this information? But how can I, considering the circumstances I left under? I try to think of who would be able to help me. Maybe Robert would be able to help me.

I look at flights to Goa, but I don't really want to go there. It's too dangerous.

Jai messages later in the day. He says he needs to buy gym shoes for two thousand rupees. I say it's fine; it will go onto his credit. He asks if I have had lunch, which is a standard line.

He asks if I am OK being alone. I say, "Yes, it's fine. I am glad to have some space to myself. I need to clear my head and figure out how I am going to get out of this mess."

I phone my Mum and tell her what's happened. I try to explain the process to her. She is shocked but says it will all work out. I tell her not to worry and say that I have friends who will help me. She asks where I am staying, and I tell her I am back at the apartment.

Strangely I am feeling calmer after speaking to my Mum. She says a prayer while she is on the phone. She makes me feel loved, which is what I needed.

That night Jai stays at his parents'. Again, I am fine with this. The words between us are getting fewer and fewer, although he does message me, asking if I have had dinner and telling me his body is in pain. I tell him I need to sleep as I only had four hours' sleep last night. He says, "Love you. Take care," and we both say good night.

I too said, "Love you", but the words feel empty and meaningless.

The next day Jai comes back to the apartment. He says that he knows someone who can help with the FRRO exit permit process. It's early afternoon. We set off in the car. It's crazy traffic. Jai manoeuvres through some side street to beat the chaos. It doesn't work; we still end up in the gridlock.

He makes a phone call, to someone official by the sounds of it. He explains that his friend who is an NRI (non-resident Indian) has visa issues and has to apply for an exit permit. He says "sir" a lot and speaks in both English and his language. He hangs up and says his contact has told him about a travel agent who is an expert in visa issues.

He receives a text message with contact details of this visa expert. He speaks to the visa expert, advising him of the situation. He says we'll be there in one hour. Jai turns to me, saying we'll go to the place now and speak to the visa expert, whose name is Darshan.

We arrive at the place, which is a travel agency, and are guided to the second floor by the security guard. We wait and are offered drinks. Small cans of Coke are put in front of us.

Darshan comes and greets us, and we explain the situation. He says that immigration and FRRO have become very strict with any visa issues, especially in Gandabaan, where a lot of Africans and Arabs come and deal in drugs.

He explains the process to us in more detail, saying that I will need evidence of where I have been staying for the last six months. I will also need to have some sort of police check done. He asks where I have been staying.

From this point onwards I cannot give too much information or too many details about who provides evidence to support my exit permit application. I want to ensure that the people who helped me are not incriminated. I do not want to identify people and put their security at risk.

However, you could argue that I am doing exactly that with Jai, putting him at risk. But he is vital to the events that have happened from the very beginning, and this whole account has turned into some sort of twisted and bitter love story where he is the yin to my yang. Who is the light and who is the dark is still up for debate. Therefore, he remains central on this stage of my nightmarish adventure.

Darshan advises us that he will complete the online application once we have given him some further information, a rental agreement, copies of receipts, a copy of my passport, and two passport-size photos. He also advises that I book a return flight for the next week so I can show that I am ready to go home, but the date may need to be changed depending on when the interview with the FRRO is scheduled.

Darshan tells us the cost of his service. Jai has a mini meltdown when he finds out how much it will cost. He tries to negotiate a deal. Darshan advises that he has already given a significant discount as I was referred by some eminent contact.

We arrange to meet Darshan tomorrow. This will give us a day to sort out the evidence.

Jai drops me off at the apartment as he has family commitments, a nephew's birthday. He wants to take his grandfather to buy a bicycle for the boy.

On the way back I fancied some cake, so we popped into bakery. I needed something to make me feel better. Chocolate cake is always a girl's best friend when everything else is falling apart.

So, I am left to my own devices in the apartment. I phone up to see if I can get my original flight changed. They say yes, but it will be an additional cost of about £200. I change the flight to Monday, 13 March.

I think to myself that I want to have my palm read and numerology done. I am feeling lost. Maybe the Universe can give me some direction. I Google a palmist in the local area, and after much fannying about with OTPs (one-time passwords), I manage to directly contact a place which is nearby. I have made the appointment for tomorrow afternoon.

I also read more about the exit permit process to get a better understanding of what is needed. This stresses me out.

My Mum phones, and I give her an update. She tells me Dad is completely freaking out. He thinks that something horrible has happened to me. He comes on the phone, and I explain the process as best I can and to try to make him feel better. I remain calm, but inside I'm also freaking out. He asks if I need money. I say, "No, I have a credit card." He says he will send some money just in case I need it, so later I message my bank details to my nephew Benny.

It's evening now, and I've been in the apartment on my own most of the day. It's been fine, but I am getting a little bored. I smoke cigarettes and watch TV.

I get a text from Darshan asking about the rental agreement.

I tell him I will call Jai. Jai is not answering. Darshan messages again, saying that maybe Mr Jai is on his way to Hindavi. I am totally confused. Why would Jai be on his way to Hindavi?

I call Jai again, and again there is no answer. I message him, saying, "Are you going to Hindavi? What the fuck, Jai? What did you tell the guy? Where are you?" I am now freaking out."

After a while he messages back, saying he was sleeping at home. Have I gone mad! I tell him I'm freaking out. Why would the guy say he was going to Hindavi? He replies that he had to go to Hindavi, but then he says he simply said it to makes things go quicker.

I tell him, "For fuck's sake, you could have told me what you said so at least we would have had our story straight." I ask him, "So do you need to go to Hindavi?"

He replies, "I cancelled because I had a lot of stuff running in my head. I saw the tickets for the flight but said 'fuck off' because the cost was too high. I have so many commitments here."

I say, "When were you going to tell me?" He replies by saying he would only have told me if he were going. I ask him why he needed to go. He doesn't reply. I say that just in general he could have told me. I mention that we don't talk any more, saying that it's not right.

My paranoia is at the maximum point now. The only reason he would go to Hindavi would be to see Anisha, his ex-girlfriend. She is the only one he is in contact with in Hindavi. But I don't say anything about this.

My priority is to get out of Gandabaan. I tell Jai to sort out the agreement. He asks if the cats have eaten his pastry. I reply, "No, it's still here."

He later messages and says that he will stay with me in the apartment tonight. In the evening we go out for dinner and to the cinema.

In the morning he leaves early to pick up some of the paperwork required for the exit permit.

I am ready when he arrives. He is also ready and dressed. We sit and talk about what's going to happen, and we confirm what time we need to meet Darshan at the travel agency. We need to leave in about half an hour as the traffic is going to be crazy.

He shows me something on his phone. He is just sitting casually and talking, and WhatsApp is open on his phone. It must have opened by accident. I glance at it and can clearly see a conversation. The last message is "See you next week. I love you, sweets."

I ask him, "What's that message?" My anger is a volcano, and I am fuming. He looks at his phone. I ask him again, "What is that message?" It's to Anisha. I try to grab the phone. He moves it away. I grab his arm. I say, "Show me your fucking phone," and he says no. He has a smirk on his face. I slam my fist down on the armchair. I say, "Show me the fucking phone."

He says, "No. I need to have my privacy. And it's only one message."

I say I want to see the full conversation. He says no. I am fucking fuming and call him a liar. *I want to see the phone!* He refuses. I call him a liar and a cheat. And he says no. He stands up. My blood is boiling. My voice is low, but I stare at him with death in my eyes.

"*I want to see the fucking phone!*" I tell him. "*I want to see the full conversation!*"

He says, "No."

I want to see what they have written and said about me.

He changes the subject and says we need to go. I say, "*Show me the fucking phone!*"

He says, "No!" He says that his friend's mum is sick and that he is providing support. He says that Anisha is married anyway. I don't believe him. If she is having problems, why isn't her husband providing support?

I'm beginning to feel sick with rage. But we have to leave to meet Darshan.

I have never felt so alone and betrayed in all my life. I am stuck here in this foreign country, and the man who is supposed to be my boyfriend and is meant to be supporting me is sending "See you next week. I love you, sweets" messages to another woman.

He was planning to go and see his ex-girlfriend as soon as I left the country. What am I, just a bit of entertainment while I am here? As soon as I leave, I will be replaced by a younger, prettier, more suitable model?

Where has my support been? Yes, he has been here physically, making sure I have food, taking me to the cinema, and helping to sort out this exit permit. But where is my emotional support? Where are my "I Love You, Sweets" messages?

Now that I have set him up financially, he will use my money to go and see his ex. I feel completely used. I feel ashamed and disgusted with myself for having let this happen. Did my love make me completely blind to him? Was I that desperate to be loved or to love?

The message is burnt into my eyes. That's all I can see. I want to smash Jai's face with his phone.

We get into the car and set off. I don't speak. He says he is sorry. I start to cry silently, looking out the window, the scenery now becoming familiar.

He says, "It's nothing. I love you. There isn't anyone else."

I say, "I've just seen the fucking message: 'I love you, sweets.'" He says it's nothing; it's just a friend.

In my book there is a difference between just saying "love you" and saying "I love you." It's the intention of the words, the intention of the word "*I*" in "I love you," which gives it its power. There is a depth of feeling in that "*I*" that cannot be taken away. The "*I*" comes from within. It's not a surface-level "Love you".

And I have just seen it with my eyes, the intention of "*I*".

I tell him, "Just help me get out of this situation and the country." He can do what he wants after I have left.

I just want out of this turmoil, this nightmare.

We arrive at the travel agency, and we go inside to the reception area. Darshan arrives and greets us. Drinks are placed in front of us.

Jai hands him the paperwork that he has gathered, but Darshan is not happy with it, as it doesn't make sense in terms of the timeline, which calls its authenticity into question. Some of the copies are not clear. But we go through the script of what needs to be said at the FRRO interview.

This I can do. We rehearse the story, Darshan acting as an official. In my best Queen's English, I answer the questions from the script.

Following our meeting, and after I've paid the remainder of the outstanding amount, Jai and I head back to the apartment. Jai is acting all nonchalant as if nothing has happened. I say very little.

He needs to do some chores, so he drops me off at the apartment. I am still deeply hurt and angry. I don't want to be around him.

When I get upstairs, I message him, saying, "I'm not finished with this, and I am seriously fucked off!"

He replies, saying, "Please, Sabbie Boss, stop it. I have a hell of a lot of tension. Please don't start. I am only happy with you, and I don't want you to be a pain also." I tell him we will talk later.

It's now just after lunchtime, and I am left to stew in the apartment. My head is already smashed from all the exit permit stuff, and now I have to deal with the "I love you, sweets" message, which I cannot remove from my vision when I close my eyes.

My mind is spinning, and I think about everything that has happened and the money that I have lent to Jai. Has it all been a lie? Have I been manipulated and deceived for the last six months, since stepping foot in Goa?

I think about the fifty thousand rupees that I transferred to Jai's uncle's account. What has he done with that money?

Has he used it to spend on his ex-girlfriend? All the times when I couldn't get a hold of him, was he with her? My mind is spinning!

I message Jai's uncle and ask him if he still has the fifty thousand rupees. He replies, saying, "No. Jai took it the next day from my account." I say OK. He asks if there is a problem.

I say, "No. I am just doing my accounts." I don't want him to know that I am in a meltdown over everything.

It's nearly time for me to go to the palmist/astrologer. I pull myself together and get ready. Then I go downstairs and order an Ola (the India equivalent of an Uber).

I had mentioned to Jai that I was going, but I didn't want him to go with me. I am glad he is not here. He had snorted and asked why I was simply wasting money, but it is my money. Plus, they had quoted me only RS800, which in the grand scheme of things is not a lot. I need some sort of sign. Inside I am lost and directionless. Maybe the universe/God can give me some answers.

I arrive at the astrologer's place, and it's near to where Jai's family live. I had told him where it was. I am greeted by a couple in their late twenties or early thirties. They ask me to sit and to complete a form with my date of birth. They need to know what time I was born, so I call my mum. I can't tell her it's for an astrologer—she will think I have gone mad, which I feel like I have—so I tell her it's for the visa people, who want to know every detail. Mum tells me I was born around 1 a.m., which I didn't know. I had never asked her before.

I ask the woman how much this is going to cost me. She says it will cost RS800 for the consultation. I say OK.

After a short while, the man takes me next door, and I wait there for the astrologer/numerologist. I look around. There are varies books on shelves. There are posters and charts on the walls, and picture of various Hindu gods with the seven chakras and energy flowing from their bodies. It's a small room with a desk. I pick up a leaflet showing the astrologer's credentials and accolades. It all seems very legitimate and authentic.

A few minutes later a tall old man with grey hair appears. He greets me in perfect English, and we both ask, "Are you well?" He sits and looks at the form I had filled in and some sort of printout.

He starts by asking what it is I want to know. I tell him I want to know what is going to happen in my life. He asks, What specifically?" I say I want to know about love and marriage initially, and also about finances, work, health, and finally family.

He asks to look at my right hand and murmurs something. He says that in relation to work, I have not fulfilled my potential, and that if I put my mind to something, I will have great success. He explains the lines on my hand, showing me that there are two lines, but saying they are broken. I cannot remember exactly which lines he was referring too.

I ask about love and marriage. He looks again at my hand and says that there are some blockages (which I have been told in the past), but he can see that there will be someone, or there is someone, who will come into my life and will be the perfect person for me. This individual will be kind and intelligent and will have a good heart.

I know what you're thinking, that this all seems like a cliché, but at this moment, I just need a glimmer of hope, some kind of word that there is a future for me with someone else. At this time, my heart is breaking. I need to know that my search for love is not in vain.

We talk more about family and health and whether he sees children in my future. I tell him my age. Again, he looks at my hand and says, "Why not? We live in a modern world now."

I ask him about my personality, saying that I am generally a chill person, but when I lose my temper, I really blow my fuse. He laughs and says he is the same, telling me not to change. I find this reassuring.

He goes on to say that the planets and stars have a direct

link to who we are as people, and that the moment we are born the planets begin influencing us.

The conversation turns metaphysical, and I explain to him my beliefs and views on the law of attraction, energy, and the universe. I tell him that I believe in God, but not in the sense of a white-bearded man. I see God as an energy that flows in and around us. I believe in that energy, and I also believe that we are God. He agrees with me.

He shows me the chart that was printed out, which shows which planets are in the sphere of my influence. He says that Jupiter is a strong influence which impacts my head more than my heart. He explains that this is potentially why I have had bad luck in the past with relationships.

He explains some other aspects but doesn't go into great detail. But now I am feeling despondent in that I am not really getting a lot out of the meeting. I don't know why, but this astrologer is not answering my innermost questions.

He then goes on to say that they have ways to unblock these blockages with energy stones and affirmations. I say OK. He asks which religion I would prefer the affirmations to be in, Christian or traditional Hindu. I say I will take both.

His son, the young man from earlier, is now in the room too. The conversation has come to an end. We say our thank yous and goodbyes, and I am led back in the previous room.

To be perfectly honest, I don't feel as if I have received any wisdom or guidance, and I am just as lost as before.

While I am in the reception room, the son shows me some small stones that will work with the affirmations. He asks if I want to take them. I say OK. At this point I am desperate. I want anything that will take the pain away. The woman totals up the cost, and it comes to RS14,000 (approximately £150). I am shocked at the amount and ask her what this covers? She tells me it's for the consultation.

My head is up my arse at this point, and I try to make the payment on my credit card, but it doesn't work for some reason.

Jai has my Indian debit card. I check my phone and see there are messages from him asking where I am. I tell him I'm at the astrologer's place and tell him to come there with my card.

He eventually turns up, and I get my card off him. We don't say much to each other. I still can't look at him. He gives me the card, and I pay. I ask the son where I can get a taxi. He says he will call an Ola for me. But after twenty minutes nothing arrives.

It's now starting to rain heavily. The son rings for another Ola, and that one doesn't turn up either. It's now getting dark outside. He says he will try to get an auto rickshaw. He spots a friend of his with a rickshaw, and he flags him down. He asks how much it is going to be, and the rickshaw operator says RS600.

I say that is too much and that I only paid RS150 to get here. But the rickshaw guy doesn't budge. The whole household is now standing outside with me, trying to negotiate the price. But still he doesn't budge. Reluctantly I get into the back of the rickshaw as it's now dark and raining.

It takes nearly an hour to get to the apartment. The traffic is crazy as it's rush hour, and the rain is coming down hard now. I try to light cigarettes in the back of the rickshaw, but the matches keep blowing out in the draft.

I feel completely emotionally exhausted. And every time I close my eyes, I see "See you next week. I love you, sweets." I feel sick thinking about it.

When I arrive back at the apartment, I message Jai to tell him I'm back. He replies and asks if I am hungry. I say yes, and he orders dhal and roti to be delivered to me at the apartment. Jai is still out.

I want to get this situation with him sorted. I message him again, asking, "Where are you? Are you coming back or what?" He messages back, saying he's coming. He's with Jalil. It's the last twenty minutes, he swears.

Eventually, at 11 p.m., he arrives. I let him in, and we sit on the armchairs. He is looking sheepish. I turn and face him and ask, “So what is happening? Why did you want to go to Hindavi, and why did you send that text if it didn’t mean anything? And why wouldn’t you let me see the full conversation?”

He says, “I’m tired. Leave it.”

I say, “No. I want to hear what you have to say.”

He says, “She is just a friend. It was nothing. Her mum is sick, and I was just being a support for her.”

I can see him starting to get agitated. A frown appears on his face.

I ask again about Hindavi: “Why would you go there?”

“I was just checking.”

I say, “So as soon as I left, you go to go to Hindavi?”

He says, “No. No.”

My voice is not raised, but I am being firm. I ask him what he has done with the fifty thousand rupees that I transferred into his uncle’s account. He says it’s still there; he hasn’t touched it. He asks if I spoke to his uncle. I said, “Yes, I did.”

He is now angry, asking why I have contacted his uncle and why I have gotten his family involved. The argument is between me and him. He gets angrier and says that he is just starting to rebuild his life here and that if things get fucked up, he will have to move again.

He says that I might as well contact Madhav and Harry and tell them that I am here. “But it’s OK. I will leave. There are twenty-seven other states in India where I can move to.”

He asks, “What is my uncle to you that you have to get him involved?”

He is fuming now. I say, “If you had shown me the message conversation, things would not have gotten this far.”

He says that he should never have brought me to Gandabaan, that he should have left me. He regrets everything. He is now crying, and his pained expression gets to me. He starts to hit his own head with his fist. He says that it’s his fault that he brought me here.

I try to stop him from hitting himself, but he moves his arm away. He is so angry. He is hitting himself. I say, "Stop hitting yourself."

He says he brought me here because he likes me. I say, "Like?"

He retracts that and says, "Love." He adds, "How can we go on when there is no trust?"

I say, "Exactly. There is no point in continuing the relationship. We cannot trust each other." I say that it's probably for the best that when I leave India we not speak to each other.

It's now 1 a.m., and we're both emotionally exhausted. For the first time since we've been in the apartment, he stays in the other bedroom. He moves all the clothes out of the way and pulls the covers over his body. I can still hear him weeping from my bedroom.

I go in to try to console him. He keeps saying, "Go away, Sabbie Boss." He is still upset and hits the headboard of the bed. It's not like I fear for myself or that he will hit me. I know he would never do that. But even though I console him, all I can see is "See you next week. I love you, sweets" when I close my eyes.

I go back to my bedroom. But sleep is not coming. Multiple times I get up and smoke a cigarette in the living area.

I must get only one hour of sleep that night. My head is splitting. Jai gets up. I hear him. He says, "Lock the door behind me," when he leaves around 7.30 a.m. I don't say anything as he leaves to go to the gym.

We have an appointment with Darshan at 12 noon that day. Darshan texts me to remind me and to say that an appointment with FRRO will be set for either Monday or Tuesday next week. I screenshot the text and send it to Jai. He replies, saying he will be back by 11 a.m.

I lie down for a little while and decide to take a painkiller to help with my head. The painkillers take effect quickly. I shower and get ready for when Jai arrives.

He arrives just before 11, and I let him in without saying

anything. He acknowledges, "You're ready," then asks if there is any tea. I say no, but I make us both a milky chai tea. He seems a lot calmer now. We both drink our tea while watching TV.

I'm perturbed at how cheery he seems and that the emotions of last night do not have seem to have affected him. I ask him why he is like this and if he is still upset. He says, "Last night was last night. I was angry last night."

We leave to meet Darshan. In the car he asks me what the astrologer said. I don't tell him all of what he said, but I reply, "He said I am not fulfilling my potential." I tell Jai that I asked about children and that the astrologer replied, "Why not!"

He tries to make small talk, but I am not listening. I am still hurt, and I don't say much. I want to stay focused on the meeting with Darshan.

We arrive at the travel agency and again sit at the reception table. Darshan joins us and says that all the online paperwork has been submitted and an appointment has been made for Monday, 13 March. He talks us through the process and tells us about the layout of the office, including where to register and where to wait.

We run through my script again, which I am more than comfortable with. I feel more like myself as we run through the script. I feel like it's something I can control. I have lost control of everything else that is happening around me.

I make the final payment to Darshan, and then Jai and I leave and head back to the apartment.

On the way back, we stop to get some lunch to take back with us. While I am waiting in the car, my mum phones. She has been calling every day since the original date I was meant to leave. She says Dad has transferred money into my account. At this point Jai returns to the car. He is talking on his phone, but he hangs up when he sees me on the phone. I speak my broken Punjabi to Mum, letting her know everything is OK and that an appointment has been set for Monday. I tell her I will check my account when I get back. I hang up.

Jai says that was his uncle on the phone and that he hung up because he might have heard me talking. I say OK.

We arrive back at the apartment and sit down to each lunch. I'm starving as I hadn't eaten much in the last couple of days.

He then asks, "How much did the astronomer cost?" I tell him fourteen thousand rupees. He is shocked! He shouts, asking why I am simply wasting money. I tell him about the stones, adding that when I originally called, the woman said it was only going to be eight hundred rupees. He says, "Let me see the stones," and I show him. They are like little pebbles.

He looks at the stones and shouts, "These are worth nothing. Those people have conned you out of your money. They are cheap people who will say anything to NRIs to get money out of them. Give me the number of that place." I give him the number. He again asks me what they said to me.

I said they had originally quoted RS800, but when I came out they offered the stones, and the bill came to RS14,000. He calls them "fucking cheap cheating people".

Dialling the number, he is still fuming. I watch as if I'm having an out-of-body experience.

He speaks to the young man I had met with, saying that I did not realise how much it would cost and that I don't want the stones any more. He says that I want my money back. The conversation started politely in English, and then they started speaking in the local dialect. Jai says, "I know people also, and I know where you are. I live in the same area."

It sounds like he is threatening the astrologer. Jai says he will go to the shop to get my money back, adding that he will be there in an hour.

In one way, I feel like my life is not my own here. But on the other hand, I feel safe that there is someone who does have my back, even after everything that has happened over the last couple of days. Everything is a paradox.

Jai gets off the phone and says that he will go to get my

money. But then he says sweetly that if I want to keep the stones, I can.

I just say I don't want them anymore; they have too much negativity associated with them now. He says that I should have spoken to him about this before paying the astrologers. I say I wanted to do this, but I didn't know how much it would cost, as they only told me RS800.

I feel like the last couple of days and this drama has taken the soul right out of me. I feel like my mind is not my own. I feel completely out of control. I think about how I was at home, how competent I used to be, knowing my path and following it with determination and focus.

Here I have nothing. Everything has been taken away from me, including my finances, which are being drained. All this is down to one person, who is supposed to be the man I love and who is meant to love me. Well, maybe two people. The other is me, for letting this happen to myself.

If this is love, I want to die without it.

I am in an alien world surrounded by leeches, with no one I can trust, no one I can talk to. How can I explain any of this to my family and friends back home, who think I am so brave to have come on this adventure, which has turned into a grotesque existence in a world where I have become a shell of my former self?

Jai leaves, and I lie down on the bed and try to sleep. The cats come and join me, snuggling up to me. Lollipop comes and lies on my stomach as she often does. Brutus lies against my legs. The ache I feel for them is the only real thing I feel. How am I going to leave them?

Jai has said on occasion that I love the cats more than I love him. And he is probably right considering the last couple of weeks. The cats have been the most authentic and honest creatures that have been with me since I've come to India. I know that when they come to snuggle up to me, it's real. There are no ulterior motives. They only want to be with their Mama, who has fed them and looked after them since they were tiny. I know that when they show emotion towards me, it's genuine and not a disgusting trick to take me for my mind, soul, and money.

I try to sleep but end up just resting my eyes. I may have drifted off slightly, but I am awakened by my phone ringing. I look at it. It's Jai's uncle, who is calling me via Facebook. I answer the call out of curiosity. What does he have to say to me?

After the general greeting of "How are you?" etc., he asks about the stones I bought off the astronomer. I relay the story to him, and he says that I should have consulted Jai before I made the payment, adding that these people take advantage of NRIs. Maybe they do, and being in a vulnerable mindset, I was one of them.

He then asks about the visa situation. I tell him the circumstances of how it happened, adding that it's now under control and that I have an appointment on Monday to get the exit permit.

He seems like a reasonable man. But who are these people really? How can I trust any of them? Jai, the man I loved, is meant to be a reasonable man, or so I thought.

We finish the call, but I cannot sleep. I get up, make myself a tea, and sit and smoke a cigarette

I open my laptop and look for places the cats can stay, i.e. a cattery. I Google catteries in Gandabaan. I find a few and read the reviews. I find one which looks OK. The guy running it sounds like he passionate about animals. I message him on Facebook. He replies and gives me his number, so I contact him on WhatsApp. We arrange for me to go to the place tomorrow and check it out.

Jai messages, asking what I'm doing. He asks if he should check the times for the movies tonight. I tell him I was sleeping until his uncle phoned, and I say, "Yes, check the times." Surprised that his uncle has phoned me, he asks, "How did he phone? Had you swapped numbers with him?" I say, "No, he phoned via Facebook."

He asks what he said, and I tell him he was calling about the stones and asking how much I paid for them, adding that I should have spoken to Jai. I also say that he asked about the visa stuff. I say it's another issue blown out of proportion.

Jai replies, "Oh God, another? What now?"

I tell him, "It's fine. Nothing new has happened."

That evening we go to the cinema to see the new King Kong film. I had wanted to see it previously as the trailers looked good. I should have seen it back home in the UK, but now Jai says that I was meant to see the film here.

We have a chilled evening. I still feel closed off, but I can tell that Jai is trying. I am stressed about the exit permit process and the interview, as well has the residue of all the other events of the last couple of days.

I am still having flashbacks to "See you next week. I love you, sweets." Jai still hasn't shown me his phone. But what can I do?

That night we sleep in the same bed. He is being all nicey-nicey. He cuddles up to me and says, "What happened? What else, Sabbie Boss?" I tell him my boyfriend has been a dick. He laughs. I browse my phone for a little while, and we both watch a video of something or other. His phone is plugged in to charge next to my pillow, so I put mine next to it.

The cats come and crawl under the covers in between our legs. Lollipop appears in between us. Jai takes her in his arms and says, "Look at the camera." I take my phone and snap some pictures of Jai and Lollipop next to me in bed.

For a short moment, it feels like when we were in Goa, in my little house, snuggled up in bed with the cats jumping on us, the room filled with our laughter and love. But it doesn't feel that way here. It's just a fleeting moment of a memory.

In the morning Jai leaves to go to the gym, and I lounge around for the morning as per usual. I have arranged to go see the cattery, which is on the other side of Gandabaan city. I'll take an Ola cab so I don't have to rely on Jai. I'm getting more comfortable travelling on my own now as I'm more familiar with the city.

After getting ready, I leave to go to the cattery around mid-afternoon. The Ola cab arrives, and it's a driver who has picked us up before. As I get in, he says hi and starts to chat, saying that he took us somewhere once. He's pleasant enough. We make small talk about where I'm from. The usual observation is made, that I have an Indian face. I relay the standard response: my family are from Punjab, yada yada. Ha ha!

En-route Jai messages, asking what I'm doing. I tell him I'm on my way to the cattery. He asks if I rang to confirm and to as if I got a micro cab (instead of one of the bigger cabs, which cost more). I tell him yes and yes. He says he needs to take good care of me. I ask why. He says because this is not the UK, and if he were in UK, I would take care of him. I reply, "Of course." I say, "It's a jungle, and there are too many predators."

He replies, "In that there's one man who can get freedom, the king is back," which I think was a strange thing to say, and don't quite understand his meaning.

I reply, "My king?"

He says, "Yup!"

But things have gone too far now. If I am honest, I am now just playing the game of "being in love". I still don't want to give up those forgotten flames. I want to hang on to them for as long as possible, even if I am burnt to a cinder.

I tell him I need to print my ticket for my flight. I forward my email to his email address, and he says he will print it out for me.

It's now past midday, and it's hot outside. The cab is approaching my destination. There is some roadworks happening on the narrow street. I get out as near as possible to the cattery. On my map app I locate the place, but there are no signs. I wander up and down the same small backstreet a few times.

There are kids playing outside and old men and women standing on corners. People are staring at me because I look nothing like anyone else there. Firstly, I'm wandering around looking at my phone, and secondly, I am dressed in Western clothes, in my knee length jeans and a T-shirt. The area is very native but seems clean and homely enough—well, as much as it can be for an Indian suburb.

I have called the guy at the cattery, but he has not answered. There's no point in me leaving now, I am so close to it.

I stop outside a building, which the map app states is the place. But again, there is no signage. There is a young woman in a burka getting off her scooter. I ask her where the cattery is. She replies in very good English, "It's on the third floor." I ask if it's OK to go up. She says yes.

I walk up the narrow flight of stairs. I know it's the right place because the smell of the cats reaches the stairwell. I walk onto a dodgy-looking balcony and loudly say, "Hello?" Through the outer window wire I can see an enclosure with about five cats all lounging around. They are of varying sizes and colours, but they are all Persian types. They all have dirty, manky eyes. And the smell emanating from the enclosure is horrible.

I shout "hello" again, and at the far end of the building is a man in his early thirties, handsome but looking as if he needs a good wash. He acknowledges me and says hi, and motions for me to come in through a side door in the stairwell.

We say hi again, and I say I was calling him. He replies that he was dealing with the cats. I look around and see that there are more Persian-type cats in the second room, which is beyond the one I saw through the balcony.

He starts to tell me about himself, mentioning that he trained in engineering at the degree level, but his real passion is cats. He says he set up this place a couple of years ago. I ask him about the rates, and he tells me it will be about fifteen thousand rupees for both cats for a month. I'm not too concerned about the money. I just want the cats to be well looked after.

I have a good look around, and all the cats seem healthy enough, but it's very cramped. There must be at least fifteen cats, some in cages and others just roaming around in the bigger playroom. I'm not impressed, and I cannot see my Brutus and Lollipop staying here.

At one point one of the larger Persians starts a scrap with one of the others. There is almighty screeching and flying of fur. The guy hands me the kitten he was holding and jumps in between the two fighting cats. He grabs the larger one and throws it into the enclosure with the balcony.

He turns his attention back to me and says that sometimes the dominant male likes to make his presence be felt. But it doesn't happen often. I'm not convinced, as there is literal fur from the weaker cat on the floor. This makes up my mind for certain. My fur babies are not coming here.

Maybe my standards are high as even the lower-end catteries at home adhere to a better standard than this. I cannot risk my kitties getting into scraps with other cats and potentially getting injured. And it's not as if I can come quickly to check on them.

I am running out of time to find somewhere for my cats to stay. Jai will need to take them with him. But I don't want to leave things down to Jai. Once he starts work, he will not have time to take care of them. Previously I had wanted him to take them, but since I've come to Gandabaan, doubts have taken root in my mind, not just about our relationship but also about whether he is responsible enough to take care of them. But what option do I have now?

I say bye to the guy, adding that I will be in touch, with no intention of following through.

On the way out, I check my phone. There is a message from Jai again, asking if I have reached my destination. I tell him I have been to the place already and that I didn't like it; it was smelly and there were too many cats. I'm not leaving my cats there. He says to go to Forum Mall and visit a salon. I had seen the mall on the drive in. It is a ten-minute walk from the cattery, so I decide to walk there instead of getting an Ola cab.

I feel liberated that I am on my own. I am free to do what I want. I enter the mall, and it's on a par with any at home. It has all the modern shops, including MAC Cosmetics, Vero Moda, and a department store.

I go into the department store first and have a good look around at the clothes. I feel free just to browse around without Jai's judgemental gaze. I buy a nice blue blouse with a Buddha pattern. I find the Elle designer store. I spot a nice black shirt dress. I try it on, and it looks perfect. I can wear this to the FRRO interview tomorrow.

I spot a salon and go in and ask if they do manicures. The young guy behind the counter says yes and asks me to take a seat. He shouts something in the local language, and an even younger, short, skinny, camp-looking guy comes out and greets me. He takes me around the back of the salon and sits me down in a booth.

I choose a colour, black, and sit and get pampered for the next forty minutes. Again, the conversation goes like this: "Where you from?"

"England."

The manicurist gives me a confused look. "But you look Indian."

"Yes. My family is from Punjab," etc.

While I get my nails done, I watch Indian dance videos on the TV in the front. I'm feeling relaxed and even a bit happy. I feel like myself! My nails are finished. I like them a lot. For the next ten minutes I wait for them to dry.

Jai messages and asks if I will get him some trackpants from Jack & Jones because his other ones have falafel grease on them. I say, "I'll see if they have any."

I tell him I have had my nails done, and he says, "Show me." I send him a pic. He says, "Nice."

I pay and leave the salon. I go to Jack & Jones to see if they have any trackpants. They do have some, but I decide I'm not going to get them. Jai is getting too used to asking for stuff. Plus, I don't want to get them, and he doesn't like them anyway.

My phone battery is low. I book an Ola cab and go wait outside. It arrives within a few minutes. I'm really loving this Ola app. I could see the car as it approached the pickup point. I get in the cab, and we head off into the Gandabaan traffic. It's now early evening, and it's getting dark.

Jai is in his area and says he will see me back at the apartment later. He is with Jalil, having dinner. I'm glad I have the apartment to myself again.

The next morning is the appointment with the FRRO. We need to get up early, so I turn the light off. Sleep comes easily.

I am awakened by a phone buzzing. I check and see it's Jai's phone. There is a WhatsApp notification from Anisha. The phone buzzes again. She is messaging him at six o'clock in the morning.

I nudge him awake and say that Anisha is messaging him. Suddenly he is wide awake.

I just say that he is a fucking piss-taker, that I have had enough, and that he can do what he wants. He says, "No, it's not like that." He doesn't know why this female is messaging him at this time.

I say, "Fuck you," and sit up to get out of bed.

He says, "Come back. I will show you the messages." He takes his phone but doesn't not unlock it. He swipes to show the full message on the notification screen.

Her message reads, "I guess you're still asleep. I will call you after work." The following messages say something about her mum's medication. At that point I lose interest.

I say that Jai thinks he's so clever just showing me the notifications and not the full conversation. He is full of shit!

I get up, go into the kitchen, and put the kettle on to make tea. Jai is shouting "Sabbie Boss" from the bed. I ignore him. While the kettle boils, I put food out for the cats and clean their litter tray.

He's saying something from the bed. I ignore his pleading. He gets out of bed and stands in the doorway. He says that he will call Anisha so I can speak to her, adding that she knows about me because Madhav had called her and told her about me when Jai had left Goa, leaving his phone behind.

I say, "OK, I will speak to her."

I sit and have my tea and toast. He goes into the bathroom.

The morning passes without much being said. I want to focus on the exit permit interview at the FRRO. We are due to be there by 9 a.m. My stress levels are through the roof.

We leave the apartment and head to the appointment. On the way there, Jai says that my leaving gift is to break up with him. I just look at him and don't say anything. He says that he knows I am hurting, and that hurts him because he loves me. At that point I look away. I don't want him to see the tears welling in my eyes. I just say, "We'll see what happens when I got home, once I'm settled."

He knows exactly what to say to get to me. It kills me that he has that type of power over me. Am I that desperate for his love, whether his love is real or just an act?

We reach the building by 8.30. We will meet Darshan here before I go to the fifth floor, where the FRRO offices are located.

We sit in a big restaurant on the ground floor of the same building. Darshan joins us about ten minutes later. Jai and Darshan order breakfast, South Indian dosa. I only manage to each a bit of it, it's so greasy. I just have coffee and then go outside for a cigarette. Jai and Darshan continue talking in English and the local dialect.

I come back inside and take all the paperwork from Darshan. He asks if I am OK with the script. I say yes. They both walk me round to the main entrance of the building. I say goodbye to them booth and wait for the lift to take me to the fifth floor. They both take a seat in the foyer.

The entrance to the FRRO is straight ahead of me as I get out of the lift. There is a security checkpoint with a metal detector, and two uniformed security guards at the entrance. As I approach, one of the guards stands up. I show him my passport, and he waves me in.

There are ten to fifteen people of varying nationalities sitting on the seats round the perimeter of the room. The check-in reception is empty. I sit down next to a white man to the right of reception. This seems to the queue before approaching reception.

Fifteen minutes later a young Indian woman sits down at the reception desk. She gets herself settled, turning on her computer and a couple of other things, and calls the first person over to the reception desk.

She looks at each person's documents, asks them to stand in front of a small digital camera, and then hands them a ticket with the section letter and number of where the applicant is to sit.

The queue moves along swiftly, and within fifteen minutes I am at the front of the seated queue. The woman calls, "Next, please." I approach the desk, hand her my paperwork, get my picture taken, and am given the ticket for where I am to sit, to the right of the reception area.

The room has five rows of seating with about fifty seats in each row. The room can probably accommodate two hundred people, but at the moment it's quiet. There must be only about twenty to thirty people who have arrived early to beat the rush, I am assuming.

I sit and wait for my number to be called out. I message Darshan and Jai to give them an update on my progress so far.

Now I don't want to go into every little detail of this process, as it would bore the shit out of you. It was boring enough for me. The process took most of the day, and I had to relay my story to at least three lots of officials.

The last lot of officials look quite senior. I have to go into a little side office partitioned off from the main area.

They ask why I have been in India for so long, whom I have been staying with, and which places I have visited. Then they ask about my family background, my work back home, my education, and how many times I have been to India. One of the senior official checks my passport.

I tell them about when I first came to travel in India and how I'd done volunteer work in Goa and fell in love with the place. The same official who checked my passport asked if I travelled alone. I reply, "Yes. I am fully independent woman." He raises a little smile at this remark.

They then go off on a tangent and started asking about Brexit and the British economy. I reply that I cannot comment on the outcome of Brexit in terms of the economy as I'm not an economist, but I say that on a social level I think there will be long-lasting effects and that a division has been created between the population who voted either to remain with the European Union or leave it. I say that I feel that the UK would be stronger within a more unified Europe.

I ask, "What happens now?" They say that I can go home. I am overjoyed and thank them both. I tell them that my dad has been freaking out because of all of this.

I thank them again. I know that I have charmed them with my intelligence and personality.

I suppose the aim of this was to ensure that I wasn't some sort of drug trafficker, and I think it helped that I am of Indian origin. But I will never really know. I go and sit back out in the main area.

It's now getting busy, and the noise levels are getting higher. I sit down and message Darshan and Jai. Now I just have to wait for my actual exit permit. Jai messages back saying that the police checks are being done and that calls have been made to the various people who helped me out.

He asks if anyone has said anything. I say, "No. No one has

mentioned anything about the police checks, but the interview with the senior officers went well. They said I can go home."

The time is now nearly 2 p.m., and it looks like all the staff are downing tools for lunch. I approach one of them and ask when the exit permit will be ready. He says that the system is down now and that everyone is going for lunch for an hour. I ask if I can go and come back later. He says, "Yes, that's fine."

I call Jai and tell him I am coming downstairs. He says to wait outside the restaurant. He will come pick me up as they had left to do something else.

Jai pulls up after a few minutes of me waiting. I get in the front passenger seat. Darshan is in the back seat. He says he needs to go back to his office. We drop him off. Jai and I go to lunch at a place nearby. I am still very stressed, and I don't have an appetite. I tell Jai I'm not hungry. He says I must eat, so I order stuffed paratha. Jai orders his usual chicken biryani.

While we wait for our food, he goes outside for a cigarette and makes a phone call. I watch him and try to determine from his face and body language whom he could be talking to. I can't make out anything.

He comes back, and I glare at him but don't say anything. The food arrives, and I eat half the paratha. Jai only eats half his food too. We don't say much to each other, but he tells me to relax things, saying that will be fine. I'm close to tears again.

It's weird; when I was in the FRRO, I was fine waiting on my own, but being with him brings all emotions to the surface, along with the stress, the betrayals, and the hurt. I just want to go home now.

We don't stay long as I want to get back within the hour in case I am wanted for further information, but from all counts everything is now sorted. It's just a case of waiting for the exit permit to be issued.

We get back in the car, and I light a cigarette while he manoeuvres the car into traffic.

I get back to the FRRO and sit in the designated area. The

staff at the desks have returned from lunch. I approach the counter where I had first been interviewed with my paperwork and ask the guy if there are any updates. He says, Not yet, madam. Please take a seat."

I am now getting impatient. Another hour passes. I browse on my phone, but it's the same cached data from this morning. I go up to the desk again and ask the same guy for any updates. He asks my name, and I tell him. He starts to go through some papers on his desk. He says, "Yes, madam. Please sign here."

I can't believe it. I ask, "Is this my exit permit?"

He replies, "Yes, madam." OMG, I am so happy!

I sign two copies where he has indicated, and he gives me one of the copies. I beam at him and say, "Thank you so much." I ask if I can go, and he says yes and smiles meekly back. I am overjoyed. I virtually run out of the building and call Jai.

I say, "I have got my exit permit." He says OK, and again picks me up outside the restaurant.

I get in the car, and I shriek with joy. I say, "I can't believe it ... I got it!" He is smiling and saying that I am now leaving. I am so happy! We head back to the apartment. I say to him, "I feel like partying." He laughs and says we can have a party.

I shriek again and let out a long breath. It really feels like a weight has been lifted and that the dark cloud that has been hanging over my head has turned into bright sunshine.

On the way home, I say I want to get something for the friend who helped me with all the documents. Jai says he likes sunglasses. We decide to go shopping for sunglasses at the mall near Captains Road, but they are expensive. Jai says we'll go to a shop near his area.

Jai also says that his leaving present is that I'm breaking up with him. I look at him and let out a little laugh. I say, "We'll see what happens when I get back home and get settled." He also says that I am buying a present for his friend and nothing for him. I say, "Excuse me? Who is funding you here?" I mention all the credit I have given him. He laughs.

Jai calls his friend, and we meet him outside one of the shops. He asks how everything went. I tell him I have been issued the exit permit, so I will be leaving India on Wednesday. He says, "That's really great news."

I say, "Thank you for everything that you have done."

He says, "No need for thanks."

I had met him at the impromptu BBQ we had on the apartment rooftop terrace. He is a sweet guy.

We go into the shop, and the three of us try on sunglasses. None of them seems to suit Jai as he has a big face; all the glasses he tries on are too small for him. His friend selects a pair, and I pay as a thank you.

As we leave the shop, Jai says he needs to go back with his friend, asking if I am OK with taking a rickshaw back to the apartment. I say, "Yes, that's fine." He flags one down for me and tells the driver where he needs to go. I head back on my own.

As I'm being driven back in the rickshaw, I really look at the scenery and take everything in. I feel like my heart is going to explode with joy and the relief of knowing that I will be going home in a couple of days. I am still sad about leaving the cats, but I am hoping for the best. And Jai will start the process of getting them home to me in the UK.

But at the moment I am enjoying the ride back to the apartment.

Once back at the apartment, I call my mum to let her know that I have received the exit permit and that I will be home by Thursday. She is just as relieved as I am. She goes on to say that Dad made himself sick with worry, and that he has not eaten much since I told them that I couldn't leave. She says she will phone him and tell him the good news. She thanks God and says a little prayer.

I too thank God with a little prayer.

As I am on my own, I decide to get rid of more of my clothes so as not to get charged extra again for excess luggage at the airport check-in. I make a pile of clothes that I will ask Jai to keep for me for when I return (if ever I do), and I make another pile of clothes that can be given to a charity. I decide to give my black hoodie to the room boy. He doesn't say anything but gives me a wry little smile. I'm not sure if this is a thanks.

I now have a much lighter suitcase, and the black holdall bag contains half the clothes as before.

Finally, I can relax and give a sigh of relief. I go lie down on the bed, and the cats join me for a cuddle.

It's late evening, and Jai messages to ask if I want vodka. I reply and say yes.

A couple of hours later he says he will be another hour. It's now around ten o'clock in the evening. He asks if I am sleeping. I tell him, "Nearly."

The next minute he messages, "Open the door." Ha ha. It's one of the little tricks he played on me when we were in Goa, messaging me from outside the door, saying he is delayed. I open the door and chuckle at him, saying I had forgotten his little trick.

We sit and have a couple of drinks. He asks if my packing is finished. I reply, "Mostly. I've kept out just the bits I will be using the next couple of days." I ask him to make sure he will be OK with looking after the cats until they are ready to be sent to me.

He replies, "Yes, don't worry."

The atmosphere is not as tense as previous nights. We both sit and watch TV with little conversation. It's now getting late, approaching midnight, and I decide I'm going to bed. He stays up a little longer, browsing on his phone. I leave him to it as I've reached the point of not caring what he's doing.

There is still residue lingering from the big fight night, for me anyway. For him, he seems to be acting as if nothing has happened. Maybe he doesn't care, or perhaps his emotions do not affect him. I personally believe that he knows that if things are on bad terms, I will no longer be his "cash cow" and he won't have his financial support.

I mean, he was really upset, crying and hitting himself at the thought that I may have betrayed him. Was it all an act to garner sympathy? If so, then wow, that guy needs an Oscar.

But for me, my emotions stay with me, and everything is still very much on the surface, writhing not only under the thin layer of my skin but also deep within the core of my being. I feel as if my whole body has been infected by some parasite of deceit, betrayal, and confusion, all mixed in with a deep senseless love I cannot understand.

What have I done in my former lives to deserve this?!

The next morning, Jai gets up early to go to the gym. Before he leaves, I say I feel like having pancakes for breakfast. He says OK, he will get some after the gym. After he has gone, I look at places where he can pick up pancakes and send links to his WhatsApp.

In the meantime, I drink coffee and smoke cigarettes. The cats are sleepy today and are still lying on the bed. I look at the poor little innocent creatures who have saved me from myself. What will happen to them? Will they be in gentle caring hands while they are here? I don't know.

After a couple of hours, Jai returns with pancakes with various syrups and chocolate sauce. He got himself a sandwich. The pancakes smell and look delicious. I unwrap them and pour on some of the syrup. I'm thinking, *Fuck the diet and my weight. I will get healthy when I get home.*

I take the first bite, and my taste buds are overwhelmed by the sweetness. The pancakes are way too sweet for me. I take a couple more bites, but I cannot eat them. I tell Jai they are too sweet. He tries a mouthful, and says they seem OK to him.

I'm just not used to this over-sugary syrup. I try a bit without the syrup, but it's too late. I'm going to gag. So, I leave them. That was a waste of money.

I just stick with my coffee and cigarettes.

Jai says that we'll go out today as it's my last full day. We'll go to some bars and have a little party. I say, "OK, but it can't be a late one. I don't want to be hung-over for my flight tomorrow."

He says, "Don't worry."

He is going to meet Lagan, his cousin, whom I met at the BBQ. He says he will meet him and then come back after a while to pick me up. I agree: "OK, fine."

So, he has a shower, gets ready, and leaves. I sit around for a while longer and then also shower.

It's late afternoon, and Jai messages to ask if I am hungry. He also says he is late because Lagan wanted to score. He has bought half a kilogram of grass. I reply, saying that he shouldn't have and adding that I have to get up in the morning. He says, "Don't worry."

He says to order food off Swiggy.com as he is going to be some time. I tell him that I'll eat when we are out as it will take time for food to arrive anyway.

After a couple of hours, Jai arrives with Lagan. They put a massive bag of weed on the table, and I laugh, saying, "OMG, I've not seen this amount of weed before." We sit and chat, and Lagan rolls a joint. We smoke the joint, and I feel a little more relaxed. But I don't want to be so stoned that I cannot function.

Jai goes into the bathroom to freshen up, and Lagan and I are standing around chatting. He says we'll take the weed with us. I say, "No. What if we get caught by the police and we get arrested? I don't want to be an international criminal and (1) get caught and (2) miss my flight." We both laugh.

Although I think secretly Jai and Lagan would be impressed to be associated with an international criminal. Jai has previously said that he has always wanted to date a gangster's daughter. I sometimes wonder about his sanity and his criminal ambitions. He says these things as a joke, but many a true thing is said in jest.

Jai comes out the bathroom. We gather our things, minus the bag of weed, which we leave on the table. It stinks, and

I express concern: "What if the building manager smells it?" They both tell me not to worry, saying it will be fine.

We pile into Lagan's SUV. I sit in the back seat. We head off towards Gandabaan centre. On the way we pick up Patrick, a friend of Lagan. They both went to University of Southern England.

Jai sparks up a joint as Lagan drives. I am a tad stressed about this. I don't want to be caught by the police. But again, they both say it's fine. Apparently, their family have influence in the area, and they will just pay off the cops, as they say. The SUV windows are blacked out, so that is some comfort.

The joint gets passed around, and I have a smoke. Lagan has put music on. I relax and watch the scenery passing us by.

Patrick is sitting next to me in the back. The three lads chat in their language. Lagan laughs at what I had said earlier. I look at Patrick and tell him I don't want to be an international criminal. We all laugh.

The first place we go is Social, which is a really cool place Jai had taken me when we first arrived in Gandabaan. There's lots of young, hip, trendy Indians sitting around and chatting. There is a small group of young guys on laptops at a big oval desk.

It's around 3 p.m., and I still haven't had lunch, so I am starving. Lagan orders a selection of bites for the table, including a veggie option for me. Drinks are ordered too.

We are sitting at a high table. Lagan and Patrick are sitting opposite, and Jai is sitting next to me. The guys are chatting in their language. I don't understand a word of it. I feel uncomfortable, so I go to the outside balcony for a cigarette. I don't feel stoned either.

On my return, the drinks have arrived. I have my standard vodka and soda, which Jai had ordered for me. The guys continue to chat, and the odd question is asked of me. I don't speak to Jai much.

After the food has been eaten, we relocate to the open terrace area, where we can smoke. Lagan intermittently asks if I am OK, which I think is sweet of him. I think he has noticed that I am a bit tense.

The guys talk about when they were in Bristol, and I join in the conversation as they are speaking in English. We talk about cricket, and I ask about match fixing. Patrick replies that most of the Indian cricket league are involved in corruption.

It's nice on the terrace. I look around, people watching.

We stay in Social for a couple of hours and then decide to move on and go to another couple of places. We end up in a little bar which is run by a friend of Lagan. Jai and I had been there previously. I don't remember the name though.

We drop Patrick at home on the way to the next place. We park up and walk onto the main street. We stop off to get some ice cream. Lagan and I walk on ahead. Jai is loitering behind, making a phone call. I leave him to it.

Lagan and I stop at a kulfi (Indian ice cream) stall. He says this is one of his favourite places to get ice cream. We order and wait for Jai.

There is some commotion on the street. A car is being towed away. We stand and watch the mini drama while eating our ice creams. We have a giggle at the bloke trying to secure the car to the tow truck. It's nice to just hang about with someone other than Jai. Lagan is a cool guy, and I like how he keeps checking to see if I am OK. Jai has not asked once after my well-being.

We arrive at the next place and sit on beanbags. There is a low table with a shisha on it. Jai asks one of the waiters to set it up for us. By now it's getting late, and I am getting stressed again. Lagan notices again and asks if I am OK. He says I must be stressed. I say, "Yes. I need to be on the flight tomorrow."

He says, "Don't worry, it will be fine."

Jai asks Lagan to plug his phone in to be charged. The socket is in between me and Lagan. After a short time, Jai says something to Lagan in their language, and Lagan turns the phone face down so the screen is not showing. They think I have not noticed, but I stare at Jai. I don't think he knows why.

What is wrong with him? Does he really think I am so stupid that I don't know what he is doing? He doesn't want me to see the screen if "anyone" calls. My mood takes a turn for the worse, and I don't talk for the rest of the evening.

I feel sorry for Lagan as he is trying hard to engage with me, but I don't want to talk.

I am feeling tired and ask if I can order a coffee. Jai calls the waiter over, and I ask for a coffee with cold milk on the side. I wait nearly half an hour for a coffee, and when it turns up, they have given me hot milk. I complain to Lagan and Jai, and they call the waiter over again, explain the situation in their language. The waiter takes the hot milk and the cup away.

I wait for another half hour. The coffee still doesn't arrive. I'm getting frustrated and annoyed now. I say to Lagan and Jai, "What the hell is happening? All I want is a coffee. How hard can it be to make a coffee?" After a while the owner, who is also the head chef, comes over and asks what the problem is. I tell him, "All I wanted was a coffee with some cold milk on the side." He apologises, makes some lame excuse, and says he will bring it over.

So, an hour later my coffee arrives!

It's now approaching 11 p.m., and we're all getting hungry again. Rather than eating at the restaurant, Jai suggests we pick something up and take it home. I am happy with that. Lagan drops us off at the apartment and then leaves.

Another hour later, with the food picked up, we're sitting and eating dinner in the apartment. I am quietly eating. Jai pipes up, "Are you still not talking to me?"

I just reply, "I am eating."

He says, "This is the last night. At least talk to me." I don't say anything. I don't want to get into another argument.

He continues by saying that I am very insecure and paranoid. I say that it's because he calls other women. He says that he will speak to women up until he gets married. I reply, "So it's OK for you to call married women? You are such a hypocrite."

He says, "OK, leave it," adding that he doesn't want to fight on my last night. I don't say anything.

We sit in silence for a while, finishing our dinner, drinking vodka, and smoking cigarettes. I get up and play with the cats for a little while. They are running around as usual for their night-time craziness. They don't come to me and hide under the bed.

It's not yet 1 p.m., and I decide to go to bed. A short while after, Jai comes to bed too.

He comes close and says he's sorry for everything, adding that he doesn't want to fight on our last night. He pulls my face to his and tries to kiss me. I reluctantly kiss him back, but my heart is not in it. He pulls me in closer, and I start to melt a little.

The cats have jumped onto the bed also.

I want to be with him, but my body is not letting me. But as luck would have it, it is over before it starts.

He gets out of bed and is annoyed with himself. I just lie in bed and let him do what he needs to. I do not have the energy or inclination to placate his dented male self-importance.

I cuddle Lollipop as she has climbed up near my head.

Jai comes back to bed, and I turn my back. He loosely puts his arm around me, and we fall asleep.

I wake up early in the morning. I want to get to the airport well in advance just in case there are any issues. My flight isn't until the evening, but I want to be at the airport about 5 p.m.

The usual lazy morning ensues. I just have a few last things to pack, but I'm ready to leave when the time comes. I still feel upset about leaving the cats, but I am not distraught this time round as I was before.

I think to myself, *Maybe this is the universe's way of bringing the truth to me. I had to be delayed to find out what Jai has been doing behind my back, messaging other women, especially his ex-girlfriend Anisha. Maybe the universe is saving me from more heartache down the line. I mean, God knows what he will be doing while I am back in the UK. He might be saying one thing and doing something completely different.*

In Goa, when I was with him and he would receive phone calls, he would be all coy and lie about where he was, telling other people he was just at home, when in reality he was with me at my house. And what if at those times I were the woman on the other end of the phone, and he was with someone else, not even in Gandabaan but Hindavi or anywhere else? No matter how much love I feel, there is no way I could trust him.

I sit, drink tea, and smoke cigarettes while I mull things over in my mind. He is still asleep with the cats sprawled around him. I watch the three of them sleeping without a care in the world in their respective dreamlands.

Again, the emotional minefield pulses in my belly. How did it get to this point? I came out to India to make my own Goan dream a reality, something which I had planned for the last three years, but the dream has turned into a living nightmare, leaving me in a state of utter confusion. I have run away, leaving behind the shards of a perfect future that was maybe never meant to be.

Jai stirs in bed. His phone is buzzing. He ignores it. I get up, sit on the edge of the bed, and gently nudge him to wake up. “Five more minutes,” he murmurs. I leave him.

I watch TV, but I’m now getting restless. I have plenty of time, but the urge to get things moving is making me edgy with anticipation.

Brutus is awake and stretching in the living area. Lollipop follows behind. I clean their litter tray and put food out for them for the last time—until when, I don’t know. I have already packed up their food and litter into a box, which is in the kitchen.

I make another coffee and sit aimlessly watching TV.

Half an hour later Jai awakes and checks his phone. He says, “Good morning, Sabbie Boss.”

I reply, “Morning.” He lights a cigarette and goes into the bathroom.

He has left his mobile on top of the fridge, and it’s buzzing again. I leave it, but I want to know who is calling. He comes out of the bathroom and says that it's OK to answer his phone if he is not there. I just look at him. I say that it stopped ringing anyway. He looks at the phone and says, "It's Jalil. He is going to meet us at the airport as he works somewhere in customs."

He comes and sits next to me on the armchair. He says, "Your last day, Sabbie Boss."

I say, "I know." He seems sombre. Maybe it's hitting him too. I say, "You'll be free to do whatever you want now."

He replies, "Hey! What will I do?" He asks, "Is everything packed?"

I reply, "Yes, apart from my shower stuff."

I tell him about the different piles of clothes, one to leave and another to be given to charity. I ask if he will please keep the bag containing my clothes, along with the box containing all the cat stuff. He says OK.

He says that he will come to the UK soon, as soon as he has his paperwork ready. I don't say anything.

By late afternoon, I am showered and ready to go, but I still have a couple of hours' wait until we leave for the airport. I finish off the last off my packing, putting away my toiletries and make-up. I make sure I have all my paperwork ready in my laptop bag.

I am standing in the other bedroom, tidying the last few bits, and Jai comes and stands in the doorway.

I say to him, "Please look after the cats."

He says, "I will. Don't worry. Even I have been with them since they were little." I can feel the tears welling up. I go to our bedroom, and he follows me.

As I stand there, he comes and hugs me, and I loosely hug him back. He says, "You don't have to go. We'll speak to Darshan about staying longer."

I say, "No, I must go. My dad has been freaking out."

He says, "I know you are ready to go now." He asks, "Are you crying?"

I say, "No." But inside the waves of grief are lashing.

Its 4.30 p.m. and I'm ready to go. I ask Jai to call an Ola cab and request that my bags be taken downstairs. I don't show him my face, and I daren't look at him in case I cry.

I try to catch the cats to give them one last hug. They don't want to be caught. Maybe they know that I am leaving them and are punishing me for abandoning them. I tell them I will see them soon.

The heartache ripples through my body.

Jai and I go downstairs, and the taxi arrives a few minutes later. The room boy loads up the car, and I sit in the back seat. Jai sits in the front passenger seat, and we head off towards the airport.

On the way Jai chats to the driver, and I sit quietly in the back seat. After a while, as we approach the airport, he turns to me and says, "You're happy to go home, Sabbie Boss?"

I reply, "Yes, I am."

He says, "You must be very happy." He says he will come to the UK soon and that I cannot say no now. This is the last time he will say it.

I reply, "Yes. OK," just to shut him up.

By now all previous feelings of leaving the cats, and to some degree Jai, have subsided. These feelings have been replaced with a slight nervousness. I just hope nothing goes wrong this time.

The taxi pulls up at the departure gate, and the driver takes out my luggage. Jai has brought over a trolley. I load the luggage onto the trolley, and we both walk towards the entrance.

Jai says he'll wait until I get through immigration and tells me to call him once I am through. I say OK.

We get to the entrance. I say bye to him without looking at him. He says, "Bye, Sabbie Boss," and I enter the double door, check in, and get through immigration without a problem.

I am going home!

Chapter 14

THE AFTERMATH AND POSTMORTEM

I have been back home nearly two months now. I wrote the last three chapters a good while after the events happened. So, writing and thinking back to the time before I left Goa has been a very painful reminder of the time that has passed and a present reminder of how everything has changed.

Obviously, the main change and the common thread from the outset has been Jai entering my life and the whirlwind of events of which he has been at the core.

I think not only of his initial help with setting up LOM, but also of him having been my constant companion, friend, lover, and confidante up until the time I left India. I have been the same to him, with the one added element of being his reluctant financier, which has been a black storm cloud over our heads throughout.

So now that I am back in the UK, we have tried to sustain some speck of a long-distance relationship amidst very difficult circumstances. Things have been as much of a roller coaster as they have ever been.

The same issues keep coming up and again and again, and

they have been slithering away under my skin even though I have tried to exorcise them.

Trust has been a major factor, i.e. the lack of it on my part. Especially since the last month in Gandabaan. But even with these trust issues, I have tried to cling to Jai and the memories of better times. He has been there with daily phone calls, but I can feel him drifting away from me.

The contraction of emotions, holding on and fighting to let go, has made my head spin.

I feel like I am back to square one in terms of the feelings I had left behind to seek a brighter future. Feelings of loneliness, emptiness, and sometimes even despair and desperation—these are the overriding emotions that I am now facing.

All these feelings have flooded back into my existence as if a renewed tsunami has swept over me. Sometimes I am drowning under the torrents. And there is no lifeguard to save me from myself.

I feel like I am grieving the intensity of the last seven months, but I am alone in this grief. The only person who could come close to understanding is also being grieved for, or maybe it is the person that I had built up in my mind. The truth will never be known to me. I am grieving for the potential of something that could never be or never was.

It's been turbulent to say the least. I have been fighting to escape this long-distance relationship, but Jai won't let me go. He says that he is always going to be there and that I will always be his girl. I just want to break free from the emotional angst of the separation and the physical distance. But even so, the emotional ties keep me pulled in.

Another two months have passed, and the roller coaster continues. I am sick of the ups and downs, but now mostly they are downs, more than they have ever been. The love that once blinkered me to what was happening right under my nose has evaporated, and I can now see clearly.

Now that I am halfway across the world, I only have my

senses to rely on, and they have been spot on. I have gone beyond the feelings of being high on love, and now I feel only resentment, bitterness, and complete distrust.

The anguish and confusion that Jai has caused has made me doubt my own sanity at times. For this I can never forgive him. He has driven me to the point that I cannot trust anyone.

He is not the person I thought he was. Inconsistencies in his behaviour sent my instinct into overdrive and set the alarm bells ringing. The red flags have been flying at full mast when his words have not matched his actions. The lies and deception continued. These were revealed to me by a source I cannot expose, and by my own detective work, which confirmed my suspicions.

He had the audacity to say he lied to me to keep me happy. How distorted a view of the world, and more precisely of me, does he have? I cannot believe anything he ever said or says to me again.

My behaviour, once he found out about it, has in turn made him lash out at me. Accusations have been made on both sides. We have each felt betrayed. But in my defence, this all stems from his lying. I stand my ground and try to make him see what he has done. I don't know if any of the long phone calls have had an impact. But at least I've tried.

However, one thing I have learnt from all of this is that the universe, or God in a more metaphysical sense, is always trying to talk to us. If something doesn't feel right, it most likely isn't. I prayed, and I was given the answers to understand the cause of my distress and why I was feeling like this. Because something wasn't right.

The universe is on my side.

All this has occurred because I want to bring my cats home to me in the UK, but he has used the cats to extort money from me. He has kept them hostage because of my emotional attachment to them. Money remains unaccounted for, and I am threatening to go back to Gandabaan to sort this out myself.

He is the sweetest liar. I bide my time until I must make my move. The nightly phone calls still take place, but I am getting stronger by the day as the truth has been revealed to me. He is trying his hardest to convince me that he will do all the "cat work" and that he has not cheated me out of money. He tells me he loves me and that his feelings go beyond just the money.

But I still reserve full judgement until I have evidence of where all the cat money has gone.

So, I bring this tale to an open-ended close. There is no happy ending where we both ride off into a Goan sunset on a scooter with me holding tightly onto his body and with the wind blowing in my hair.

The reality is that I don't know what our ending will be, whether there will be an ending at all or whether our lives across continents and oceans will be forever entwined.

I know that you must be thinking that there are too many unanswered questions, but that is how it is given the current state of play. Even I do not know the answers.

But one thing is for sure: up until the time when the cats are safe here with me and the credit has been paid in full, I will be like a devil on Jai's back.

And maybe the reason we are both in each other's lives is that we are both scared to let go, even now. For him, I have the power to turn his world upside down, and he is keeping his frenemy close. For me, I am waiting to be paid back the money I lent him.

I don't have any regrets, as one thing Jai did show me is that I have the capacity within me to love completely. I will never forget how we were at one while in Goa, how it was just me and him battling the outside world. And that gives me hope, hope that one day I will feel like that again.

For this one reason, I do not hate him or wish him harm, but I will love him in some way forever, my God of the Sun.

About The Author

First generation of British Born Indians. Parents and Grandparents came to England in the late 60's.

Having been born in English, the author grew up going to English Schools and watching British TV.

She was the eldest sibling with three younger brothers who were all born within 5 years of each other. There were also Cousins who were all like brothers and sisters too. All growing up, having fun and hanging out together. It was restricted but a happy and innocent time!

However, from a very young age the Author knew what was expected of her regarding cultural norms and values. What was planned for her future, and how it would come about.

But she had a wild side, and a strong sense of independence. She would fight back and argue.

Eventually as her rebellious side really kicked in when she was in her late teens, the family gathered and conspired and decided it was time for her to be married to save face and shame from the community.

She managed to escape the cultural traps and built a life for herself. Having put herself through high education and University, and then working her way into to a successful corporate career within IT Projects. Over the years romantic relationships has started and ended, causing emotional layers of hurt and betray to be laid.

However, it wasn't all bad. Being the rebel that she was, she partied hard and laughed a lot since the Escape. Music was her one relief. She danced her way through her life. She'd made life long friends who supported and comforted her during the hard times and played as much as she did. She had built a good life.

But there was always something missing!

It took nearly 20 years and most of her adult life to realize the deeply embedded subconscious trauma was a result of what had happened to her. All her decisions and relationships stemmed from those moments of betrayal and grief inflicted on her from the people close to her.

Having experienced the most brutal of another betrayal, which opened and bought to the surface everything that she had buried, she realized that she had been running away from herself most of her life. She was disconnected from her own soul.

But now after an intense and painful period of self-discovery she is finally at peace with herself.